Praise for A DRIN

It's rare for me to find a book that is bo
insightful. Roy has brilliantly and cour
relationship addict and offers his wisdo
addiction. His advice may not always be ......, you want to hear, but in
my book, he's brilliantly defines the doorway out of profound loneliness
and back to love.

—Diana Chapman, 42, Santa Cruz, CA.

After meeting Roy and choosing him as my life and relationship coach, I
read his book *A Drink with Legs*. What an eye opening look into my
dating relationship patterns and mistakes! Along with spiritual
enlightening tools to excavate our authentic selves, his book is
lighthearted with a serious approach to the love relationship path. I would
highly recommend reading *A Drink with Legs* if you are serious about
ending dating nightmares, and creating a true, spiritual, love relationship.

—Amber Weiss, 37, Boca Raton, FL.

Rarely, when reading a book, do I find myself laughing out loud while at
the same time having the thought, "this is profound." I had this
experience regularly while reading *A Drink With Legs*. *I* found the book
to be a roadmap for navigating the treacherous terrain of relationships.
Roy seems to understand the "real world" of difficult relationships and
able to help me/us find our way through the maize to the possibility of a
truly wonderful connection with another human being that is not, at its
core, co-dependent. Quite frankly, I think the book is a must (and fun
read) for anyone who serious about creating a profound connection with
another human being.

—Jim Dethmer, 57, Chicago, IL

After coming to the conclusion that my marriage was unfulfilling, Roy's
book, *A Drink with Legs,* gave me insight and courage to move forward
with the next chapter of my life. His easy to read, but meaningful story,
is a breath a fresh air amongst a lot of heavy books in the same genre. I
continue to re-read this book; it is not only helping me understand the
anatomy of my past experiences, but it's helping me to shape the future
choices I make in order to live my best life.

—Kathy Lake, 33, SanFrancisco, CA.

A Drink with Legs is both a dynamic and powerful tool anyone can use to get started on their own path to creating a Spiritual Relationship with the partner of their dreams. While so many books today are still locked in blaming, keeping score and the 'psychology' of the relationship between men and women, Roy, in a most unique way, cuts through all that and focus's on each person's spiritual perspective and brings them back to the truth of their own consciousness again and again. Using his own true life stories and adventures (both the seemingly good and bad), Roy sets up a system for success leaving no steps out along the way. *A Drink With Legs* is a very honest and compelling read and spoke to me on a number of areas I needed to examine within. My life changed dramatically for the better after reading and using the concepts Roy shares. I heartily give *A Drink With Legs* two thumbs up!

—Kelly Brown, 47, Orlando, FL.

Roy, I just finished reading *A Drink with Legs* and I absolutely loved it! It spoke to me deeply. I am committed to a new path and will use all your tools to discover more about myself. I believe all you have said in your book is completely life-altering for me and I think everyone should read it. When I was 3/4 of the way through the book I felt like everything in my life fell into sync, the world was clear and bright and I had shape-shifted into a new me. I really appreciated your down to earth sense of humor, personal authenticity, spirituality and how you blend it all together in such a new and inspiring approach and philosophy. I am going to be recommending it to a lot of my clients.

—Mheyah Bailey, 45, Vancouver, Canada

Reading *A Drink With Legs* was like holding a microscope up to my personal life and relationships. Each time I turned the page I saw my own mishaps in love being acknowledged and brought into full view. I believe this book made it possible for me to change some useless habits and live in a state of happy anticipation of a successful loving relationship. Thanks, Roy, for putting yourself out there to encourage others to open the door to more satisfying relationships.

—Victoria Lloyd, 54, Altamonte Sprs., FL.

A Drink with Legs

From Being Hooked to Being Happy —
A Spiritual Path to Relationship Bliss

ROY BIANCALANA

Foreword by Gay Hendricks, Ph.D.

This book is published by Roy A. Biancalana

This is a non-fiction book. Everything in the book is true, though most names have been changed in respect of their privacy. There is no disclaimer in this book as to the path it recommends. If you follow the principles outlined in this book you will transform your life.

Library of Congress Cataloging-in-publication data available upon request
ISBN 978-1-4507-2570-5

www.coachingwithroy.com

Printed in the United States

First Printing: July 2010
Second Printing: September 2010
Third Printing: January 2011

To Eric—

**If, as it's said, "The apple doesn't fall far from the tree,"
then I hope this book will help you find your spiritual
liberation and the love of *your* life. I love you, Son.**

—Dad

CONTENTS

Acknowledgements, 8

Foreword by Gay Hendricks, Ph.D., 11

A Note From The Author, 12

PROLOGUE, 13

INTRODUCTION, 22

PART ONE
"Wasted away again in Margaritaville"
The Devastation of Dependence

1. The Buddha on Babes, Boys and Bliss, 37
2. You Are Under Arrest For LWI: Loving While Intoxicated, 42
3. How I Finished Last in the 2003 U.S. Open, 52
4. Committing to Your Relationship Revolution, 62

PART TWO
"Searchin' for my lost shaker of salt"
Exploring Our Thirsty Hearts

5. Bar-Hopping My Way Through Life: Golf, God, Girls, 71
6. Jerry Maguire Was Full of Shit!, 80
7. Rivers of Living Water, 87
8. Exorcizing the Demon of Loneliness, 98

PART THREE
"Some people say there's a woman to blame"
From the Darkness of Drama to the Dawn of Intimacy

9. The World's Oldest Profession, 109
10. From Insanity to Intimacy, 120
11. Stuck Between a Rock and a Hard Place, 128
12. Casanova: The World's Greatest Lover, 136
13. Loving a Love Junkie, 145
14. The Difference Between Sex and Relationship Addiction, 154

PART FOUR
"But I know it's my own damn fault."
Leaving Margaritaville

15. The 12 Steps To Relationship Bliss, 161
16. Step One: First Things First—Hit Rock Bottom!, 167
17. Step Two: Commit to Navel Gazing, 172
18. Step Three: Choose to Be a Stupid Dog, 175
19. Step Four: Retain a "Rude" Relationship Coach, 179
20. Step Five: Go Public With Your Personas, 183
21. Step Six: Complete With Former Lovers, 186
22. Step Seven: Go Cold Turkey, 192
23. Step Eight: Date Yourself, 196
24. Step Nine: Have an Affair—with Mother Nature!, 200
25. Step Ten: Live *As* the Eye of the Hurricane, 203
26. Step Eleven: Get A Life!, 208
27. Step Twelve: The Ingredients for a Delicious Love Life, 212

EPILOGUE
The Love of *My* Life, 227

Appendix I
A Chronological Timeline for *A Drink with Legs,* 230

Appendix II
Affirmations for Freedom, 233

About The Author, 234

Acknowledgements

I am so grateful for the teachers, mentors, friends, cheerleaders, supporters and "mirrors" that have been a part of my evolutionary path. Words can not adequately express how much each of you has impacted my life. I love and appreciate you all so very much.

MaryMargaret, you are a beautiful woman and I am crazy in love with you. You are an amazing wife, lover, friend and spiritual partner. I completely enjoy the luscious, authentic woman that you are, as well as the playful and passionate relationship we have created. It is an absolute joy to begin each day by looking into your eyes.

Jim Dethmer, you have made an unspeakable impact on my life—by simply living yours. Though your presence and wisdom have greatly influenced me, it is your commitment to your spiritual evolution that has made the most profound impression in my life. You are like an evolutionary magnet, drawing me, not toward you, but toward who I truly am.

Diana Chapman, you are so much more than my coach and mentor. I feel like we are soulmates! You have been with me in my darkest moments, always giving me the space to be, yet never allowing me to be less than I am. You are a gift from God to me. Our relationship is one of the most treasured things in my life.

Gay Hendricks, thank you for your guidance with this project and your help in getting it out into the world. Having you in my corner has been a dream come true.

Mom, Dad, my sisters **Sally, Nancy** and my brother **Jeff**, each of you has loved me and supported me through out my life and I am so grateful for each of you.

Eric Biancalana, I love being your dad. From the day I brought you home from the hospital, you have not stopped teaching me what it means to live authentically, tenaciously and tenderly. It has been the greatest joy of my life to watch you grow into the young man that you are.

Michael Wright, whether we are having a beer at *Friday's*, walking the fairways at the U.S. Open or talking about what it means to live consciously, I treasure each and every moment of our friendship. It's hard to imagine two guys being through as much as we have! Your consistent support, your sense of humor and your desire for spiritual growth means more to me than you'll ever know.

Grace Caitlin, you also are a gift from God to me and I will always appreciate your coaching. When we first started working together, I was closed off to my deepest feelings and unable to express them. But your loving guidance taught me how to live congruently with my feelings and that has truly changed my life.

John Phelps, though are friendship has had some bizarre twists and turns since we met back in college many years ago, I still consider you my friend and you have made an incredible impact on my life. You had a front row seat for almost everything written in this book and I will always appreciate your support.

A number of other people have made huge contributions to this project. **Kim Collier** and **Jamie Ziegler**, thank you for your work on the manuscript, your thoughtful insights and your amazing encouragement every step of the way. You are both very creative and intelligent women and your feedback has been invaluable to me.

Ryan Evans, thank you for creating my websites and setting up my information systems. **Mike Brucher**, thank you also for working on my websites over the years and for your work on the cover. Designing a drink with legs was no easy task!

Finally, there are three amazing women who appear prominently in this book and each of you has had an immeasurable impact on my life. I have attempted to tell our stories truthfully (the truth as I see it anyway) and yet honor you in the process. I hope I have succeeded, for I have deep admiration and respect for each of you.

Laurie (her real name and my ex-wife), you are a wonderful woman and mom. We spent 21 years together and you have done an absolutely fabulous job raising our son. For that I will always be grateful. The friendly relationship we have forged since our divorce is one of the things I treasure most in life. Thank you for being who you are.

Pam (not her real name), our brief relationship was the turning point in my life and I will always appreciate our time together because of that. You have a loving and honest heart and I wish you and your sweet son nothing but the best.

Julie (also not her real name), words can not express how much I appreciate you and our relationship. It was an incredible 30 months together and I treasure every minute of it. Our relationship truly changed my life. I am a better man for having been with you and I have absolutely no regrets about our time together. I wish nothing but love and happiness for you and your two amazing boys.

Foreword
By
Gay Hendricks, Ph.D.
Author of *Conscious Loving, Five Wishes* and *The Big Leap*

A Drink with Legs is one of the most insightful and entertaining works I've read in a long time. In it, you'll go on an odyssey of healing perhaps like none other you're likely to encounter. The real-life hero, Roy, is indeed a real-life hero of a very special kind. He is a master of ruthless yet compassionate observation, willing to look at the darker side of ourselves that very much needs illuminating. And he does it in a way that allows us to laugh at his foibles, and by so doing, take ourselves a little less seriously.

A Drink with Legs comes along at a particularly opportune time. The recent relationship troubles of Tiger Woods, the world's best-known and richest athlete, have been the subject of millions of words of print and many miles of television footage. With all the energy and attention expended on this subject, though, are we really any wiser? There has been very little reflection on, or deeper inquiry into, what actually drives a person's obsessive behavior in regards to love, sex and intimacy. You'll find that in this book and a great deal more. Roy has been there and back in the territory in which Tiger has stumbled and fallen. Now, with Roy's book, we have a map for the territory, along with a very entertaining story.

Now, turn the page and let the adventure begin.

A Note from the Author

Dear Reader,

I know what it is like to be utterly devastated and broken-hearted by love. I have been through it and it is one of the most agonizing things in life. But I have discovered how to create a wonderful and blissful love life. *A Drink with Legs* shows you how you can do the same.

This book is structured much like a weight loss commercial, meaning, it has before and after "photos." The before "photo," the Prologue, is a true story that depicts my love life when it was an absolute, drama-filled, outrageous, sickening mess. *It is written from the perspective of the "hooked" and dysfunctional man I was at the time and it is definitely not a pretty picture, though it is an honest one.*

The after "photo," the Epilogue, is also a true story, but it depicts my love life completely transformed by the principles presented in this book. The chapters in between describe how I went from one to the other, and more importantly, how you can too.

If you can open your heart and see yourself in the pages that follow, you too will be able to experience what your heart most deeply desires—relationship bliss.

Roy Biancalana
Orlando, Florida
January 2010

PROLOGUE

Rock Bottom
The Caribbean, October 2006

So whenever your relationship is not working, whenever it brings out the 'madness' in you and in your partner, be glad. What was unconscious is being brought up to the light. It is an opportunity for salvation.

—Eckhart Tolle

She was as little as her name was short. Barely over five feet tall, and all of 115 pounds, Pam was 45 years old and had a body that most 25 year-olds would die for. She had sparkling light green eyes, a devious smile and shoulder-length auburn hair, all of which made her quite easy on the eyes, to say the least. However, she had a hyper, yippy personality that simply grated on my nerves and drove me nuts. She was a lot like a cute little Schnauzer—on caffeine. But I overlooked her Schnauzer-ness because she fulfilled my only real requirement in a woman: *she liked me.*

We met on-line, *Match.com*, if memory serves. I'm not absolutely sure because I was on three different dating websites at the time. Pam was the third date of the week for me, all with different women, of course. That wasn't so bad, it was only Thursday. Besides, she was the only date I had planned for that day. Sometimes I would have three dates in a single day; a lunch date, an after work meet-for-a-drink date and then a dinner date. It all seemed perfectly healthy to me. Frankly, I thought cutting back to one date a day was a sign that the relationship coaching I had been in for the past six months was finally starting to work.

Pam and I met in late May of 2006 at an expensive steakhouse in the western suburbs of Chicago. Before this first face-to-face date, I had the usual thing going with her—flirty phone calls and funny emails. I think she was already falling for me, which frankly, wasn't all that unusual. In fact, I remember meeting a woman on-line who actually told me she loved me before we even met! No, I am not kidding. Things did not work out, though. I think she had some sort of relationship addiction problem and I did *not* want any part of that.

Anyway, Pam and I met, as I said, at the steakhouse for drinks and an appetizer. No *Starbucks* for me. That was not part of Casanova's play book ("Casanova" is the name I've given my "hooked on love" pseudo-self). And, of course, my Casanova-ness would never let a woman pay her share, even if the odds of this turning into something special were about as likely as the Chicago Cubs winning the World Series. I remember it cost me about $60, which was about average for my dates. You can imagine the amount of money I was spending every week on my love life.

I'll save you the gory details of the date and simply tell you that I played my best card twenty minutes in: I leaned over and kissed her. Yes it was bold but Casanova is a great kisser. You don't believe me? After our second date, I moved in with her. Yes, you read that right. She took me home, made mad, passionate love to me—the schnauzer on caffeine thing wasn't *all* bad—and after that night, I simply never left.

Well, things progressed as you might expect. After about three months we were at each other's throats. It was all her fault, of course. She had issues. So I broke it off and moved out. And again, I did what you'd expect. I went looking for my next "drink." But there was a small complication. I had planned a trip to an exotic *au natural* resort in the Caribbean about a month into my "drinking binge," um, I mean my relationship with Pam. No problem, though. We would simply cancel and get our money back, right? Wrong. The cancellation date had passed. No refunds.

So, I had three options. First, I could pay Pam for her part of the trip (we did split the cost of the trip—Casanova must have had a sober moment) and find someone else to go with me. I actually gave this serious consideration. I thought Trish might go if I asked. (I'll tell you more about her in a minute.) But, unfortunately, the plane tickets were not transferable. So my last two choices were either to waste the money by not going, or, well.................. I *could* go with Pam.

I dismissed the option of wasting the money in about a second. There was *no way* I was going to waste thousands of dollars. Besides, I had never been to an exotic romantic resort in the Caribbean, much less one of the naked ones. I wanted to go!

This was the trip of a lifetime. I imagined it would be like being on the set of a porno movie filmed at the Playboy Mansion! Gorgeous people, wild sex everywhere, and I'd be the star.

So, yes, you are reading this correctly. I actually decided to go on a week-long romantic trip to a beautiful, *au natural*, all-inclusive resort in the Caribbean and stay in a top-floor ocean view suite with one King size bed—with a woman I couldn't stand and had broken up with. (Stop laughing. It's not polite.)

And just as I was unwilling to waste thousands of dollars by not going, I sure as hell was not going to be on the set of my porno movie—celibate! I could not imagine such a scenario. And so, you see my predicament, don't you? Even though we weren't a couple any longer (we'd be broken up for about six weeks when this trip was scheduled to happen) I wanted to go *as if we were a couple and madly in love.*

The only way I knew how to create that was to tell her that I wanted to give "us" another shot. So I met with her and told her that I wanted to go on this trip as an intimate couple and see if it rekindled our romance. I remember it went something like this:

"Pam, sweetheart, I've been thinking. Maybe our break up was a mistake. Our whole relationship began so quickly. We met on-line, we fell head over heels; we began living together after our second date. It was all so fast. Maybe I overreacted about our personality differences. We have such incredible chemistry. I want to go on this trip as a couple, as if we never broke up. I think that the trip might rekindle our romance and get us off to a more "normal" start. (Yes, I did use the word "normal.") There is a chance, I suppose, that when we come home from the trip we might go our separate ways, but then again, who knows? I think it's worth a shot, though. What do you think?"

Well, she loved the idea. Why? Who knows. Maybe she truly loved me. Maybe she was as screwed up as I was. It didn't matter. She agreed to go as a couple and see if the trip brought us back together again. You may not believe this, but I actually *did* think this was possible. (Casanova was talking and even I believed him!)

Well, the first five days of our trip went great. We frolicked on the beach, naked of course. We ate naked, drank naked, sunbathed naked, canoed naked. Naked. Naked. Naked. And we had sex all the time and everywhere—in the ocean, on the beach, in the pool, in the hot tub, in the room—it *was* like being in a porno movie. By the way, while the whole porno movie fantasy came true, the Playboy Club part definitely did not. Pam and I were the only people at the resort, it seemed, under 70 years old! (Sorry to make you visualize that.)

The frolicking fun came to a screeching halt the evening of day five. She began questioning me about our relationship and its future (the nerve!) and speaking as if we definitely had one. I tried dancing around that subject, doing my best impression of Fred Astaire. But her Schnauzer-ness continued. Finally, in an attempt to shake her loose from my pant leg, I told her that, "I just don't think we have the personality fit to make something work long term."

Hearing that our relationship was going to end sooner than a gallon of milk would spoil in the hot Caribbean sun, well, let's just say it caused a bit of drama. We argued all night. And when I say "all night" that is not hyperbole. We literally stayed up and argued from ten o'clock in the evening until seven the next morning (naked, of course). We didn't sleep for a minute and we didn't stop arguing for even a second. No exaggeration. It was an all-night fight. She said I was "a lying piece of shit", and that I manipulated her, used her and played her. I reminded her, in an I-told-you-so kind of way, "Pam, I said all along that there was a chance we'd go home and not see each other again." (I think that having sex with her at least 10 times over the last five days communicated something else to her. Go figure.) She was really furious. The argument ended as I left for breakfast at seven a.m., neither of us having had a wink of sleep.

Of course we spent the day apart, but we really couldn't break up. I mean, I couldn't just get in my car and drive away like I could if we were in Chicago. We were in a foreign country at a resort in the middle of nowhere. And remember, we were staying in a room that only had one bed! ("What a tangled web we weave...") And that evening, when we were forced to be in each other's presence again, we were like a couple of prize fighters coming out of our respective corners for another round. We picked up right where we left off. She resumed saying I played her and I continued to say I never committed to anything. Blah, blah, blah.

Remember the movie, *Groundhog Day*? We were having the same *exact* argument. So, either out of boredom or because I was addicted to drama (you choose which one, I haven't a clue) I decided to trade in the Fred Astaire persona for my Johnnie Cochran one and prove that I was innocent of her nasty charges. I told Pam that not only had I not committed to a future with her, *I had not even committed to being exclusive with her.* I told Pam that during our month apart, the time between when we broke up and now, I had started seeing a woman named Trish. (Ladies and Gentlemen of the jury, I rest my case!)

Let me pause for a moment and tell you about Trish. I met her on-line too. She was a couple of years older than me, which was alright because she was fun, made a ton of money and she was gorgeous. In fact, there was a radio station holding a contest to find the "Hottest Cougar in Chicago." The voting was done on-line and she won! And that's not even the best part. Though she loved her job, her real passion was helping women to get more in touch with their feminine sexual energy by teaching them to pole dance! *So I was dating a rich cougar who teaches pole dancing!!* Even though I still had something going with Pam, how could I let *The Cougar* get away? Come on! Be serious. Besides, it was a month until the trip. What was I supposed to do…go without a relationship for that *whole* time?

Getting back to Pam and me, last night's argument was nothing compared to what was in store for this fine evening. The cute little Schnauzer on caffeine was transforming into a raging Pit Pull on steroids. About two hours into round two, I realized that there was nothing left to talk about. I turned on the television, hoping to put an end to our pointless "discussion." She hated me and we were through. That was obvious. My thought was, *let's get through the next two days and be done with each other.*

Evidently she didn't share that thought. She turned the television off. She was not through screaming. I turned it back on. I was. She turned it off and I turned it back on. Off, on. Off, on. Off. on. This childishness went on until she finally took the remote and threw it out the window! *Wow, nice,* I thought. Not to be outdone, I walked over to the television. and turned it on by hand. I looked at her and said, sarcastically, "Now what are you gonna do?" She came over, fully embodying her Pit Bull persona

17

now, went behind the television and unhooked the cable from both the wall and the set, and threw *that* out the window too! (Thank God the TV was bolted down!)

I stood there, staring incredulously out the window and laughing about what she'd just done. It was unbelievable. This whole thing was unbelievable. When I turned around to ask her if she had completely lost her mind, she hauled off and slapped me nearly into next week! I mean she cracked me good. I'm six feet tall and 180 lbs. and I saw stars. I'm not kidding. I have never been hit that hard in my entire life. My eyes welled up from the pain. The left side of my face felt like it was on fire.

In total disbelief, with my hand on my face, I just stared at her, dumbfounded and speechless. I'd had arguments with women before and I had been through my share of break ups. So I was not unaccustomed to some drama. Hell, I went through a divorce! But never had it gotten physical. I was in as much shock as I was in pain. Finally, taking my hand away from my face and checking it for blood, I said slowly and calmly, "I don't care if you're a girl or not. If you hit me again, I'll drag your naked ass out of this room and lock you out all night."

Her eyes were red with fire. It was as if she were channeling *Cujo*. She didn't seem a bit concerned with my threat. ("Hell hath no fury like…") We stood toe to toe, like two boxers in the middle of the ring getting pre-fight instructions from the referee. Neither of us was backing down. We stared defiantly into each other's eyes, seeing who would blink first. For a few seconds there was utter silence.

Then with a quickness that I don't believe I will ever witness again, she hit me—believe it or not—harder than the first time and in the exact same place! After my head snapped back from the force of the blow, I must have had fire in *my* eyes because she took off across the room toward the bed. Enraged, I chased her and grabbed her by the ankles just as she scrambled onto the bed. This was the first and only time I ever laid my hands on a woman in anger, and although it didn't feel right, I started pulling her off the bed anyway. *"Your ass is out of here!"* I screamed. I recklessly snatched her off the bed and her body smacked loudly against the cold, hard tile.

It was now a full blown *Jerry Springer* moment. As her body slid screeching across the tile, making the sound of gym shoes on a basketball court, she wildly clawed and kicked and flailed, attempting to get free from my grip on her ankles. I had to twist her legs like a pretzel in order to weaken and immobilize her. As we continued to wrestle toward the door, screaming and cursing at each other, I had one of those moments that is hard to put into words. It was as if I became a fly on the wall and the fly asked me, "Roy, what the hell are you doing? Look at yourself, dude? Look at what your life has become!" Immediately I let go of her ankles. I walked away from her, though I kept her in my sights. And for about the next hour I owned up to everything I had done to create this mess. I told her the unvarnished truth about my lies, my manipulation, my deceit, my motives and my relationship with Trish. I did not sugar coat it, make excuses or blame her in any way. I simply told the truth. And I wish I could tell you that it felt great to come clean, but it didn't. I actually felt horrified at what I was hearing come out of my own mouth. It was as if I was still the fly on the wall, listening to my own confession. It made me sick to my stomach.

You also might think that hearing my confession calmed Pam down. Wrong. She took my honesty as an invitation to verbally abuse me as much as humanly possible. And damn, she had a way with words. Normally I would not let someone dump on me like that, but I think the fly on the wall told me to shut up and listen to what she had to say. She was in incredible pain and I was greatly responsible for this mess. I felt like I needed to stand there and let her swing at me—with words only—for a time. Not only did she say she hated me with all her guts and that I was a pathological-lying-manipulative-deceptive-slimy prick and that she never wanted to see me again as long as she lived, she also told me that my mother didn't love me, my coach didn't respect me, my friends thought I was a loser and that I was a complete joke and failure in my career. She made fun of the way I dressed, she said my spirituality and enlightenment was laughable (that part was true) and she told me I was an awful father, setting a horrible example (also true) and she hoped I got killed in a car accident on the way home from the airport! Then she dropped the big one. She told me that of all the men she had ever been with, I was the worst lover—with the littlest dick!

Anyway, after about an hour of being abused, I told her that I'd heard enough and I was going to take my stuff and leave. There was no way I was going to sleep in that room with her. I actually feared closing my eyes. She liked golf and she had her

19

clubs in the room. I believed it was entirely possible, maybe even likely, that if I closed my eyes she would bash in my head—reenacting the shower scene from *Psycho*, only this time using a 7-iron instead of a knife.

I began gathering my things and putting them in the suitcase. Actually, it was her suitcase. I didn't own a suitcase big enough to hold seven days worth of stuff. So I borrowed an extra one of hers for the trip. (I don't know why I brought so much stuff. I never wore any clothes.) As I began putting my stuff in the suitcase she attacked me from behind, hitting me and screaming, telling me not to touch *her* suitcase. I had a hand full of clothes, and turning toward her, I straight-armed her in the face, keeping her away from me. Grounding the clothes into her face, I said, forcefully, "Enough! I'll leave the suitcase. If you come at me again, Pam, so help me....Now stop!" She did.

So I took two pillows out of their cases and put all my stuff in them. And along with a pillow, I took a sheet, my bathroom case, my shoes, wallet, phone and passport and walked out the door. I went to the pool and made my bed on one of the lounge chairs. It was three o'clock in the morning.

I could no longer run from the reality of my life. It was impossible, even for me, to explain this away, lay the blame on her or just ignore it. *My life was out of control.* There was no other way to spin this. The fly (my deepest Self, I now know) told me to take a good look at my life in this moment. And with sober awareness, this is what I saw:

I saw a man lying in the damp night air with all his stuff like some kind of homeless person. He had a hand print on the side of his face and he was clutching his passport, fearing she'd come steal it in the night. (If that happened, he'd have a hell of a time getting home.) Both his lack of integrity and his out-of-control addiction to relationships and drama had landed him on a pool-side lounge chair, literally fearing for his life should he fall asleep, for Pam and her 7-iron, were not far away.

There were no tears; there were no sobs. This went far deeper than mere sadness. With muted despair, his eyes stared into the black night like those of a dead corpse—open, yet blank and devoid of life.

In his mind, though, and in living color, his love life flashed before his eyes, seeing the destruction and the debris that he left in his wake.

He saw the crushed, pain-stricken face of his then seven year old son the day he told him that he and his mom were getting divorced. He also could feel, like it was yesterday, the breathless moment when his fiancée, Julie, almost exactly one year before this moment, put her engagement ring back into his trembling hand, telling him it was over. And he saw the confused, grieving faces of the women he used to get over that break up, the last of which was Pam. But maybe most heart rending of all, he saw the faces of his coach and friends. What would they think, seeing him like this? They loved him and they had been trying to get through to him for many, many months— to no avail.

So, maybe it was the voice of their spirits, or maybe it was God or maybe that fly on the wall had followed him out there by the pool. Either way, as the sun was rising and people were headed to breakfast, staring at the poor, homeless son-of-a-bitch on the chair, a voice said, "Roy, wake up! Wake up, Roy!"

Before this moment, I knew I had issues with women. I really did. That may sound funny having read what I just wrote. But I knew I had a problem. I was working on it with my coach. But as any addict will tell you, there are moments when you know you have a problem, and then there are moments when you *KNOW* you have a problem. And now I *KNEW* I had a problem. This was Rock Bottom.

INTRODUCTION

The Mayor of Margaritaville

To really lose yourself is like holding a gun to your head
and pulling the trigger-it takes courage.
Facing the truth means tying a bag over your head
until you suffocate-it takes faith.
You have to be brave to follow God's tracks into the unknown
where so many new things overwhelm and panic you.
But trust me and plunge the jeweled dagger into your heart.
This is what it takes to lose yourself.
There is no other path to God.

—Hafiz

In *The Chronicles of Narnia: The Lion, the Witch and the Wardrobe*, Lucy, one of the main characters, accidentally discovers a portal to another world while hiding in a closet. It is a world of enchantment, magic, adventure and beauty—Narnia.[*]

Narnia takes her breath away, and for a while, she is completely lost in the wonder of the magnificent place. But soon she thinks of her friends and she feels compelled to show them what she has found because it is just too spectacular to keep to herself. So she returns to her friends and invites them to follow her through the closet, the portal, so they too can experience Narnia.

Without meaning to sound too grandiose, I feel like Lucy. For I too have found a portal to another world, only this is a world of enchanted *love*, magical *intimacy* and beautiful *communion*. I've found *Relationship* Narnia.

---

[*] Fans of *The Chronicles* will note that Narnia was also a scary and dangerous place, especially early on. I ask that you grant me a bit of poetic license, as I use Narnia simply as a metaphor for a place of heavenly bliss, which for C.S. Lewis, it ultimately was.

Narnia is a "place" where the deepest longings of our hearts are fulfilled. It's a place where two people experience love's divine intensity and presence. It's a place where two people are seen and cherished for who they truly are. And I have written this book to show you, not only what I've found, but to invite you to come with me to Narnia, this magical place of relationship bliss.

Now, my guess is you are a bit suspicious after reading that last paragraph. Perhaps your shelves are lined with books that have made similar claims, yet your love life is still as disappointing as ever. I know, I've got the same books on my shelves and they didn't transform my love life either. But here's why I feel so confident that this book can make a real difference in your life: My love life was an absolute, utter disaster—and now it's not.

If you read the Prologue you know I'm not exaggerating about the disaster part. And although that relationship was the most spectacularly dysfunctional of all my relationships, it was only the last of many disappointing, drama-filled and failed intimacies.

But now I have a relationship to die for. I really do. My wife and I are open and honest with our feelings; we rarely argue, criticize or blame one another; we understand and honor our many differences; we support each other's creative path; we encourage each other to fully express our most authentic selves, and our sex life is wonderful—passionately and playfully celebrating the beauty that is our relationship.

How did that happen? Well, that is what this book is all about. I want to tell you how I transformed a love life characterized by heartache, pain and disappointment—better known as drama—and instead created deep, authentic intimacy—what I call relationship bliss.

My premise is simple: If I can do it, you can do it. For although we may have different genders, beliefs and past experiences, when it's all said and done, you and I are the same. We are just human beings who want to love and be loved.

Love, Life and the Pursuit of Intimacy
I want to have an open, honest and deeply personal conversation with you about our love lives—whether you are currently in a relationship or not. This book is not a psychological, clinical, shrink-speak treatise on relationships. Though I am a Certified Relationship Coach with years of

experience and considered to an expert in this field, I don't want to write to you from my head. I want to write to you from my heart and from my experience. So think of this book like this: It's you and me sitting together in a quiet, intimate setting and having a heart-to-heart talk about love, life and the pursuit of intimacy.

The Core Issue

I have noticed something about life that seems strange to me. Maybe it will seem strange to you as well. Over the last hundred years or so, there have been drastic improvements in almost every area of life—*except relationships.* Think about it. Medicine, civil rights, transportation, technology and communications—they have all radically evolved. Yet the divorce rate is not changing much, if at all. Two reasonably sane people still can't seem to be happy with one another for any significant length of time. What's up with that?! Don't you find that strange? Everything is improving except love. *What's wrong?*

Well, after a failed marriage, a break up with my fiancée and a bunch of internet dating disasters, the last of which left me homeless in the Caribbean, I started asking myself that very question: What's wrong? But because I was confused and in pain, I asked a more personal question: What's wrong—*with me?* What was *my* problem? I never set out to understand why the rest of the world's love life sucked. I wanted to know why mine did. What was going on with me that led to so many disappointing and drama-filled relationships? That's what I was after—fixing my own love life.

With the help a relationship coach, I was able to discover the core issue that was responsible for *all* of my relationship pain. Although I had been in a bunch of relationships with very different women, all of the drama and heartache was coming from one single root issue which was this: I was relying on the attention and the affection of my partner(s), to make me feel special, alive and whole. In other words, I saw a relationship as the means to alleviate my feelings of loneliness, to be the source of my happiness, to validate my masculinity and to secure my self-esteem.

Forgive me for using a corny, overdone cliché, but the truth was that I had an unconscious belief in a concept that the movie *Jerry Maguire* made famous: "You Complete Me."

24

Now, I loved that movie. And I cried when Jerry said "You complete me." I really did. Hell, I *still* cry whenever I see it. It moves me and touches me because I'm a hopeless romantic. Who doesn't want to hear that said to them? Who doesn't want to feel that way about their partner? I do, as does anybody who has a beating heart in their chest. We human beings (even men!) are very romantic creatures.

However, if you asked me if the "You Complete Me" mindset was technically healthy and appropriate, I would have said flatly, "HELL NO!" My brain would have said that another person isn't responsible for my happiness. That's my job. And my brain would have also said that it's not my partner's job to alleviate my feelings of loneliness or to make me feel special or whole. But while my head might have said that, my life was saying something altogether different.

In reality, I *was* relying on my partner(s) to meet those emotional needs. And, of course, what partner can do all that or even come close? Do you see why I experienced so much disappointment and drama? Unfortunately, that was the story of my love life. (My guess is that it's the story of yours as well.)

Hooked on Love

So there it is. It took me about a year of coaching to finally see this. The core issue that was responsible for all of my relationship pain and drama was that I was relying on a partner's attention and affection to make me feel special, alive and whole.

And let's not sugar-coat this, shall we? The word "relying" is simply a nice, politically correct way of saying I was *hooked* on love and relationships. It was like an addiction. Am I overstating things just for dramatic effect? I don't think so. Consider the following:

- I was unable to be alone.
- I felt empty and unhappy when I wasn't in love.
- When one relationship ended, I'd jump into another one immediately.
- When I wasn't hooked up (pun intended), I joined numerous Internet dating sites, occasionally having more than one date a day.

- I'd go out with women I had previously broken up with, or, continue to date women I knew weren't right for me—all because it was better than being alone.

But maybe the clearest sign that I was hooked on love was the way I reacted when one particular relationship ended. I'm going to tell you much more about Julie, my ex-fiancée, as the book unfolds, but I'll briefly touch on it here because it was this relationship that gave rise to the title of this book.

When she broke off our engagement, which, as I said, happened a year before my disaster with Pam in the Caribbean, I came completely unglued, experiencing panic attacks, sleepless nights, heart palpations—the whole nine yards. I knew I was in bad shape, so I sought out the help of a relationship coach, a woman by the name of *Diana Chapman*. In our first few sessions, while I thought we were merely processing my grief, she saw what was really going on. I was experiencing withdrawal symptoms. I was hooked and addicted to Julie and our break up was akin to me being cut off from my "drug," hence the symptoms.

During one particularly memorable session, Diana was gently trying to help me see this, but I wasn't getting it. So she tried a more direct approach. She told me, bluntly, that Julie was "a drink…with legs." I was like an alcoholic, only my "drink" wasn't booze, it was babes, and in this case that babe was Julie.

That startled me. I was confused and fell silent. After a long moment, she went on. "Roy, if Julie was a drink, what kind of drink would she be?" (She was channeling Barbara Walters.) My mind was spinning, but after a few moments I stammered, "Well, she was sweet…sexy…and, well, kinda salty." I paused and then it hit me. I blurted, "She would be a Margarita!"

That was the moment when all my relationships, and the drama I had experienced, started to make sense. It all fit. My divorce made sense, my relationship with Pam made sense, the compulsive Internet dating made sense and my reaction to losing Julie made sense. It was all the result of one thing: Relying on my partners to make me feel special, alive and whole. It dawned on me that my *entire* relationship history had been one long "drinking binge" in Margarita-ville!

My core problem was that I was a relationship addict. I was hooked on love and my partners were "drinks with legs." And when I got caught up in my addiction, as happened many times and most profoundly with Pam, I called that being "wasted away again in Margaritaville." So I use the term "Margaritaville" throughout the book to describe being hooked on love.

The Portal to Narnia

You know where I'm going with this, don't you? Yes, believe it or not, I'm about to tell you that *your* relationship disappointment, heartache and pain is because you too are hooked on love. Your partners have been "drinks with legs" and you too have spent your love life "wasted away again in Margaritaville." Now, don't get all bunched up when I say that. Give me a chance to explain. I know you bought this book hoping to feel better about your love life. And being told you might, to some degree, be hooked or addicted to love might not be what you had in mind. But I promise that not only will you experience a better love life, you will experience Narnia—relationship bliss—*for recognizing that we are hooked on love is the portal to Narnia!*

That's right. The entry point to the world of enchanted love and magical intimacy is *through* your addiction. It is the *portal* to profound spiritual growth and the creation of authentic intimacy. And even if you do not think, in any way, shape or form, that you are addicted to love, and I'm guessing you don't, I'm asking you to keep an open mind, because the realization that I was hooked on love totally changed my life.

The incredible relationship I now have with my wife would not be possible if it were not for what I learned from my addiction. My spiritual awakening, my growth as a man, the purpose of my life as a writer and a relationship coach—all of it, would not have occurred apart from my relationship addiction. *With all of its pain and misery, my addiction has been my salvation.* It can be yours as well.

But I know that no one wants to think of themselves as being hooked or addicted. It conjures up images of someone living underneath a bridge, wearing tattered clothes, smelling like garbage and clinging to a bottle like a two year old clings to a toy. We don't want to think of ourselves like that. But the good news is this: *I'm **not** referring to that!*

I am talking about something so common, so widespread and so absolutely a part of our culture's consciousness that we don't even know we're suffering from it! Yet, in my opinion, it is ruining more lives than alcoholism ever will. We are a culture completely obsessed with, hooked on and addicted to love and relationships. It's the primary reason why love is so difficult and the divorce rate is so high. Except few see it.

So when I use the word "hooked" or "addicted" to refer to myself, you or anyone else, I don't mean that we're pathetic people who are psychologically damaged and imbalanced, unable to function and lead productive lives. Quite the contrary. I'm speaking about normal, mature, responsible, intelligent men and women, single or married, with thriving careers and lots of friends. I'm talking about high-functioning people who simply believe that life is found *in love.*

Now, of course, I could choose softer words like "dependent," "compulsive," "needy," "attached," "clingy" or "obsessed," for they are all synonyms for what I'm talking about. But as inflammatory and polarizing as words like "hooked" and "addiction" are, I'm going to stick with them because the moment I stopped sugar-coating my issue and owned up to what was really true about me, was the minute my true healing began.

That night by the pool in the Caribbean was the night I dropped the idea that I was "dependent" or that I was a little "obsessive" concerning women and relationships. That was nonsense. I was an addict. Plain and simple. And my life began turning around the moment I dropped the euphemisms and told the unvarnished truth.

Losing Yourself

It may make sense now why I chose to start this chapter with the poem, *Lose Yourself,* by Hafiz. I would encourage you to reread it right now...

Do you see its relevance? Your entrance to Narnia will not be easy. The journey we are about to embark on—from Margaritaville to Narnia, if you will—is often going to feel like you're putting a gun to your head or plunging a dagger into your heart. This journey will ask you to find the courage to really look at yourself. And let me tell you right now that much of what you find might not be pretty. You will have to face your dark side, your crazed ego and your deeply embedded unmet emotional needs. But if you can find the courage to continue when the journey becomes difficult and scary, and I'm forewarning you it will, the result will be a relationship with yourself and with a partner that is beyond your wildest dreams.

"Convince Me!"

The first thing we need to do then, if you're willing to look at yourself, is to determine the degree to which you are hooked and addicted to love, for I realize that you may not be fully on board with the idea yet. Even though you've had your share of pain, heartache and drama, whether or not that means you're a relationship addict is quite another matter—in your mind. I get that. So I want to make a few preliminary comments about addiction in general. Then I want to define exactly what I mean by relationship addiction, because, as I said, most people grossly misunderstand it at first glance. Then the fun begins. I have a thirty question self-test to help you gage just how hooked and addicted you are. And then lastly, I'll tell you how this book will unfold, preparing you for the journey ahead.

Degrees of Love Addiction

So, first of all, as I said, there are varying degrees of relationship addiction. For example, I went crazy with Internet dating, had sex with a bunch of women to try to forget the pain of my break up with Julie (which doesn't work, by the way), went to the Caribbean with a woman I didn't like and had already broken up with, and wasted a year of my life whining about women in general.

But, of course, it can be much worse. Relationship addiction can become a dangerous problem when a person repeatedly calls, harasses and stalks a former or potential lover. Remember the NASA Astronaut who drove 900 miles in a diaper to confront her former lover's partner? That would be a fairly extreme case of love addiction, wouldn't you say? Yet it can go even further than that: think—*Lorena Bobbitt* (ouch). And finally, the most extreme and pathological cases of love addiction are where someone wants to kill the other person so that no one else can have them.

So, there are degrees. And I would guess that about 90% of those reading this book are hooked only to the degree I was, or less. I call us normal, everyday, run-of-the-mill relationship addicts. We're not weird; we're not doing anything illegal or dangerous. Yet our love lives are difficult, disappointing and painful. Even though calling that "addiction" seems a bit over the top, I have found that it gets my attention and makes "recovery" my central priority.

Defining "Hooked"

Addictions, in general, can be broken out into two broad categories: chemical and non-chemical.

We are all familiar with chemical addictions, some of the most notable being alcoholism and smoking. But we can become addicted to non-chemical things like work, exercise, shopping, fame, conflict, power, approval, security, competition, the Internet, suffering, pornography, food, and yes, even intimate relationships.

In my view, there are many, many more non-chemically addicted people in our culture than there are chemically addicted people. In fact, the more materialistic, hedonistic, capitalist and egocentric a society becomes (ours, in a nutshell), the more prone it is to suffer from non-chemical addictions. As we try to find our value, significance and aliveness *externally* through things like money, pleasure, success or even love, it is a recipe for addiction, dependence, obsession and drama.

Sometimes at parties or gatherings, I like to spice things up a bit by asking, "So, what are you addicted to?" (I'm a really fun guy.) The question is somewhat unnerving because it *assumes everybody has an addiction.* And in my view, except for (maybe) the most enlightened among us, we are all addicted to something. Sometimes it is to a chemical, but more often than not, it is to something non-chemical.

However, chemical and non-chemical addictions, as different as they are, share two important similarities. First, both of them give a powerful "chemical hit" and an actual high. When I was involved in Internet dating, there was a palpable rush that I felt meeting a new woman. And secondly, when the non-chemical addict is cut off from his or her "drug," there are real withdrawal symptoms like panic attacks, sleepless nights, obsessive thoughts, just to name a few.

Non-chemical addictions are just as real as their chemical counterparts and even more prevalent in our society today.

Obviously, being hooked on love and relationships lies in the non-chemical category and I define it this way:

> *Relationship addiction is any reliance on another person to give you a sense of your self, alleviate a fear, create a feeling of aliveness, or to validate your worth.*

Put another way, if you are lonely and you think a relationship would fix that, or if you believe that a partners' love will make you feel better about yourself, or if you think you would be happier if you were in a committed relationship, those are signs of being hooked and addicted to love, as I define it here. The essence of relationship addiction is the *reliance* on a person to give you that which you cannot, or will not, give yourself. Drama is the guaranteed outcome of such external reliance, because when you feel that your partner's affection or attention is inadequate, "withdrawal" sets in and drama begins.

Any time we are unaware of, or disconnected from our deepest Self, the Ground of All Being, we invariably turn to *external* things to give us that which we *seem* to lack internally. This turning away from ourselves is the essence of non-chemical addiction and dependence. In other words, to look within is to find you are everything you need; to look without, in order to fulfill a *perceived* need, is to create addiction and dependence, which always leads to drama and suffering. *Relationship addiction is your ego's attempt to find itself in another person.*

The Moment of Truth

Below is a self-test. Answer "T" if the statement is true and "F" if it is false. Think back over the last few years and/or your last few relationships and answer with your first instinct. (Better yet, if you really want the truth, get your best friend to answer for you! I dare you.) Then, at the end, add up your "T's" and score yourself.

1. _____ I am on two or more dating websites and I check my email for matches or responses daily.

2. _____ I have dated people after it was clear to me that they were not right for me.

3. _____ I have ignored or downplayed "red flags" in others because they were hot, handsome and/or the sex was great.

4. _____ I've gone on some dates because it felt better than spending a weekend alone.

5. _____ My friends complain that I disappear when I begin dating a new person.

6. _____ I *think* I can be without a relationship, but it seems I never am.

7. _____ My friends have told me that I move too fast with my new partners.

8. _____ I am a magnet for partners that have been emotionally unavailable or are commitment phobic.

9. _____ I have experienced panics attacks and/or sleepless nights when a relationship has ended or was in serious trouble.

10. _____ I've had so many rebounds in my life—I should be in the NBA!

11. _____ I have taken medication—specifically—to help me deal with a relationship issue or a break up.

12. _____ When a relationship ends, I'm afraid that I'll never find "the one" or that I'll end up alone.

13. _____ I recycle with partners, going back and dating them again.

14. _____ I try my best not to do or say things that would hurt somebody's feelings, especially my partners'.

15. _____ I get stressed out, overwhelmed and over committed because I don't know how to say "NO."

16. _____ I don't express anger, because I'm afraid if I did, others couldn't handle it, or worse, they might leave me.

17. _____ My therapist, coach or friends have told me that they think I have boundary issues.

18. _____ I think a lot of relationship problems are caused because couples don't know how to compromise.

19. _____ My partner has said that no matter how much attention and affection they show me, it's never enough.

20. _____ In relationships, I focus on what the other person wants.

21. _____ *If* I know what I want, I usually don't speak up about it.

22. _____ The ideal relationship is where two people take care of each other and make each other happy.

23. _____ If I could not give my partner what's most important to them, (e.g. sex, money, attention), I fear they would leave me.

24. _____ It's politically incorrect, but life was better in the 50's when "men were men" and "women were women."

25. _____ I have cheated on my partner, or, being single, I have a friend with "benefits."

26. _____ Sex is one of the most effective ways I relieve stress or escape from all that is on my mind.

27. _____ I've told others that I am single when I am actually married.

28. _____ I view pornography weekly and/or go to strip clubs when I can.

29. _____ I "veg-out" by reading romance novels, watching soaps or relationship reality shows like "The Bachelor".

30. _____ I can stop doing any of the things I marked "T"—any time I want.

Total _____

Self Scoring

All of the questions above are expressions of being hooked, addicted or dependent on relationships to one degree or another. Later in this book, we'll take a closer look at them. For now, though, find the range that you fall into.

0 You are either reading this book on top of some mountain in Tibet while taking a break from meditating, or you are canoeing down a river called "De-Nile."

1–7 While your relational life has not been a complete disaster, you've experienced your share of drama. You are really going to enjoy this book because it will not only help you make sense out of your past and present relationships, but you will also be able to assimilate the ideas in this book quickly and experience wonderful results. Read on and enjoy!

8–20 If you fall in this category, take heart. In my estimation, this is where 75% of people are, *if* they are self-aware and honest. You, undoubtedly, have had a lot of pain in relationships and you may be wondering if it's even possible for two human beings to be with each other and not drive each other crazy. Are you willing to do whatever is necessary to clear up the "issues" that have created the messes you've experienced? If so, read on. Real, deep, authentic and healthy intimacy awaits you.

21-30 You, my friend, are my comrade, my "homie!" Welcome. We are cut from the same cloth. Your road will not be easy. You, most likely, will relapse, taking three steps forward and two steps back. You will want to give up, telling yourself lies like, "People never change." I know. I've been there. But if you press on, you will transform your life. You will have to pay special attention, though, to the final section of the book where I discuss the 12 Steps to *Narnia*. You will have to commit to them as an alcoholic would to the 12 steps of AA.

Our Path

Because Jimmy Buffett's term *Margaritaville* has had such profound meaning in my life, I've built the four parts of this book around the four phrases that comprise the final chorus of the song. They just so happen to perfectly describe the journey from relational "drunkenness" to "sobriety," from Margaritaville to Narnia. You may have it memorized, as I do, but here are the words anyway:

Wasted away again in Margaritaville,
Searchin' for my lost shaker of salt.
Some people claim that there's a woman to blame,
But I know it's my own damn fault.

In part one, *Wasted away again in Margaritaville: The Devastation of Dependence,* we'll see that my story is your story and that our story is the very story of human experience. We aren't alone in *wasting* our lives in our thirst for love.

In part two, *Searchin' for my lost shaker of salt: Exploring Our Thirsty Hearts,* we begin digging into what the relationally dependent person is really *searching* for.

In part three, *Some people claim that there's a woman to blame: From the Darkness of Drama to the Dawning of Intimacy,* we not only look closely at who is to *blame* for our pain, but we also begin the healing process by discovering the deep shifts in our consciousness that must take place in order to create healthy, blissful intimacy.

In the final section, part four, *But I know it's my own damn fault: Leaving Margaritaville,* we get extremely practical by focusing our attention on specific practices and actions that are necessary to "sober up" and permanently leave Margaritaville once and for all.

A Final Word

What I have learned about being hooked on love has not come from mere study, research and training, though I've engaged in each extensively. And although I coach people with this issue, my insight is not based on what I've seen work for *others.* I've practiced this in my own life. And I desire to share that with you *because I think it will work for you as well.* I invite you, not to believe what I say, but to *try* what I say, and see if it works for you.

This book is about how the "Mayor of Margaritaville" sobered up, left town and found authentic, blissful intimacy. There is an old saying that captures the essence of this book and my role in writing it, and it is this: "I'm just one beggar telling another beggar where to find bread." Come. Let me show you what I have found.

PART ONE

"Wasted away again in Margaritaville..."
The Devastation of Dependence

CHAPTER 1

The Buddha on Babes, Boys and Bliss

Life is suffering
—The Buddha

Life is difficult
—M. Scott Peck

Life sucks, then you die
—My ex-wife
(on being married to me)

Around the year 544 B.C., Siddhartha Gautama, the man who was to become The Buddha, was thirty-five years old and having a mid-life crisis.

Frustrated and confused by the suffering of life, he wisely decided against medicating his pain with a brand new red chariot and a hot, scandalously-young blonde babe, and opted instead to sit under a Bodhi Tree until he discovered the meaning of life. About six weeks later, the eyes of his heart were opened and he became enlightened, taking the name Buddha, which means, "enlightened one." Under that tree, four truths came to him in stark clarity, the first of which was "Life is suffering."

That part of the story is very well known. But what is not so well known is what happened to him *immediately before* he committed to sitting under that tree.

He had a huge fight with his partner.

I bet you didn't know that, did you? It's true. Where do you think the insight, "life is suffering," came from anyway? The guy had to be in a relationship!

Sid and his partner had conflict and drama, it seemed, since the day they met by the well. Occasionally things were good between them, but more often than not, their relationship was filled with arguments, power struggles, blame and hurt.

She complained that he spent too much time with his buddies watching the camel races every Sunday afternoon and not enough time sharing his feelings with her. He complained that she spent

37

too much money at the Mirage Mall and wasn't interested in sex enough.

But this particular fight was the straw that broke the camels' back. He walked out of the hut not knowing where he was going. He wasn't really mad at her; he was mad at, well,—IT—love, life, relationships in general. "Why are they so hard!" he screamed at the heavens. "All I want is a decent relationship! Is that too much to ask?

Wandering in despair and wondering if love was even worth the effort, he came upon a beautiful Bodhi tree and sat beneath it. He was at the end of his rope. He decided then and there, that he was not leaving that tree, he wasn't going home, he wasn't even going to eat until he discovered why life and love were so damn difficult.

Out of answers, out of hope, depressed and desperate, Sid sat under that tree, meditating and waiting. And then the eyes of his heart were opened and he became the "Enlightened One."

And now you know... *the rest of the story.*

Okay, truthfully, almost all of that is complete fiction. But did I have you going? If so, it's because you know better than anyone that love/life *is* suffering. Isn't that an accurate way to express your experience in relationships? It was for me.

I wanted to be in love. I wanted to be with someone special, someone I looked forward to being with every moment, someone I could talk to, make love with and connect with for the rest of my life. I know that isn't the kind of thing you hear from a man everyday, but trust me, we men want that. Men want to be living in a romantic comedy with a sappy, happy ending too. But it wasn't that way for me. My relationships may have started out in romantic comedy fashion, but they always ended up with tragic, painful endings. My guess is that you can relate.

So, if both men and women want to love and be loved, what's the problem? Why are healthy, fulfilling, lasting intimate relationships so rare? I mean, if we both want the same thing, if we both want each other, why can't we seem to hook up and find the bliss we so desire?

Think of Adam and Eve. They're a perfect example. These two had it made. They were literally made for each other. Their compatibility and chemistry were off the charts. On top of that, there was no career to worry about, no children to raise (at first), no bills to pay. They had no clothing budget, they had no mortgage to pay and gas prices didn't matter. And—this is my favorite part—they were told to have sex as much as possible! But that's not all. Neither of them had in-laws, nasty ex's, dating history or childhood wounds. There was no baggage! They were two healthy people with zero responsibilities. Their only concern was what part of the garden to christen next!

And with that set up, all it took was one landscaping issue (some silly disagreement over a tree and its fruit) along with some wise-ass snake to make all hell break loose! One simple issue comes up and these two perfectly matched lovers living in paradise are at each other's throats! They blame God, each other, even their pet snake. "You did this!...No, it's your fault....You tricked me!"—and my personal favorite, "Actually, God, since you made her for me and she gave me the apple, technically, it's *your* fault!"

Buddha was right. Life *is* suffering.

So, as much as we boys and you babes want bliss, the reality is we are suffering. So again, I return to the sixty-four thousand dollar question: Why do we experience so much drama and pain in our relationships? Well, let's go back and visit our friend Sid, um...The Buddha, one last time.

As we've seen, his first realization was that life is suffering because human nature isn't perfect, life is impermanent and unpredictable, and everything eventually dies (a cheerful thought, huh?). In today's vernacular, this deep spiritual truth is translated as, "shit happens."

The second realization explains *why* life is suffering. It dawned on him that if you *attach* to that which is imperfect, impermanent, unpredictable and subject to death, you will suffer. Relying on, craving for, clinging to or becoming obsessed with anything in the external world, will produce suffering. It's so obvious and simple, isn't?

In other words, if you try to find life from life—suffering happens. We see this everyday. If you are attached to your finances, and the market crashes, you suffer. If you are attached to your athletic ability and you can no longer perform, you suffer. If you are clinging to your youthful appearance and you get old, you suffer.

Everything that we can see, touch, taste, hear and smell; everything and everyone in the visible and external world of form is imperfect and impermanent. If we cling to any of it, if we are dependent on anything external as a life-giving source, we will be constantly and deeply disappointed.

So, here is the answer to our sixty-four thousand dollar question as to why relationships are so painful and drama-filled. We are attached. We're hooked. We've made our partners, or potential partners, our source of meaning and life. That is what I did with women and that is the essence of addiction, for attachment is a synonym for addiction. Recall our definition:

Relationship addiction is any reliance on another person to give you a sense of your self, alleviate a fear, create a feeling of aliveness, or to validate your worth.

Let me explain further.

Have you ever gone skydiving? I never have, but if I did, I would definitely do one of those tandem jumps where you get physically attached to an experienced, expert jumper and ride on their back as you both float (hopefully!) to the ground.

Before the jump, I would be obsessed about whether our connection was secure and if the parachute would operate perfectly. And when we actually jumped, I would choke the life out of my tandem partner, clinging to him or her as if life depended on it, for my relationship with my skydiving partner is my connection to life itself. If our connection were to be severed, I would not simply be sad, I would freak out! I would panic and I would be screaming and yelling and flailing, trying to reconnect with him or her (or anyone nearby), for without that connection, my life is over.

That is how we relationship addicts feel about love, our lovers and our need for a partner. It's more than wanting companionship, it is like life and death. We believe that our partners are essential to our well-being. That belief drives us to attach to them, to hang on for dear life, for apart from them we feel like we would free fall to our death.

And when we are attached and addicted to our partners, being dependent on them as our source of life, what happens when they don't give us the attention and the affection we need, or worse yet, what happens when they leave us? To put it mildly: drama. Drama with a capital "D."

40

Conflict, chaos, pain and suffering happen because we rely on another person to make us feel alive, worthy, safe or special, which, of course, they can never consistently and reliably do. Welcome to Margaritaville.

Sober Up!

Here is a short homework assignment. (Don't worry, there won't be any math.) It's a challenge to "Sober Up!" At the end of almost every chapter, you will have the opportunity to apply what you've learned and make real changes that will revolutionize your relationship experience.

This first assignment is easy. I simply want you to list your partners by name, your "drinks with legs." Who have you attached to, tandem-style? There may only be one, or if you're like me, there may be quiet a few. I'll let you know where we're going with this later.

1. _____

2. _____

3. _____

4. _____

5. _____

CHAPTER 2

You Are Under Arrest for LWI—Loving While Intoxicated

'Cause every time my boyfriend and I break up
My world is crushed and I'm all alone
The love bug crawls right back up and bites me and I'm back
Can't help it, the girl can't help it

—Fergie
Lyrics from *Clumsy*

For about a seven year span, I worked two jobs in two different cities. I played professional tournament golf in the Orlando area during the winter months and then during the summer months, I'd go to Chicago and be a golf instructor.

Not long after Y2K, during my annual pilgrimage south for the winter, I was going to stop in Huntsville, Alabama to play a golf tournament. On the way, I stopped to visit one of my best friends. We played golf together and then went to *Hooters* (where else?) for a couple of beers before I continued on to Huntsville. Two hours later I was pulled over by the Georgia State Police.

As the State Trooper walked to my window, my mind raced. Why was I being pulled over? I knew I wasn't speeding. I was on a two-lane road in fairly heavy traffic. I couldn't speed if I wanted to. Maybe my tail lights weren't working properly.

I rolled down my window, handed him my license and asked, "Officer, is there a problem?" He stood there silently, looking at me and my license with one hand on his gun. Then, leaning in as if trying to get a look inside my car, I heard him inhale deeply through his nose. He said, "Bwwoy, ubeeeendraaankin'?...cus I smell al-co-hollll on yer breattth?" "Step outda veeecle, puleassse." (It took him about twenty seconds to say that sentence.)

I'm pretty sure my heart stopped. I was stunned. Of all the reasons I could have been pulled over, driving while intoxicated never crossed my mind. It was outrageous. It came out of nowhere. It didn't fit.

"What?...Drinking?...No, no officer...Well, I had a couple beers about two hours ago with a buddy of mine, but I'm not drunk."

"Son, I gonna assu one...mer...tiiiime. Step outda veeecle."

I did.

He and his partner proceeded to put me through a gamut of road-side sobriety tests. I stood on one foot with arms outstretched and counted to thirteen; I touched the tip of my nose with each hand; he had me follow his finger from side to side without moving my head; I walked heel-toe-heel-toe up and down the sidewalk; the whole nine yards. I won't bore you will all the gory details, but suffice it to say, it was a big ordeal, and in the end, I was acquitted by a jury in twelve minutes.

But while I was not *driving* while intoxicated, I have been guilty of *loving* while intoxicated. I have spent quite a few years "wasted away again in Margaritaville," enjoying one "drink with legs" after another. What I needed was the Love Police to pull me over and put me through some *relationship* sobriety tests! I would have failed them miserably. I would have been arrested, cuffed, booked, jailed and had the proverbial key would thrown away.

Roll Play

Thoroughly understanding our addiction, what I call, Margaritaville, is essential to evolving beyond it. It's the first step in the spiritual liberation process that leads us to *Narnia*. To that end, let's have a little fun and role play.

Imagine that I just pulled you over, and as I approach your window, you say, "Officer, is there a problem?"

"Miss (or Mr.—make this work for you), I am Officer Biancalana of the *Margaritaville Police Department*. I have been following you and I notice that your love life is swerving all over the road."

"What do you mean? I thought I was loving just fine, Officer."

"Miss, I've witnessed the following: Every time a relationship in your life ends, you immediately jump into another one because you're so afraid of being alone. A few miles back, I witnessed you having the same fight with your partner over and over and over again. And more recently, you have either pursued men that aren't interested in you, or you dated men that you had previously broken up with. And to top it off, even though you know the guy you're currently with isn't "The One," you're still continuing to see him."

"I'm sorry, miss, I believe you may be guilty of LWI: Loving While Intoxicated. I'm going to have to ask you to step out of the car. I want to put you through four road-side relationship sobriety tests: *The Self Test, The Fear Test, The Aliveness Test and The Worth Test.* These tests should reveal if you are, indeed, Loving While Intoxicated."

The Self Test

Back in the mid 1980's, one of the biggest names in professional sports and certainly in professional golf, was the Spaniard, Seve Ballesteros. If you aren't familiar with golf, Seve was the "Tiger Woods" of his day. Like Tiger, he had incredible skill, an infectious smile and magnetic charisma. He was the best and most captivating player in the world. I loved him. He was my idol. I modeled parts of my game after him.

One of the highlights of my competitive career was getting to play three tournament rounds of golf with him in March of 1986. Even though we didn't speak much to each other (his English wasn't good and he was all business), it was an incredible experience.

Three months later I qualified to play in the U.S. Open Golf Championship, and of course, he was in the event as well. As I walked across the practice range, I passed Seve and our eyes met for a second. I quickly looked away. I didn't think he'd remember me, but if he did, I didn't want him to think I was stalking him! The instant I turned away, though, I heard this Spanish sounding voice, like that of Antonio Banderas, saying, "Roy, Roy!" I turned around. Seve was looking right at—*me.* I looked over my shoulder, sure that someone else named Roy was standing right behind me. But no one was there. He motioned me to come over.

He said hello to me as if we were old friends and we shook hands. I just stared at him as if he had a treat and I was a puppy. He said, "Watch, I ask you question." Did I hear right? Did Seve, the number one player in the world, just ask me for help? I thought I was being punked. This was incredible.

Let me put this in a context that may help you appreciate how freaked out I was. Imagine you are a young, aspiring singer trying to break into the music business and you happen to bump into

Mariah Carey in some recording studio and she asked *you* to help her with *her* voice. Do you feel me now? This was outrageous. For the next fifteen minutes, on the range of the U.S. Open, in front of hundreds of spectators, officials, caddies and players, the number one player in the world proceeded to ask my advice on his swing.

Finally, we wished each other luck in the tournament. As I walked off the range toward the putting green, I had to pass through scores of on-looking fans. I'll never forget the way they looked at me. It was as if I was Moses, having just returned from the presence of God (I wondered if my hair had turned white). My chest swelled, my shoulders pulled back, my chin lifted and a cocky smile grew on my face, one that said, "Yea, folks, you saw right. Seve and me are tight!

The king of golf noticed me. He knew who I was. I was special and I felt different about myself.

Though dramatic, this is an example of what it means to get your sense of self from another person. My sense of I/me was enhanced by my relationship to Seve. He knew me and I knew him. I was now special. That connection gave me a sense of my self, it gave me self-esteem.

For a variety of reasons, some of which we will touch on later in this book, we relationship addicts come into our adult years without a sense of ourselves. There is a *perceived* void at the core of our being. We don't know who we are. It's as if the lights are on, but nobody's home. Though we have skin and bones, emotionally we feel empty, invisible and undefined. So we look for "Seve." We look to attach ourselves to a partner whose attention and affection makes us feel whole, someone whose presence in our life becomes our North Star. In short, we turn a human partner into our Higher Power.

Do you fail this relationship sobriety test? Do you rely on another person to give you a sense of your self? And can you see how drama is unavoidable when you ask a human partner to be your Higher Power? What person could reliably meet that need?

The Fear Test

The second relationship sobriety test focuses on how we rely on another person to alleviate fear, particularly our fear of being alone or being abandoned.

At the beginning of this chapter, I quoted lyrics from Fergie's hit song, *Clumsy*. She sings the national anthem of relationship addicts. Read her words again:

'Cause every time my boyfriend and I break up
My world is crushed and I'm all alone
The love bug crawls right back up and bites me and I'm back
Can't help it, the girl can't help it

When one relationship ends, another one begins. This is the quintessential sign of relationship addiction and I call it the "Tarzan Syndrome." We swing from one vine to another, never letting go of one vine unless there's another one to grab on to. Not being in a relationship, for an addict, is akin to a fish being taken out of water. It's more than uncomfortable, it feels life-threatening.

I am not saying being a Monk or a Nun is the highest form of enlightened living. In fact, I believe, that except for a chosen few, we are all made for relationship. But there's a big difference between the natural desire for a partner and craving a relationship because you *fear* being alone. How do you know the difference? Your body will tell you.

When a non-addicted person experiences a break up or a divorce, they will most likely feel incredibly sad and grief-stricken. Their heart will ache; they will cry their eyes out. That's a natural and healthy reaction to loss. But when a relationship addict experiences a break up or a divorce, they *panic*. We don't feel sad as much as we feel danger, peril, and doom. Think skydiving. This panic leads to obsessing over our last "drink" to the point that we make fools out of ourselves trying to get a "refill." And if we can't get "served," we immediately and desperately search for a new "drink."

But in addition to panic, there are other withdrawal symptoms. We experience heart-palpitations, trembling hands, shortness of breath, inability to concentrate, the relentless voice in the head, night-sweats and a constant racy, queasy feeling in our stomachs.

When my fiancée, Julie, broke up with me, surprisingly, I wasn't all that sad. In fact, I barely cried. But, oh God, did I panic and go through withdrawal! When my connection to her was severed, I felt like an untethered helium balloon, in danger of floating away, never to be seen again.

The Fear Test asks you, "How do you respond to a break up or divorce?" Do you become "Tarzan," grabbing on to another "vine"? Do you panic? Do you go through withdrawal? If so, you're loving while intoxicated.

The Aliveness Test

This relationship sobriety test seeks to discover if we are relying on a partner to make us feel alive, happy, radiant and filled with life.

Madison Avenue, the home of geniuses in the field of advertising and marketing, know that they don't sell items like beer, shoes, cars or cosmetics—per say. They sell a *feeling*. They sell how a product can make us feel.

Madison Avenue sells *aliveness* because they know that's what we're really after. They know that more than anything, we desire to feel vibrant, turned-on, happy, powerful, attractive— alive! Madison Avenue does not tell us that we have the very life of the universe within us—if we'll only turn our attention inward to discover it. They tell us, instead, that aliveness is found in the external world of stuff. And let me say something that may surprise you: This is usually not that big a deal. Let me explain what I mean.

If a guy buys *Axe Body Spray* because he falls for the not-so-subliminal message that using the spray will result in beautiful women spontaneously attacking him in public, is that a big deal? And ladies, if you buy *Prada* shoes because wearing them makes you feel sexy and special, is that the end of the world? Of course not. There's no danger and no one gets hurt.

But it *is* dangerous and people *do* get hurt when we believe that a romantic relationship can make us feel alive. And that is exactly what our culture promises through its movies, music, fairytales, novels, advertising and commercials when it speaks of love and romance.

This is not to say that everyone who feels the euphoria of the early stages of a relationship is an addict. The romance phase is an exhilarating time of excitement, wonder and joy. Science has even found that there is a chemical reaction in the body that occurs in the romance phase. But there is a huge difference for us addicts.

The addict doesn't feel alive *without a relationship*. A "sober" person may welcome or even desire a relationship, but he or she feels quite vibrant and alive without one. The addict, however, *needs* one to feel alive. This is why people settle, ignore red flags and recycle with old partners. Any love is better than no love. Love makes us feel alive. Nothing expresses this better than the fairytale, *Sleeping Beauty*. In that fairytale, a beautiful young woman has been cursed and lies asleep, dormant and lifeless. Her only hope of aliveness is the kiss of her soulmate, Prince Phillip. She is "dead" without him and she needs him to resurrect her, to bring her back to life. This may be difficult to admit and own, but can you relate to the story of *Sleeping Beauty*? Are you looking for the love of a prince or princess to make you feel alive? If so, you fail the aliveness sobriety test. But take heart; you're not alone. Of the four tests, this is the most common one. In my experience, it's nearly impossible to find someone who would pass this test.

The Worth Test

This final relationship sobriety test seeks to discover if we rely on our partner, or on a potential partner, to make us feel like we have value, that we're worth something, that we're special.

I have never liked the Christmas song, *Rudolph the Red-Nosed Reindeer*. In fact, to be perfectly honest, I *hate* it with a passion! Go ahead, read the lyrics and see if you can tell why it drives me insane.

Rudolph the Red-Nosed Reindeer, had a very shiny nose,
And if you ever saw it, you could even say it glows.
All of the other reindeer, used to laugh and call him names;
They never let poor Rudolph, join in any reindeer games.
Then one foggy Christmas Eve, Santa came to say:
Rudolph with your nose so bright, won't you guide my sleigh tonight?"
Then how the reindeer loved him, as they shouted out with glee,
Rudolph the Red-Nosed Reindeer, you'll go down in history.

One day they're laughing at poor Rudolph, calling him names, making fun of his goofy red nose; and the next day, Christmas Eve, when the weather is bad, all of a sudden they're Rudolph's best friends! I often have said that Rudolph should have told Santa and his nasty Reindeer to go fuck themselves! But, in the

48

show, Rudolph laps it up. He's so excited that Santa needs him and wants him.

I am Rudolph! Every relationship addict is Rudolph. We've spent most of our adult lives waiting for "Santa"—insert your version of Santa here: a beautiful, smart woman or a handsome, successful gentlemen—to tell us we're special and that they need us and want us. We think, "Wow, if my version of Santa wants *me*, then I must be valuable and worthy!" I know that sounds yucky, but it was so true of me.

I remember back in the early '90's, there was a woman in the church I led who was my "Santa." She was beautiful, open, sexual—and married. So was I. We were emotionally close, but things never became physical. I remember thinking that if I could get this beautiful woman to *want* me, just to *want* me, I would feel validated as a man. I didn't want to have sex—I was too afraid of the ramifications of that at the time—*I just wanted to be wanted.* If this beautiful creature wanted me I would feel valuable, I would feel worthy as a man.

This final relationship sobriety test asks if you rely on your partner, or a potential partner, to make you feel valuable, special and worthy.

If you failed *The Self Test* because you rely on "Seve" for your sense of self; if you failed *The Fear Test*, panicking or becoming "Tarzan" when dumped; if you failed *The Aliveness Test,* waiting for your prince or princess to bring you back to life; or if you failed *The Worth Test*, seeking a "Santa" to validate your worth, then I, as an officer in the *Margaritaville Police Department*, will have to place you under arrest for LWI: Loving While Intoxicated.

Identifying Your Addiction Type

You may be familiar with personality type systems like the *Enneagram* and the *Myers-Briggs*. These, and others like them, are good tools used in the effort to "Know Thyself." Knowing the truth, Jesus said, would set us free. But as helpful as it may be to know your personality type, for relationally dependent and obsessive people, knowing your addiction type is crucial.

Real transformation becomes possible when we can pinpoint exactly what we want our "drink with legs" to give us.

In order to help you identify your addiction type (one has probably already resonated with you), I'd like you to revisit the self-test in the Introduction. Each of the thirty True/False statements are real life expressions and demonstrations of one of the four addiction types.

The Self Test is expressed in statements 1-7, *The Fear Test* is expressed in statements 8-15, *The Aliveness Test* in 16-21, and *The Worth Test* in 22-29. Statement thirty stands alone.

In which category did you answer "True" most often: Self, Fear, Aliveness or Worth? The section with the greatest number of "T's" is the primary need you're looking for your partner to fulfill for you. So, go ahead and label yourself. Which one are you?

For me, frankly, all four of them apply. Each statement in the True/False test has been true of me at one time or another in my life (except for #'s 7, 13, 21). But if I had to choose, it's clear that my primary issue has been "Worth," followed closely by "Fear."

Sober Up!

So, what type of relationship addict are you? Are you a "self" addict, a "fear" addict, an "aliveness" addict or a "worth" addict? As I said, I am primarily a "worth" addict (though I could make a case for all of them). Now, here's your introspective homework assignment.

Write a "what I have been up to" sentence. Combine the person you identified as your "drink with legs" in the last chapter with the addiction type you have identified in this chapter. For example, mine would read:

1. I used <u>Pat</u> to make me feel <u>worthy and special.</u>
2. I used my <u>ex-wife</u> to make me feel <u>worthy and special.</u>
3. I used <u>Julie</u> to make me feel <u>worthy and special.</u>

Write one sentence for each person you listed at the end of chapter one. The value in this is that you're beginning to take responsibility for your relationship history and pain. This is a crucial part of the spiritual liberation journey we are on. You can't enter *Narnia* without it. It's like your passport. So here is an example way to write each one.

- I used TOM to give me my identity and a sense of self.
- I used CINDY to alleviate my fear of being alone and abandoned.
- I used JIM to make me feel happy and alive.
- I used LISA to make me feel worthy and special.

1. _____

2. _____

3. _____

4. _____

5. _____

CHAPTER 3

How I Finished Dead Last in the 2003 U. S. Open Golf Championship

If you don't fix your life, you're gonna put a bullet in your head.
—Julie
My Ex-Fiancée

Consider all of the creative talent we've lost due to drugs and/or addiction: Jimi Hendricks, Janis Joplin, Elvis Presley, Jackson Pollock, Edgar Allen Poe, Charlie Parker, River Phoenix, Andy Gibb, Bruce Lee, Len Bias, Kurt Cobain, Chris Farley, John Belushi, Heath Ledger and Michael Jackson. All were in their 30s or 40s when they died, lives only half-lived.

What a waste. What an incredible waste.

Can you imagine if they were still around? Think about it for just a second. Imagine Hendricks and Cobain continuing to create music that exposes and challenges our culture as it did years ago? And what if Farley and Belushi were doing skits together on *Saturday Night Live*? Or imagine the poetry and the art that Poe and Pollock would be creating today. But they're gone and we will never know what other amazing contributions they would have made to the world.

When I hear stories about lives being wasted on drugs and addiction, I actually feel angry. It's such a terrible waste. Although they each made a lasting impact on us, they could have done so much more with their lives if they had not wasted it on their version of Margaritaville.

And then it dawns on me. I feel angry and depressed because *I am* Hendricks, Belushi, Ledger and Jackson. I mean, I see myself in them, for I have lived my life in a very similar fashion. I have wasted my life on my version of Margaritaville. I too have experienced the devastation of dependence.

Don't misunderstand. I am not comparing my talents to theirs. Nor have I killed myself with my addiction. But I have wasted golden opportunities to use my gifts to achieve my dreams and make a lasting difference in my life and in the lives of those around me. I squandered those opportunities; I let them slip through my fingers. One such opportunity was when I qualified to play in the *2003 United States Open Golf Championship.* I wonder today what might have been had I not played that event "drunk," "wasted away in Margaritaville." Let me tell you about this particular "drinking binge."

A couple of years before the 2003 U.S. Open was even on my radar screen, I faced a critical fork-in-the-road moment. I had been married to a truly wonderful person, Laurie, for about sixteen years, but our marriage had become a functional, co-parenting, platonic relationship. While we cared deeply for each other, we were roommates, living together as brother and sister. There was no passion between us and it had been this way for the vast majority of our relationship. I was deeply, deeply frustrated and disappointed.

We didn't fight often, but if we did, it was always about our sex life. And it was always the same fight. I can remember sitting in bed with her, year after year, complaining and whining about us rarely having sex, pleading with her about how much I needed it and blaming her for not being a good wife. We went to a number of therapists over the years but nothing worked.

In those days, I had no idea that I had an addiction issue, and that I was relying on her to make me feel like a man and to make me feel special. In my mind, she had the problem. Looking back, though, I now realize that I was after more than the physical act of sex. I lacked an inner sense of my own value and worth and I was looking for Laurie to give that to me by constantly wanting to have sex with me. I now believe that at some level, deep in her cells, she knew this. And her body shut down because of it.

But without getting what I needed from her, and not knowing how to turn inward and give it to myself, I felt completely trapped. Divorce was not a step I wanted to take. I had a five year old son and I didn't want to put him through that. So with divorce off the table, but still craving the attention and the affection of women, I turned to strip clubs. And even though I was paying for attention, it felt good to have a woman at least *act* as if she wanted me. Or at least it did for a while. The buzz from that "drink" quickly wore off and I needed something stronger.

So my fork in the road moment came as I sat on my best friend's porch one warm summer evening in Chicago two years before the U.S. Open. Three things were crystal clear to me.

My wife and I were never going to have a sex life together. Secondly, I didn't want to get divorced. Third I was not going to live the rest of my life without sex. So in an amazingly "drunk" moment, I came up with the brilliant idea of leading a double life. Now, I must stop here and say that I am not the least bit proud of what I'm about to tell you. Nor am I proud of the episode I shared in the Prologue, which, by the way, took place five years *after* this moment.* As I sit here today, I am amazed at how cowardly I acted. I know that I will never follow that path again. But I also realize that I was simply acting from the level of consciousness that I had at the time, which, of course, wasn't very high!

So here is the idea I concocted. With my wife and son living year round in Orlando, and me spending the summer months alone in Chicago teaching golf for a living, I had the perfect situation in which to create a double life. I could have a no-strings-attached sexual fling in Chicago and then spend the winters in Orlando with my family. And the next summer I could find a new girl and do it all over again. Sweet, huh? God, I was lost.

I had no luck that first summer. I was pretty scared to approach women. But the next summer the plan worked like a charm. I met a nice woman and we dated and had sex all summer. I broke it off in September when I went south. It was great.

I should mention that not only did I not tell my wife of my double life, I didn't tell any of the women in Chicago either. I told them I was divorced and available for a relationship. I believed that in order to have sex, I couldn't tell them I was married. So each and every woman I met got the same story about how my marriage became a co-parenting, plutonic relationship. Yada, yada, yada. I conveniently left out the part about still being married and being too much of a coward to do anything about it.

The only real problem with my double life scenario was if I fell in love with someone. Then what would I do? I just brushed that off. But four days after I went up to Chicago for another summer I met Julie.

A mutual friend introduced us at a local restaurant/bar and we spent the evening flirting, laughing, dancing and getting to know each other. I told her my bullshit story and she told me about her life. She was amazing. Not only did she survive some really

---

* For a chronological timeline of events in this book, see Appendix I.

difficult times, but she built a very successful career. She was open, honest, funny and quite beautiful. Though neither of us said anything, it was clear that we were very into each other. My birthday was eight days away and I playfully begged her to spend my birthday with me, saying that it would be cruel of her to allow me to be alone. We had that flirty, playful cat and mouse kind of thing going, but we both knew exactly what was happening. There was magic. There was undeniable personal and physical chemistry between us.

When I picked her up eight days later, she had prepared a gift for my birthday. Chocolate chip cookies. That was my "you had me at hello" moment. At dinner we picked up just where we left off, laughing and flirting. Our server asked us if it was our first date. That kind of startled us both, and when we said it was, she said, "Looks like things are going *really* well!" She was right. Oh shit, she was right. I excused myself and went to the men's room.

On the way, I heard a voice say, "Roy, this is no good. This is dangerous. Just walk past the men's room and head out that door and don't look back. She can take a cab home. Get out. This is trouble." But I could no more do that than I could cut off my right arm. I was falling in love and I knew it. And she was too. And I knew that as well. For the first time in years I felt alive. I felt happy. This amazing woman wanted me in every way. It was obvious. It was written all over her. It was written all over us. Even our server could see it.

We got back to her place by 10:00, made love until 1:00 and talked until 3:00. I drove home eating my cookies and having a bi-polar, manic-depressive moment, alternating between Tom Cruise on Oprah's couch and some poor bastard on his way to the electric chair.

The next six weeks, leading up to the U.S. Open, was a period of time in my life that only love stories, poetry and fairytales can describe. Name any romantic movie you can think of, *Sleepless In Seattle*, *When Harry Met Sally*, or *Casablanca* and it still doesn't come close to the movie in which I was starring. We spent at least four nights a week together and when we weren't with each other, we talked on the phone for hours. And we couldn't keep our hands off each other. I literally had more sex in six weeks than I had in the previous five years of my marriage. I'm surprised I played well enough to qualify for the U.S. Open with my legs as wobbly as they were! But I did. And that was the cherry on top of what had been the best six weeks of my life.

Playing in a major championship like the U.S. Open is an opportunity of a lifetime. I had played in four other Opens, but this one was clearly the best opportunity for me to display my talents and change the course of my life. This Open was being played in my hometown—Chicago, at *Olympia Fields Country Club*. This was my backyard. I was comfortable with the course and I was playing great, well on my way to being named Player of the Year in Illinois.

The tournament is conducted over four consecutive days and if I played my best, I was four days away from making millions of dollars and being financially set for the rest of my life. I was four days away from becoming a household name. I was four days away from realizing a dream that began when I was twelve years old. It was all right there in front of me. All I had to do was focus, concentrate and execute and all those dreams could be realized.

Because it was such a big deal to be in the U.S. Open, my wife and son wanted to fly up from Florida to watch me play. And, of course, Julie, the woman I was madly in love with, wanted to come watch me play as well. You get the picture. This is like one of those funny sitcoms where some loser is juggling two women, expending tons of energy trying to keep them from meeting and finding out about each other. Except this wasn't so funny.

I had to tell Julie that she couldn't come to the tournament. I told her that my "ex" was bringing my son up and I didn't think he was ready to meet daddy's new girlfriend yet. But there's more. I was, of course, going to be with my wife and son all the time, especially at night. So, now what was I going to do? It's one thing to come up with a reason to keep Julie away from the tournament during the day, it's another thing to come up with a story that explains why I can't spend the night with her for ten days when I haven't been away from her for more than one night since our first date six weeks ago! But I juggled things, concocted some stories and I had it all worked out.

However, handling the press was another matter. Being the only local guy in the field, the press wanted to do stories on me. I did interviews with radio and television stations and I gave a bunch of print media interviews. I worked hard not mention my wife and son. Julie and her family would be reading and watching everything because they were so excited. So I made sure not to mention them in any interviews.

After having expended a huge amount of emotional and physical energy to control Julie, my family and the press, I thought I had it worked out. I thought I could keep my double life a secret. My best friend, though, thought otherwise.

On Monday, three days before the event was to begin, I had lunch with him and he asked me, "Roy, how do you think your wife and Julie are going to find out about your double life?" (I found it interesting that he didn't ask "if" they would find out, but "how.") I said, "Jim, I think Julie will find out one way or another on her own, but I think I will tell my wife."

How prophetic I was, for just twelve hours later that very thing began to happen. In the Chicago suburban newspaper, *The Daily Herald*, this article appeared Tuesday, June 10, 2003:

Biancalana Still After His Dream: PGA Tour
By Lindsey Willhite
Daily Herald Sports Writer

If you want an individual golf lesson from Tiger Woods, you probably can't write enough zeroes on the check to make it worth his while.

But if you want a lesson from a guy who'll tee off just 20 minutes before Tiger in the first two rounds of the 103rd U.S. Open, simply come up with $100. That gets you an hour working with Mount Prospect's Roy Biancalana, who teaches during the summer at St. Andrews Golf Club in West Chicago.

Biancalana, 43, began teaching there three years ago for two reasons. Well, to be honest, one reason. While he enjoys helping golfers improve their game, Biancalana teaches to help himself. That's why *he leaves his wife and child in Orlando, Fla., from mid-April to mid-September.*

"I'm supporting my habit," he said. "So I can play full-time over the wintertime (in Florida) and afford to go through the PGA Tour qualifying process."

Biancalana, you see, still has The Dream. (Italics mine)

At 8:00 a.m. that Tuesday morning, my friend Jim called me. He said, "Roy, did you see the paper this morning?" I hadn't. "There's an article that mentions your wife and son in Florida." Shit.

At 8:05 a.m. Julie called and my world came crashing down around me.

She was devastated. And I felt like all the air in the universe had just been sucked out of existence and I was going to suffocate and die with my hand on the phone, hearing the pain in her voice. Over the next 24 hours, we spoke a few times and I told her why I had chosen to live a double life and that I was sorry. She told me that "if you don't fix your life you're gonna put a bullet in your head."

Needless to say, I was a complete mess in the tournament. I was so distraught that I literally had trouble seeing the ball lying in front of me. I had no chance of hitting it solid and straight. My friend, Jim, who was out watching me play, said that my posture looked like someone had knocked the wind out of me. I had no focus or concentration. And not only did I not take advantage of the golden opportunity that the event presented me, I literally had the worst performance of my entire professional life.

I finished dead last.

Wasted

What a waste. What an incredible waste of an opportunity.

Imagine what could have been. What if, on my friends' porch two years earlier, I had taken a hard look at myself and seen my relationship addiction? All the evidence was there. And what if I chose to address it then, instead of years later? What might have happened those four days? Would I have won the tournament and changed my life? Maybe, maybe not. And that's the point. I'll never know.

So, look at your life. What opportunities are you not capitalizing on because you are too busy bingeing on babes and boys? What are you allowing to slip through your fingers because your hands are wrapped around "a drink with legs?" What could you be doing with your life, your goals, your marriage, your kids, your career or your personal growth if you weren't so distracted and obsessed with "drinking"? For every minute, every ounce of energy, ever penny we spend "drinking," is time, energy and money we aren't spending on creating our dreams. And that brings devastating results.

These are sobering questions. And I don't ask them to make you feel guilty or to fill you with regret—I've been down those paths and they don't help. But maybe it's time you look in the mirror and consider how much life you're not living because of your relationship addiction. What are you not living, creating and being because you're obsessed, "bingeing," and "bar-hopping" for babes or boys?

I get the chills when I think of how much time I spent on-line surfing dating websites, scrolling through profiles and emailing and responding to messages. And I don't even want to think of the amount of money I wasted on strip clubs and frivolous dates. It probably equals the GNP of a small country.

That said, there is good news. We're not dead yet. We still have a chance to get up off our bar stools, get sober, live our lives to the fullest *and* create a relationship that is healthy. Jackson, Belushi and the others don't have that opportunity. We do. You can sober up and not let any more of the golden opportunities that are right in front of you slip away because you're too "drunk" to seize the day.

Are you willing to take a hard look at yourself? Are you willing to do whatever it takes to sober up? Have you experienced enough devastation from your addiction to walk out of the bar and seek *Narnia*?

Sober Up!

I'll be honest with you. This particular homework assignment is going to be excruciatingly painful. But it is absolutely essential. We have to take a look at how we've *wasted* our lives in our addiction. Part of what makes Alcoholics Anonymous effective is that they don't shy away from challenging their participants to "make a searching and fearless moral inventory" of themselves. And that's what we're about to do. I invite you to breathe deeply into your belly and allow your attention to focus on what your addiction has cost you.

This is not about shame, guilt or regret. It's about waking up. Perhaps you have seen a boxer or a football player get knocked nearly unconscious. When that happens, in order to wake them up and bring them back to reality, a trainer will pass smelling salts under their nose. The chemicals in the smelling salts are so potent that it shocks them wide awake. The following questions are designed to have that effect on you. Read them, meditate on them, "smell" them. I'll answer them first, then you'll have your chance.

1. **How much money have you spent on your addiction?**
I gave up half my net worth in my divorce to pursue my addiction. I also estimate that the cost of maintaining my day-to-day addiction was at least $500 a month. Over the five year period when I was highly active in my addiction, that comes to $30,000! (Now that will wake you up!)

Okay, your turn. How much have you spent on your addiction? Be sure to include things like the costs of on-line dating and/or porn, cosmetic surgery, jewelry, nights out at bars and clubs, visits to strip clubs, clothing to go "drinking" in, dating, gifts, trips and even bigger ticket items like cars. (I used to drive a mini-van. That had to go. What woman wants a man who drives something like that? I purposely bought a car to help me lead my double life. (The 30k mentioned above did not include this!)

_____

_____

2. **What opportunities did you squander in your "binge drinking"?**
This chapter is my answer. What's yours? What opportunities have you wasted because of your addiction? How are you like John Belushi or Jimi Hendricks? If you had put the energy into your career and life that you put into your obsession, where would you be today? Could you have started your own business, written a book, earned your MBA or a PhD? Write what could have been.

_____

_____

_____

_____

3. What price have others paid because of your addiction?
My son and my friends were abandoned to one degree or another while I was "drinking." And there were many nice, sincere women who got tangled up and hurt relating to me. Calculate how your obsession impacted your children, friends, family and lovers.

_____

_____

_____

_____

_____

_____

CHAPTER 4

Committing to a Relationship Revolution

Insanity: Doing the same thing over and over again and expecting different results

—Albert Einstein

One of my favorite movies is *Back To The Future*. You'll recall that Marty McFly, played by Michael J. Fox, was accidentally sent back in time thirty years to 1955 in Doc Brown's *DeLorean* time machine. I love the scene toward the end of the movie where Marty is jamming with the band at his parent's school dance. He does this wild piano and guitar solo that is from another time, his time—the future. When he finishes, the place is stone-faced and silent. They're appalled, staring at him like he is some sort of freak. They've never seen a performance like that before. Unable to explain himself, he simply says, "You guys aren't ready for that, but your kids are gonna love it." In that moment we are reminded that the world has changed dramatically in just thirty short years.

As I write this, my son is fourteen years old and I have moments like that every day. When I was his age, my music came on 8-tracks and 45's; he has an *iPod*. My family had one television with three channels and we used aluminum foil on the rabbit ears for reception. He has his own television in his bedroom that has 3 zillion channels from a satellite dish attached to the side of the house. And when I was a kid, the only thing that was "on line" were my clothes as they hung air-drying in the backyard!

It's a very different world.

In fact, as I look back over the last hundred years or so, the 20th century was a time of mind-boggling cultural evolution. Aside from the invention of weapons of mass destruction, the evolutionary shifts have been enormously positive. Almost every thing about life is better today than it was when my grandmother was born in the year 1900. This is a point I made earlier.

Our intimate partnerships and our marriages have not kept pace with the rest of our advancing and improving society. For example, the following statements seem to be nearly universally true:

- We are much better at honoring each other's rights, but we still don't know how to honor each other's feelings.
- We all carry a phone in our pockets or purses, but we still don't know how to speak to each other without blame and criticism.
- We can surgically open up the chest and heal the heart, but we can't open our mouths, tell the truth and heal our relationships.
- We travel and move about by car, train and airplane, but we don't know how to move our relationships from drama to bliss.

Our lives are certainly richer, easier and more productive today than ever, but our relationships are stuck in the dark ages. Intimate partnerships today function no differently than they did thousands of years ago.

Back to the Future

Let me show you what I mean. Ride shotgun in my *DeLorean* and let's go back in time together. A short, whistle-stop tour of ancient and recent history will reveal that the relationship difficulties of today have been going on for thousands of years.

Our first stop would be all the way back to our metaphorical parents, Adam and Eve. As we've already seen, they are just like any modern 21st century couple. They started out madly in love, and then something goes wrong and next thing you know, they are in a heated argument about whose fault it was that they were expelled from paradise.

Moving on, we come to the biblical stories of Samson and Delilah and King David and Bathsheba. (Did you pay attention in Sunday School? Shame on you!) Both are classic stories of relationship addiction.

If we get back in our *DeLorean* and crank it back up to 88 mph, we can come back to the future where there is no shortage of spectacular expressions of relationship addiction. Take, for instance, Bill Clinton, Elliot Spitzer, John Edwards and Mark

Sanford. These "kings" allowed their addictions to devastate their lives and the lives of those around them. We could even include John F. Kennedy in that list had the press addressed his personal matters as they would today.

But these issues are not restricted to the world of power and politics alone. Athletes, actors and musicians, and of course their families, are devastated by this addiction as well. For example, while the PGA Tour has a squeaky clean image (there haven't been any steroid issues or dog fighting scandals, nor have there been any night club shootings involving golfers), some of the tour's most popular and recognizable single and married players are wildly promiscuous, involved in sex bingeing, orgies and even wife swapping. (Tiger Woods is definitely not the only one on tour doing these kinds of things). Additionally, the strip clubs in Orlando, Florida have the busiest week of their year when the club professionals of the PGA of America come to town in January for their annual merchandise show.

So while the rich and famous make headlines, how many of us "normal" people are ruining our lives and the lives of those around us with this addiction? This brief tour of history brings us face to face with four important points about relationship addiction.

1. Relationship addiction is not a victimless crime.

As we saw in the last chapter, I paid a huge *personal* price for my addiction. I not only wasted my time, energy and money barhopping, but I squandered golden opportunities to advance my life and realize my dreams because I was too "drunk" to take advantage of them. But the devastation isn't limited to us personally. History shows that, like alcoholism or any other addiction, everyone and everything is impacted by it. Our partners are hurt, our families are embarrassed, our children are wounded, our work is unproductive and, in some cases, even our country can suffer. We don't live on an island. Our obsession has far-reaching effects.

2. We are not alone.

Have you heard the saying, "The more personal, the more universal"? Relationship addiction is a very personal issue, but it doesn't appear very universal because it isn't talked about much. People do talk about their relationship disappointments and problems—ad nauseam—but people don't speak openly about being relationship addicts, that they're "hooked and using" or in need of a "drink." So when you and I are courageous enough to admit that we are, in fact, long-time residents of Margaritaville, it is easy to feel isolated and alone. It can feel like we should be quarantined for having some sort of freakish disease that doctors have never seen before. But we aren't alone. *In my estimation, there is no addiction more prevalent in our society today than relationship addiction.* Look around you. It's everywhere. It is nearly impossible to not be infected with the "you complete me" mindset to some extent. It permeates our media, movies, magazines and music. We have been conditioned to look at relationships with a salvation mindset.

Even before Elizabeth Gilbert wrote her amazing best-seller, *Eat, Pray, Love*, she was a successful, nationally-recognized feminist author. Yet in her book she describes her relationship to David, the man in her life, in this way.

> "I was despondent and dependent, needing more care than an armful of premature infant triplets. His withdrawals only made me more needy, and my neediness only advanced his withdrawals, until soon he was retreating under fire of my weeping pleas of, 'Where are you *going*? What *happened* to us?...The fact is, I had become addicted to David."

We are indeed not alone.

3. Margaritaville is not for women only.

I have purposely chosen to use men as examples of relationship addiction in this chapter because most people think that being hooked on relationships, being love-obsessed and being needy and clingy is exclusively a woman thing. But remember, it was a man who said, "You complete me."

It's not unusual for people to look at me like I'm from another planet when I tell them I am a recovering relationship addict. It doesn't fit the stereotype. Their look says, "Men get obsessed over work, sports and, yes sex—but not relationships, not love, not intimacy!"

Well, you'll get no argument from me that the feminine is more concerned with relationships and the flow of love than is the masculine. However, many, many men are obsessed with women.

65

My experience says that is inarguable. It's just that men manifest their obsession differently. For example, if you eavesdrop on two male love addicts at a bar watching a ball game, you won't hear them talking to each other about how lonely they are and how much they want a relationship. Take it from me, though, men who are hooked do feel that way. We just don't *say* it that way. We might try to be macho and say, "I need to get laid!" The point is, men do seek the attention and affection of women to feed their egos and make them feel special. If you look beneath the surface of the male and female m.o., you'll find the exact same core belief running in the background: They are looking for another person to make them happy and complete.

4. It is time for a relationship revolution.

Loneliness, heartache and drama have been the norm in our intimate relationships since the beginning of time. Enough already! It's time for that to change. It's time for a relationship revolution!

That's not to say that we haven't tried to figure this out. During the last half of the 20th century, there was an onslaught of self-help books addressing the topic. We now know that men are from Mars and women are from Venus, yet our hearts are still worlds apart. University professors have published books that have identified essential characteristics of successful relationships, yet the divorce rate has remained basically unchanged.

What we need to do is to take Einstein's wisdom seriously. We can't keep trying the same methods and expecting different results. The methods we've tried aren't working.

Instead of recognizing that men and women are different, and instead of having knowledge *about* relationships, what if we took a completely different approach? What if we actually looked at ourselves? What if we shifted our attention away from anything outside of ourselves and made a commitment to turn inward, to "Know Thyself." That would be different. That would be radically different.

Margaritaville is the metaphor I've chosen to illustrate relationship addiction and the drama that it causes. Narnia is our metaphor for the freedom, intimacy, wonder and bliss that can be experienced in healthy relationships. The two are at opposite ends of the spectrum. *The portal, the pathway, the bridge from Margaritaville to Narnia is your spiritual awakening, your enlightenment, your discovery of who you really are.* You cannot cross over from Margaritaville to Narnia by finding the right partner. You cannot cross over by studying principles. And you can't cross over by dwelling on the past. I've tried. It does not work.

What does work is making the revolutionary commitment to turn your attention inward, seeking to discover who you truly are. When the eyes of your heart are opened, you will find the love of your life. You will finally find the one you have always dreamed of finding—YOU! *Narnia*, my fellow addicts, is you! Everything you've been looking for has been there the whole time. The love of your life is waiting for you and you don't have to go anywhere. All you need to do is to simply look inside.

Are you ready? Are you ready to end the madness, the drama, the pain and suffering that comes from relationship addiction? Are you ready for a relationship revolution?

I hope so, but I must warn you—there are casualties in every revolution. Your journey to "Know Thyself" may be a solitary one. As any alcoholic will tell you, when you decide to sober up, you often lose a significant part of your social network because many of your friends are addicts too. You may or may not know this, but your social network is filled with relationship addicts. The more you wake up to your own addiction, the more you will see this. So when you stop "drinking" and commit to a different path, the inward path, others may not follow. This is "the road less traveled." Jesus said, "For the gate is small, and the way is narrow that leads to life, and few are those who find it."

It could be that your friends and certainly your current partner (if you have one) may not applaud this inward journey, much less join you in it. No matter. Mary Oliver captures the heart of the commitment we must make in a beautiful poem called, *The Journey.*

One day you finally knew what you had to do, and began,
though the voices around you kept shouting their bad advice—
though the whole house began to tremble
and you felt the old tug at your ankles.
"Mend my life!" each voice cried.
But you didn't stop.
You knew what you had to do,

though the wind pried with its stiff fingers at the very
foundations—
though their melancholy was terrible.
It was already late enough, and wild night
and the road was full of fallen branches and stones.
But little by little as you left their voices behind,
the stars began to burn through the sheets of clouds,
and there was a new voice,
which you slowly recognized as you own,
that kept you company
as you strode deeper and deeper into the world,
determined to do the only thing you could do—
determined to save
the only life you could save.

Sober Up!

Are you "determined to save the only life you could save"? Are you ready to commit to a relationship revolution in your life? Have you hit Rock Bottom? Do you believe *Narnia* is possible? And are you open to a new approach—though it's been around for thousands of years? If so, I'm going to ask you to put your name to it, to jump in with both feet, to commit with your whole being. If you're ready, read and sign a life changing commitment:

I, _____ on this day _____, have been a relationship addict, wasting away in Margaritaville. I have experienced devastation because of my dependence and I want a new experience. Today, I make a new commitment to take a loving, yet unflinching look at myself, to turn my attention inward and to discover who I am.

Congratulations! Though nothing tangible has changed since you signed your name a few seconds ago, you have made a powerful energetic shift and it's one that the universe (or God, or whatever works for you) has witnessed. You have set yourself on a new path. Your life will never be the same again.

Onward!

We have now come to the end of Part One. We have made incredible progress. We have learned what relationship addiction is and faced ours squarely. Additionally, we have identified how it manifests in our lives and we have thoroughly come to terms with the devastation it has caused in our lives and the lives of those around us. But most importantly, we have made a clear commitment to our relationship sobriety. All life change begins with commitment and we have done that now.

In Part Two, our journey deepens. Instead of learning about being hooked and its effects, we explore our inner landscape. It's time to get up close and personal and turn our attention inward. Let's explore our stories. Let's explore our beliefs. Let's take a really close look at ourselves. What are we *searchin'* for? How did we get "hooked" like this?

Take a deep breath. I'll start. See if you can see yourself in my story.

PART TWO

"Searchin' for my lost shaker of salt..."
Exploring Our Thirsty Hearts

CHAPTER 5

Bar-hopping My Way through Life: Golf, God, Girls

Wherever you go, there you are

—Confucius

Do you remember *Madge* who starred in that god-awful, yet classic *Palmolive Dishwashing Liquid* commercial from the late 70's and early 80's? If you do, you're already smiling. If you don't, it's because you're less than 35 years old or you're having a senior moment. Either way, I'll set the scene.

There's this poor, unsuspecting woman getting a manicure from Madge. While Madge is working on the woman's left hand, the woman is unknowingly soaking her right hand in *Palmolive Dishwashing Liquid*. So they're chatting away and the woman is telling Madge how washing the dishes is ruining her hands. Madge, the sadistic manicurist from hell, tells her that Palmolive Dishwashing Liquid is great for her hands and then mentions nonchalantly, "You're soaking in it." The woman gasps in horror and pulls her hand away. But Madge reassures her that it's safe for her hands and the woman fearfully puts her hand back into the liquid.

Why do I bring this up? Well, aside from a 30 year crush I have on *Madge* (check her out on *YouTube*—oh, the hairdo!), I bring it up because I'm about to tell you something that may make you gasp and pull away too. Are you ready? The book you're "soaking" in, it's not really a book about relationships—it's a book about enlightenment.

Wait! Don't run off. Let me explain. I never liked the word "enlightenment" either. It has always turned me off. I used to view it as either a cowardly withdrawal from the real world, or believing in new age wackiness, a la Shirley MacLaine. But more than anything else, enlightenment reminded me of guys with shaved heads passing out pamphlets in airports, renouncing all material possessions and abstaining from sex for the rest of their lives! (Sign me up!)

But to my pleasant surprise, I've discovered that those are misconceptions and stereotypes. While some people *do* espouse wacky ideas and others choose poverty and celibacy, these are not requirements to experiencing enlightenment. Enlightenment simply means "to see clearly." That's all it is. It's no more complicated than that. It doesn't mean you quit your job, find your chastity belt and move to Tibet. Enlightenment is like walking into a completely dark room, stumbling and fumbling around, and then finding the light switch—you suddenly see everything clearly. You see—what is. You see truth. You see reality.

So an enlightened *person* would be someone who sees *themselves* clearly. And that is what this book is really about—seeing your self clearly. Relationship addiction (or any non-chemical addiction for that matter) exists only when we don't see ourselves clearly. Margaritaville is populated by "blind people," those who live in the dark, those without clear in-sight as to who they really are. The reliance on another person to give us a sense of self, alleviate fear, create aliveness or validate our worth—our definition of relationship addiction—*evaporates* the instant we see the reality of who we are. So our quest in Part Two is to see ourselves clearly, to become enlightened.

Now, I assure you that I am not a fully enlightened being (as anyone who knows me will attest). The only thing I have in common with the Buddha is the first letter of my last name. My soul is like yours: a mansion with many, many dark rooms in it. My personal commitment is to continue stumbling around in the dark looking for light switches. That said, I have found a few switches and I do see myself more clearly than I used to. And one of the things I've seen is that my addiction has not been limited to just relationships. It has been present in every area of my life. And the same is almost certainly true for you.

There has been an obvious pattern in my life (obvious now, that is) of relying on something external to give me a sense of self and to validate my worth. One of the first "light switches" I found in my darkened "mansion," allowed me to see clearly that I have been up to the same thing in my life over and over and over again. It did not matter if it was personal or professional; it did not matter if I was twelve years old or forty years old, I've been living the same pattern throughout my life.

I am going to tell you my story and my pattern, but as you read, reflect on your own life story and look for your pattern. It's there. What you'll notice is that what's occurring in your *love* life has been occurring in your *whole* life.

Do you remember what your addiction type was from chapter two? Were you a "Self Type", a "Fear Type", an "Aliveness Type" or a "Worth Type"? Bring it back to your awareness. It will blow your mind when you "see clearly" how your whole life has been about the attempt to meet that perceived need over and over again in multiple ways.

"Bar" #1: Golf

I grew up in an atmosphere that valued performance above all else. In my family, you were special and you got noticed when you did something well. My brother got noticed because he was (is) a musical genius. He now plays trumpet in the *San Francisco Symphony Orchestra.* My sisters got noticed for their abilities in school, dance, music and cheerleading. They excelled in those areas. I sought to be noticed through athletics. It was a good thing, too. I made a better sound blowing my nose than I did blowing into a trumpet. And I had no interest in art, music or school. If I was to be special, if I was to be seen as a kid, it was going to be through sports.

In baseball, I was a decent pitcher, but I wasn't much of a hitter. In basketball, I could shoot, but I was slow and couldn't jump. Football wasn't an option. I didn't want anyone to hit me. So even though I worked really hard at sports, I wasn't good enough to stand out at anything. I couldn't seem to find something I excelled at, something that would make my family and friends say, *"Wow! Roy is special. Did you see what he can do?* Nothing I tried was getting me seen. And internally there was a lot of angst about it. I felt sort of invisible.

I don't want to give you the impression that my parents didn't love me. They most certainly did. They didn't grind their kids into the ground with athletic or scholastic pressure, as you see some do today. They didn't tell me that if I wasn't good at something by the age of 12, I was going to be kicked out of the family! It wasn't like that—at all. There were no overt conditions placed on receiving love. There was no refrigerator magnet that said "Succeed or get out!" There was, however, an *atmosphere* that connected your personal worth and value to your performance. In my childhood, you got more accolades for your "doing" than you did for your "being." (That's fairly common, unfortunately.) So, although I loved sports and was reasonably athletic, I was nothing special and I felt like an invisible kid. But then, just after turning 12 years old, I tried golf. It's difficult for me to tell you how instantly good I was without you thinking I'm exaggerating. I was a natural. I didn't need lessons; I didn't need to be taught. I just knew how to hit a golf ball. For those of you who know golf, I made a par on the very first hole I played. That's unheard of. There are people who play for years before making their first par—and I did it on my first try—when I was 12!

I loved golf. But what I *really* loved was the way people treated me because of how good I was. Instantly I was special. My friends had greater respect for me, realizing that I was a lot better at my sport than they were at theirs. The word got around school and teachers would stop me in the hall and say, *"Hey Roy, I hear you're pretty good with the stick!"* At golf courses, grown men would stop and watch me hit the ball—and clap! I overheard my parents brag to their friends numerous times about how good I was. And I could see it in my father's eyes. He looked at me differently. Finally I was noticed. Finally I was special. Finally I stood out. Golf gave me a sense of my self and it validated my worth. I was somebody and that felt GOOD!

I have very, very little memory of my childhood *before* I began playing golf at the age of 12, a fact that has raised the eyebrows of a few therapists and coaches over the years. It aggravates my mother and astounds my siblings. It is as if I *began to exist* at 12 years old, like I was born the moment I made that first par.

The better I played, the more attention and applause I received. It was amazing. The better my score, the more visible I became. So you can imagine the passion with which I approached golf! I was obsessed. My practice habits were legendary. At 13 years old, during the summer, when my friends were sleeping in like "normal" teenagers, I would go with my mom to the golf course at 5:30 am to play before her woman's league started. Other days, when my mother wasn't playing, I put my golf bag on my back and rode my bike to the course. Upon turning 16, when I could drive, I'd practice and play all day, and then take a flashlight out of my bag and put it on the ground behind the hole and

74

practice my putting until midnight! (The grounds crew loved me.) The harder I practiced, the better I got; the better I got, the more special I became.

Golf became my first "drink." Call it a "drink with a grip." It was the first "bar" I stopped at in life to give me a sense of self.

And everything was okay for many years. I won high school tournaments, went to college on a scholarship and turned professional immediately after graduating. In a couple years time, after winning everything in sight (some 40+ events nationwide), I qualified for the PGA Tour, which is the pinnacle of professional golf. And I started out pretty well. In my first event, I was in contention to win, though I didn't. I had a couple other high finishes early that year. But then things started going south. I played progressively worse toward the end of that first year and the downward slide continued through out my second year. My poor performance made me just another no-name guy on Tour. I was not special any more. Even though I was 30 years old, I felt like I was 10 again—invisible.

Initially, my poor play made me work harder and practice more, but it didn't work. I didn't play better. My *sense of self* was disappearing and something had to be done. So I began looking for another "drink." Of course I didn't do this consciously, but my answer to my poor play and my disappearing self was to go to a different "bar." And that "bar" was God.

"Bar" #2: God

At the end of my second year on Tour, I quit golf to go into the ministry. Yes, you read that right. I quit the PGA Tour to be trained to start and lead a local church. Tour player turned preacher. Happens everyday, doesn't it? Nobody, including my wife, could make sense of it. My father, who got a lot of his sense of self from having a son on the PGA Tour, thought I was completely out of my mind. My whole life had been about getting on the PGA Tour, and now, as soon as it was being fulfilled, I was quitting...to become a pastor! Bizarre, I know. But wait until you hear *where* I was going to be trained because then it will make sense to you. My internship was at *Willow Creek Community Church.*

You may not know much about the church world, but *Willow Creek* was like *Harvard, Microsoft* or the *New York Yankees.* It was THE church. Back in the 80's, *Willow Creek* was the largest, most influential church in the United States. With its upbeat music, use of multi-media, drama and messages that speak to real-life issues, *Willow Creek* was revolutionizing the way the world did church. In fact, it was becoming so popular and successful that Willow Creek's leaders wanted to select 12 of the absolute best young spiritual leaders and communicators they could find to start satellite churches around the country. And these churches were not to be small, insignificant neighborhood churches. No, they were to be brilliantly-run, massively effective, mega-churches impacting thousands and thousands of people. They were to be the kind of churches that cause traffic jams on Sunday mornings. In whatever city these churches were planted, the pastor/leader was expected to build *THE* church in that town, eventually building sprawling, multi-million dollar campuses and garnering huge media attention—just like the mother church, *Willow Creek.*

I applied to their internship program and was chosen to be one of "The 12." Now do you see why I quit golf? I was special again. In the spiritual world, being picked to be an intern at *Willow Creek* was akin to being chosen to be a part of the president's cabinet. Even though I loved golf and was on Tour, I wasn't playing well. That "drink" wasn't giving me the buzz it once did. I needed a new drug. Being one of the 12 interns made me visible and special again. That's why I quit golf. But, as I've repeatedly said, I was blind to these motivations.

At the time, I thought God was calling me to use my life and my gifts for the greatest eternal impact possible. I was simply unenlightened as to what was really motivating me. I wasn't able to see myself clearly, that I was bar-hopping from profession to profession looking for a "drink" that would quench my thirsty ego and my need to be special.

So, for seven years I desperately tried to make *Windsor Crossing Community Church,* located in suburban St. Louis, a brilliantly-run, massively effective mega-church that reached thousands of people with a huge budget and a sprawling campus. Today, it is exactly that, but back when I was there in the 90's, it was a small, insignificant neighborhood church that met in a theater at the local YMCA. It was nothing special. I was nothing special. I was becoming invisible again. That was intolerable.

I resigned from the church blaming the congregation for rejecting my personality and leadership style. They, I thought, wanted to be coddled like sheep by a touchy-feely shepherd, rather than being led by a take-no-prisoners visionary like myself. That was bullshit, of course. In fact, it's kind of comical now. I mean, how dare they come to church and expect to feel cared about by their pastor!

The truth was, although I couldn't see it at the time, I left the church for the exact same reason I left golf: It wasn't delivering on my need to be *Mr. Somebody Special*. And, faced with the same exact feeling—that I was disappearing—I sought a new "bar" to serve me a new "drink." The cycle was repeating itself. Professionally, I returned to playing and teaching golf, and of course, I did seek my *self* in it like before, but not to the degree I did years earlier. As the saying goes, "been there and done that." It was time for a new obsession: A "drink" with legs—women.

"Bar" #3: Girls

While golf and God were consecutive obsessions of mine, my addiction to women was something that was occurring throughout my whole life, though it didn't hit full stride until I left the church. For example, I latched onto my high school girlfriend like a parasite; I had some inappropriate things happen when I was a pastor; I had my strip club period, followed by my double life episode. So, if I had eyes to see, I would have seen my addiction long ago. But I was still living in the dark concerning myself. It was only when Julie broke up with me that I *began* to see I had an issue with women. And, of course, my *Jerry Springer* moment with Pam really flipped the light switch on!

I won't spend much time on this phase of my life because that is what this book is all about. I will tell you, however, that I divorced my wife for the exact same reason I "divorced" golf and God. I relied on golf to give me a sense of self and when it failed to come through, I quit. I relied on God/church to give me a sense of self and when that failed, I resigned. And I relied on my wife to validate me as a man through her attention and affection and when she "failed", I divorced her. Same pattern over and over and over again.

At each "bar" in my life, if it didn't make me feel special and seen, I went looking for someone or something else that would. (Is the same thing happening by being a relationship coach and an author? Hummm. Great question, huh?)

Sober Up!

That's my story and my life pattern. I have been addicted to golf, God and girls. They each were "bars" I frequented, places that I went to quench my thirsty heart. What I was looking for in each of those "bars" was to be seen, to be special, to be "Mr. Somebody Special." Whether it was a "drink with a grip," or a "drink with a pulpit" or a "drink with legs," I have played out the same basic pattern throughout my life, for as Confucius said, "Wherever you go, there you are." I was relying on things external to meet my internal needs.

Now it's your turn. What's your story? What's your pattern? When you find the "light switch," and see your whole life clearly, that breaks the pattern and makes genuine love and authentic intimacy possible. Seeing yourself clearly—enlightenment—is THE critical step to the love life you most desire.

Below are a couple of questions to help you see yourself clearly, to enlighten you. Take your time with them. You may have to sit with them for a couple of days. Consider asking someone who has known you for a long, long time for their input (avoid parents or intimate partners—they may be too co-dependent or unconscious to tell you the truth).

1. What is your primary addiction type—Self, Fear, Aliveness or Worth? *(If you didn't identify this at the end of chapter two, go back and do it now.)*

_____

2. What was the primary message you received in your childhood, or, what was valued the most among your family and friends? *(Was it to be perfect, helpful, successful, significant, smart, adventurous, powerful or peaceful? Mine was that you are valued by successful performance, especially in sports.)*

_____

_____

_____

78

3. How have you required your intimate partner(s) to fulfill your addiction type? Be specific. *(Mine would be, "I required them to admire me, compliment me and have a lot of sex with me so that I would feel like a special man.)*

_____

_____

_____

4. Other than relationships, what other "bars" have you frequented? *(Be sure to look at your relationship to money, your career, your body and appearance, education, etc. This chapter has pointed out two of mine—golf and God—but there are many other possibilities!)*

_____

_____

_____

CHAPTER 6

Jerry Maguire Was Full of Shit!

The purpose of a relationship is not to have another who might complete you, but to have another with whom you might share your completeness.

—Neale Donald Walsch

My mid-life crisis began the day Julie broke off our engagement. What followed was, by far, the darkest, loneliest and most agonizing year of my life. It was 12 months of "weeping and gnashing of teeth"—sheer Hell. I was undone; I came apart at the seams. It was a one year panic attack, filled with sleepless nights, heart palpitations and a voice in the head that would not shut up, nearly driving me insane as it endlessly rehashed our relationship.

Love songs made me ache. Movies, restaurants, television shows, even stores at the mall continuously reopened the wound in my heart because they reminded me of her. And my memory constantly assaulted me too. She was the last thought of every night and the first thought of each day. It wasn't my dark *night* of the soul, it was my dark *year* of the soul. It was a mid-life crisis *and* it was the greatest gift I've ever received!

Though that year was brutal, I would not trade it for anything in the world because it gave me the opportunity to stop "bar-hopping" and take a good, hard look at my life. Golf had failed. God, or better put, church had failed. And my relationship with Julie had failed. Nothing worked; nothing delivered; nothing quenched my thirsty heart.

And that's the gift of a mid-life crisis. Strip away all the clichés about middle-aged men buying expensive sports cars and dating young blonds with even more expensive boobs, and what you are left with is a crystal-clear revelation that all your "wells" are dry. I awakened to the reality that my life-sources did not work. Golf, God, girls—none of it worked. And so I had a choice. I could stop the "drinking binge" that my life had been for decades, and do some serious soul-searching—or—I could look for a new "drink with legs." I could allow my pain to tutor me toward spiritual liberation or I could medicate my pain with another woman. To be honest, sometimes I chose to "drink." I "fell off the wagon" a number of times. Other times, though, I stayed with the pain, worked with my coach and sought my growth and enlightenment. It was a three-steps-forward-two-steps-back process. And you may find as you "sober up" from being hooked on love that you too may backslide and go on a spectacular "bender" or two. Don't be discouraged. It just means you're not done "drinking" yet. In my experience, "falling off the wagon" is all a part of the journey to rock bottom. This is what happened with me and Pam, for what I described in the Prologue was such a "bender." It happened at the very end of this year from Hell I'm describing in this chapter. When she hauled off and slapped me in the face, that pain provided me with all the motivation I'd ever need. I had a problem. I had to "sober up."

Of course, it didn't have to come to that. When golf and church failed, each of those moments could have initiated a glorious mid-life crisis and put me on a path towards spiritual liberation. But each time I chose to keep "drinking." Why? Well, when I was in my 20's and 30's, I still believed there was a chance that my performance on Tour or my preaching in church or my pursuit of the perfect woman would make me "Mr. Somebody Special." But I didn't recognize that they were lousy life-sources until my mid 40's.

The reason a mid-life crisis *seems* to occur at *mid*-life is because that's typically when we finally decide to pay attention! But make no mistake about it, mid-life crisis moments are presented to us regularly throughout our lives. The only question is this: When will we open our eyes and learn what they are trying to teach us?

For residents of Margaritaville or anyone stuck in a cycle of drama, disappointment and relational heart-ache, there is a critical message imbedded in a relationship driven mid-life crisis:

You must lose faith in love.

The central, underlying belief that allows relationship addiction to flourish, but yet is responsible for our misery, is the belief that a partner's love is going to save us, heal us, make us happy or whole. We must lose faith in the idea that love will end our loneliness and make us feel alive. We must lose faith that a partner's love will validate our worth and repair our wounded self-esteem. We must lose faith in a love "out there" that will make us feel whole, special, safe, seen and secure. As long as we have even a hint of faith in love, the very love we seek will always elude us.

Faith in love has to be shattered. It must be obliterated from your being. It is a cancer. If even a single cell of it remains in your consciousness, a happy, fulfilling relationship is an impossibility. We must understand that:

Jerry Maguire Was Full of Shit!

"You complete me"—we relationship addicts believe that crap! Of course we would never say so, because we know intellectually that it's a ridiculous notion, but our actions speak louder than our words. And please don't try to tell me that this phrase is just a sappy line in a romantic comedy and that nobody actually believes it or lives according to it. Every "True" answer on the True/False test in the Introduction is a reflection of the "You complete me" mindset.

Now, don't get me wrong, I love the movie. But the notion, as romantic as it is, that we are incomplete and that another person can complete us, is simply a gross misperception of who we are as Spirit Beings.

Soul needs *Mate? Better* needs *Half? The* needs *One?* It's all a load of crap.

Quite possibly you picked this book up because you're having a mid-life crisis of your own, a crisis brought on by another broken, disappointing relationship. In fact, you may be experiencing the horrible withdrawal symptoms I wrote about at the beginning of this chapter. If that's true, if you're suffering and dissatisfied with life, you are actually in a place of grace. Ken Wilber makes this point in *No Boundary*.

> "...[growth] and discovery begins the moment you consciously become dissatisfied with life ...It has been said, and I truly think, that suffering is the first grace. In a special sense,

82

suffering is almost a time of rejoicing; for it marks the birth of creative insight."

So, again, if you are suffering and dissatisfied with your life and relationships, I feel compassion for you, because I know how much it hurts. But you have the opportunity for what Wilber calls "creative insight." You have the opportunity to use your pain as a portal for profound spiritual growth and the creation of authentic intimacy—if you allow it to open your eyes. That's what happened to me and that's why I call my mid-life crisis a gift from God. Here are a couple things my misery helped me to see.

First, the reason our relationships have been nightmares is because we believe our partner's role and responsibility is to meet our needs, whether those needs are emotional, sexual, financial or spiritual. In a very real sense, we have a job description for them. They are to make us feel safe, special, seen and whole. And when they fail to come through for us, and meet our *perceived* needs, drama breaks out in the form of pouting, complaining, getting angry or feeling betrayed.

Haven't you heard yourself say, "My partner will not (take your pick) listen, touch, help, talk, understand, appreciate, call, support, wait, provide, console, entertain or agree—with me. I'm so disappointed that he/she isn't there for me!"

Here's another realization my mid-life crisis gave me. I had never been authentically in love—EVER, and neither have you if you're at all hooked on love. No matter how often I *felt* like I was in love; no matter how often I said the words, "I love you," to one of my partners, I never truly loved them because authentic love is a one-way street. Love asks nothing, needs nothing and requires nothing. It needs no response, no return and no reason. Love has no strings, it has no memory, it incurs no debt and needs no vow. If *need* exists, love can't. If *want* is present, love is absent. Love is not mutual. It is not a two-way street. It is freely given with no thought of reply. Love is unconditional. Always.

And the only way a person can love unconditionally is if they realize that they are absolutely *without need*, that they are full and that they are complete. In other words, the only way a person can love unconditionally is if they know who they truly are as Spirit Beings.

Did I love my ex-wife, Julie or Pam? Hell no. I *needed* them. I needed their love to meet my emotional needs for attention and affection. I had faith in love. Without my mid-life crisis, which was brought on by my break up with Julie, I would never have seen this. That's why I say a mid-life crisis can be such a blessing. Its ideal outcome is not to create cynicism toward love but to eradicate the "you complete me" mindset that is the root cause of the problem. A mid-life crisis is a personal invitation to wake up to our faith in love, the unconscious belief that has been responsible for our misery.

To lose faith in love means to no longer look to love, or your love relationship, as your Source—your source of companionship, healing of childhood wounds, emotional support, self-esteem, security or personal identity. In a healthy relationship, each person is sourcing their aliveness from within. (I will show you how to do this in the next chapter) If you are relying on your partner or a potential partner for your aliveness in any way, you're doomed to perpetually experience fear, drama, power struggle and manipulation. It cannot be otherwise.

If you think you *need* things like companionship and emotional support, it is only because you are unaware of who you are. For example, if you're at the check out line in the grocery store and discover that your wallet or purse is empty, you *need* money, right? But what if, unbeknownst to you, there was, say, $500 in your back pocket? In reality, then, you don't have a financial need in the moment, you just *think* you do because you're unaware of the resources in your pocket. In like fashion, you think you *need* companionship, sex, support, etc., from your partner but that's only because you don't know what is in your "back pocket!" You don't know who you are.

You don't really *need* companionship because you are never alone in the first place. There is no such thing as separation. You are simply unaware of the constant connectedness you have to everything and everyone in the Universe. If you knew who you were and found yourself physically alone on a deserted island, it wouldn't feel any different than being at a party with all your close friends. If you're not aware of this connection, however, you will desperately search for it "out there," in the arms of a partner.

When we awaken to who we really are, we don't *need* sex, for at our depth, our inner being is in a constant state of orgasmic bliss. We just don't realize we're having "sex" all the time. Being unaware of our own inner bliss and the orgasm-like aliveness within us, makes us *think* we need someone externally to touch us and to turn us on.

When our partners aren't "there for us" we become upset believing that we need them to listen and encourage us, but in reality, we are simply unaware that we can source incredible emotional support from within. Having the awareness of our own inner completeness keeps us from requiring anything from our partners. They can't disappoint us because we don't *need* them for anything. This is the end of drama and the launching pad for authentic intimacy.

Please understand that I am not saying that wanting companionship, sex or support from our partners is somehow unenlightened—heavens no! I have all of those things with my wife and I am very grateful for them. But wanting them and enjoying them is far different than *needing* them and *requiring* them. *Who I am is everything I need.* I am a self-sustaining, self-sourcing Being, lacking nothing.

Now, another question may be arising in your mind, which is, "If I don't need a partner for anything, if I am complete and can source all of my needs from within, why bother even having a relationship? Why would I want to have a relationship at all—if I already have it all?"

There are five reasons to have a relationship, none of which is based on any perceived need for completion and none requires faith in love. You may want a relationship for one or all of the following reasons:

1. *Love is who we are.* We have an authentic desire to express what we intrinsically are: love-beings. We want to love. It's the most authentic expression of our innermost being. It's our natural inclination.

2. *Relationships are fun.* Being in a relationship is not better than being single, but you may find that you want to live with, and commit to, another person because it sounds like something enjoyable and fun to do. (It is unless you're hooked on them.)

3. *Sexual fulfillment.* Frankly put, sex with a trusted, loving, intimate partner is better than casual sex and it's definitely better than having sex with yourself!

4. **Raise a family.** Though there is not right or wrong kind of family, a committed relationship may be the context in which you'd like to have and raise a family.

5. **Spiritual practice.** There's nothing like a relationship to surface your issues, trigger old wounds and expose your faith in love. A relationship challenges you to source your aliveness from within—or die! My wife and I are together as spiritual growth allies, agreeing to not only trigger each other, but to invite each other to greater and greater personal evolution as a result of our relationship.

In summary then, we have uncovered some bad news in this chapter. We've come to the realization that love, and our lovers, make lousy life-sources. It's been painful news to swallow, but our mid-life crisis has made it crystal clear that we must lose faith in love. But is there any good news, because frankly, we're still thirsty, aren't we? For example, if it's a hot, sunny day and I'm thirsty, and I discover that Diet Coke is a lousy thirst quencher, that doesn't mean I'm no longer thirsty! It's great to know Diet Coke doesn't work, that I'm wasting my time trying to quench my thirst with that, but I still need something to drink, right?

In like fashion, it's nice to know that a relationship will not quench our "thirst." But the truth is we still *feel* "thirsty," meaning, we are still lonely, empty and feeling incomplete. Even though we know another "drink with legs" won't help, the thirst remains. The good news is that if you look within, you will find that from your innermost Being flows "rivers of living water."

CHAPTER 7

Rivers of Living Water

Not knowing how near Truth is,
People seek it far away—what a pity!
They are like he who, in the midst of water,
Cries out desperately in thirst.

–Zen Master Hakuin

One of my biggest fears in life was to oversleep on the morning of a big golf tournament. When you are playing competitively, the penalty for being late is disqualification. You aren't allowed to play later or with another group, as you can when playing recreationally. In competitive golf, you're kicked out of the event. Your entry fee is not refunded, and more importantly, you've lost your chance at winning whatever prize was at stake, which was usually life changing amounts of money.

Since I made my living competing in golf tournaments, you can imagine the panic attack I would have the moment I realized I had overslept. I'd frantically jump out of bed, skip showering, shaving, eating, brushing my teeth and even peeing! I would throw on some clothes, grab my car keys and drive as fast as I could to make it on time.

So, picture it happening to you. Let's say it's the morning of, perhaps, the Bar exam, or an interview for a job you desperately want or a flight you have to catch for a meeting with your CEO. Insert your own "If-I'm-late-for-this-appointment-my-life-is-over," scenario.

Upon realizing you've overslept, you launch out of bed into crisis mode, right? Your heart-rate skyrockets and in your mind you begin writing your obituary. As you frantically scurry about the house, rushing to get ready, imagine further, how crazed you'd be if you couldn't find your car keys! You'd go completely over the edge, wouldn't you? Like a human pin ball, you'd ricochet through your home, desperately searching for your keys. And if you still came up empty, you'd go "postal" on anyone nearby, interrogating them and even accusing them of stealing your keys! But once it sinks in that you have no hope of making your appointment, that you've passed the point of no return, you would deflate like a hot air balloon, utterly disbelieving that this is happening to you. But it is. So as you reach into your pocket for your phone to tell whoever that you're not going to make it, feeling like a doctor calling the time of her own death, your heart suddenly explodes in joyful embarrassment as you discover that your keys have been in your damn pocket the whole time! Has that ever happened to you? It has me. In fact, that scenario is the story of my life; it's the story of any addict's life. I put it this way:

My life has been the desperate search to find what I already had.

Since the age of twelve, I've been desperately searching for my "keys," yet I was completely oblivious to the fact that they were in my "pocket" the whole time. But being unaware of that truth, I desperately searched for them in golf, God and girls, thinking that if I could be successful with any of those "drinks," I would finally quench my inner thirst. Yet all along, I was unaware that my "keys" were not lost "out there" in any of the three G's, but were always right there in my "pocket", within my very being. Everything that I thought the three G's could give me—a sense of being somebody, a feeling of aliveness and personal worth—were all present within me all along. I just didn't know it.

Imagine, then, the joyful embarrassment I felt when I began to wake up to this truth! I, as a Spirit Being, and therefore lacking absolutely nothing, was acting as if I was invisible, empty and alone! It was hilarious; my life was hilarious; relationship addiction, faith in love, the "you complete me" mindset—it's all hilarious. It's akin to...

- Bill Gates holding a sign saying, "Will work for food."
- Phil Knight, co-founder of Nike, walking around bare foot.
- Owning a Mercedes car dealership, yet riding the bus to work.
- Donald Trump living in a box—in front of his own Hotel!

Zen Master Hakuin was right about us addicts. What a pity we are! We are like those, who in the midst of water, cry out for a "drink." Madness. The only explanation of such behavior is that we have a severe case of spiritual amnesia! Somehow life has bumped us so hard on the head that we've completely forgotten who we are. We've lost touch with our spiritual identity, our Ground of Being and so we seek money, pleasure, thrills, power, status, youth, or in the relationship addicts' case, partners, to tell us who we are and quench our inner thirst. Yet everything we search for "out there" we already have "in here."

Jesus taught this very truth. In his day, there was, of course, no running water. People had to walk long distances to wells to fill their pots and then carry them back to their homes for their household needs. It was an incredible chore. But Jesus told his listeners that it was possible to live a life where "rivers of living water" would flow from *their innermost being*. You could imagine how that must have gotten their attention! No longer would they have to go to external sources to get their needs met. They, of course, thought he meant this literally, but he meant it spiritually. No longer would they (or we) have to go to anyone or anything to quench our inner thirst or to meet our inner needs. With a belly full of water, how silly it would be to ask someone for a drink! Our needs are abundantly met from within by an endless Source of "water" that is infused with life itself.

The message of Jesus, and all the other spiritual teachers throughout the ages, is to wake up from our spiritual amnesia and tap into the endless Source that flows from within. The ancient Greek philosopher, Epictetus, said,

"You are a distinct portion of the essence of God, and contain a certain part of him in yourself. Why then are you ignorant of your noble birth? You carry a God about within you, poor wretch, and know nothing of it."

Know Thyself

Gnothi Seauton—"Know Thyself"—were the words inscribed above the entrance to the temple of Apollo at Delphi. That short phrase forms the most powerful and important personal mission statement the world has ever seen. For the relationship addict, to Know Thyself must become the deepest quest and the overwhelming passion of one's life. Eckhart Tolle says, "What those words imply is this: Before you ask any other question, first ask the most fundamental question of your life: Who am I?"

Margaritaville, as I'm using it, is the metaphorical metropolis that is massively overpopulated by deeply unhappy people who are desperately searching for someone to make them happy. *Narnia*, on the other hand, is the metaphorical ghost town inhabited by a few radiantly happy people who've discovered who they are. Knowing who you are *is* spiritual liberation and the only way out of relationship dependence, drama and dysfunction. In the strangest of twists, the admonition to "Know Thyself" must become *our new obsession*.

Keep "Drinking!"

I'm going to say something that might shock you because it may sound contradictory to everything I've said up until now. But I assure you it's not.

Don't try to stop being a relationship addict. That's kind of a strange thing to say, isn't it? But don't put your attention on trying to stop "drinking." In fact, let go of any effort to stop. Don't put your attention there. "Drink" and binge on babes or boys if that's what you want to do.

My coach, Diana, never chastised me about my crazy actions. I was still heavily "drinking" during the first year of our coaching relationship. And she knew that. Yet not once did she say, "Roy, stop 'drinking'!" She knew that would have been pointless, *for thirsty people seek water.* As long as I was unaware of the Source of "Living Water" that resides within me, I would always head for the nearest well. Thirsty people drink. Actions are always congruent with a person's perceived identity.

She also knew that whatever a person puts their attention on grows. If we obsess about our obsession, we'll only strengthen its hold on us. But if our attention is placed on discovering our deepest spiritual identity, if our obsession, if you will, is to "Know Thyself"—even while you're still living in Margaritaville—then recovery becomes possible.

So in our work together, she didn't try to motivate me to find the self-discipline to stop "drinking." Instead, she turned my attention inward. We talked about my beliefs about myself; we talked about my purpose in life; we talked about anger, fear and sadness and how to handle them and we talked about the relationship personas I've developed in order to survive and get attention from women (we will talk about this extensively in Part Three). We most certainly did not talk about my use of the Internet, where I was going on Saturday night or how often I was having meaningless sex. To deprive water from a man dying of thirst only makes him more desperate.

So, go ahead and let your addiction run wild. Don't worry about your *actions*. But while you are living your love life, put your attention on discovering who you really are. Don't try to stop doing anything; don't try to stop being an addict. Rather, "Know Thyself." By looking inward, you will discover that the self you thought you were, is not really your true Self after all. And once you get even a glimpse of who you truly are, your addiction will dissolve all by itself.

Your life is a reflection of who you think you are. If you think you're incomplete, alone and empty then you will search for someone to make you complete, connected and fulfilled. But if you know who you are and that you have "rivers of living water" flowing from your innermost being, then seeking to quench your thirst with "A Drink with Legs" becomes absurd. Addiction dissolves in the awareness of your true spiritual identity.

So our life's mission, our deepest quest, must be to discover our spiritual identity. This is what Ken Wilber is getting at when he writes,

> "We are the victims of an epidemic case of mistaken identity, with our Supreme Identity quietly but surely awaiting our discovery. And the mystics want nothing more than to have us awaken to who, or what, we really and eternally are beneath or under or prior to our pseudo-self."

Dr. Gay Hendricks, in his book, *At The Speed of Life,* calls us to the same life mission.

> "At some point in our spiritual quest, if it is to be successful, we must realize that we are one with source. We must align ourselves with the source of divinity, own it completely, and begin acting from the awareness that we are made of the same stuff as the universe."

Sober Up!

We have now reached a critical point in the book. Up until now, we've been defining and describing the problem of relationship addiction. We know how devastating dependence can be, we know our addiction type, we've seen that our "bar-hopping" pattern extends far beyond relationships, we've lost faith in love and we know that our life has been a desperate search to find what we *supposedly* already have.

I say "supposedly" because you probably haven't discovered it for yourself yet. How do I know that? Because you can't be both an addict AND aware of your deepest spiritual identity at the same time. The two are mutually exclusive. Just as darkness can not exist in the presence of light, so the darkness of addiction cannot survive in the light of Awareness. So for now, your spiritual identity is just something you've heard about but not something you know for yourself personally and experientially.

Don't feel bad about this, however. I feel like I'm only aware of about 10% of my truest spiritual identity, if that. I have so far to go (though there's nowhere to go). I'm still growing and learning and discovering more and more of who I am. The good news is, you don't need to have some sort of outrageous near death experience to break free of your obsession with love. All you need is a glimpse of your essence and you'll never be the same. Listen to Ken Wilber again.

> "But even the smallest glimmer of One Taste and your world will never be the same. You will inhale galaxies with every breath and sleep as the stars all night. Suns and moons and glorious novas will rush and rumble through your veins, your heart will pulse and beat in time with the entire loving universe."

Back in the Introduction, I said I felt a little bit like Lucy, the lead character in *The Chronicles of Narnia*. Lucy, you'll recall, discovers a hidden door in the back of a closet that turns out to be a portal to another world, a world of enchantment, wonder and beauty. Narnia. Her discovery so astonishes her, so takes her breath away that she can't help but invite her friends to follow her through the closet, the portal, to Narnia.

I want to invite you to follow me through, not one, but *five* portals to your personal Narnia, five "Portals to Presence," as I like to call them. Each of these can give you a glimpse of who you really are in your essence as a Spirit Being, one with Divinity.

Now, full disclosure demands that I tell you that I only made use of one of the following five portals when I was seriously caught in the grip of my addiction. The others were not a part of my recovery process, though I wish they had been. I came to understand most of these "Portals to Presence" *after* I had sobered up and left Margaritaville. Had I made use of all five of them, I would have recovered and sobered up so much faster. I now feel like one of those people who smack themselves in the forehead, saying, *"Wow! I could have had a V-8!"* It's like, "Wow, I could have broken free of my addiction so much faster had I made use of these "Portals to Presence." So even though I didn't practice most of them as I was recovering, it would be malpractice to withhold them from you.

Portal #1: Meditation

By far (and there isn't even a close second) meditation is the most powerful portal that can reveal the essence of who you are. Ken Wilber says:

> "Meditation, whether Christian, Buddhist, Hindu, Taoist, or Islamic, was invented as a way for the soul to venture inward, there ultimately to find a supreme identity with Godhead. "The Kingdom of Heaven is within"—and meditation, from the very beginning, has been the royal road to that Kingdom. Whatever else it does, and it does many beneficial things, mediation is first and foremost a search for the God within."

I'll be the first to admit that sitting in silence and paying attention to my breath and other body sensations *seems* like a complete waste of time. Personally, I'd much rather *do* than *be*, and so I struggle to practice meditation consistently. Recently, however, I went on a ten-day meditation retreat that awakened me to the profound personal realizations that meditation can bring. I now believe that had I been meditating during my year long mid-life crisis, I may have recovered in half that time, and quite possibly, instantly.

Psalm 46 says, "Be still and know that I am God." It seems that spiritual insight emerges in times of stillness, silence and solitude. Spirit doesn't scream or use a bullhorn to tell you who you are. The mind must be quiet and free of distraction in order to clearly hear the "still, small voice" of Spirit. All the great spiritual traditions have stressed some sort of meditation or contemplative prayer for *anyone* seeking a better understanding of their deepest Self, but it is a hundred times more important for those of us obsessed with love and relationships.

The core issue for a relationship addict is that we source life externally. Meditation, even if done in a group setting, is a solitary endeavor and for that reason, is extremely challenging for us. But it's essential. You cannot discover that "rivers of living water" flow from your innermost being if you don't cut yourself off from all other external sources and face your "thirst" with nowhere else to turn. With external life sources unavailable, you'll have to turn inward and you'll be delighted at what you find. If you're committed to "sobering up," discovering your true spiritual identity and creating relationship harmony and intimacy, meditation would greatly serve you.

Portal #2: Nature

Nothing in the physical world teaches us about our deepest spiritual identity and our oneness with God more than nature does. When we peer into the infinite night sky, breathe in the salty ocean air, gasp at a towering rocky mountain or ponder a simple flower, somehow our soul is opened and our loneliness dissolves. This is the one portal that I did practice and it is discussed in some detail in chapter 26.

Portal #3: Children

I was recently in line at *McDonalds* (hey, don't judge me!) and standing next to me was a child who was about two years old. Small and adorable, he was clutching to his mom's leg like a little Koala bear, waiting, I'm sure, for his *Chicken McNuggets*. Eventually, my gaze caught his attention and we locked eyes. His unblinkingly gentle presence held me captive for what seemed like an eternity. I decided to not turn away but to stay open to this little portal and feel deeply into the moment. As I continued to gaze into his bright blue eyes, I saw simplicity, peace and unmistakable Presence. He didn't *have* those qualities, he *was* those qualities and in that moment he reminded me that I was too.

I am in the middle of my life, far removed from where I came from (about 49 years removed at this writing), and far removed (hopefully!) from where I'm going. In that moment, though, this little guru, fresh from eternity, reminded me of who I am—a Spirit Being—and silently encouraged me not to get too attached to this life, for it's over in the blink of an eye.

Spend time around young children. Watch them live; watch them love; watch them laugh. Still unpolluted and unstained by the world, they will reconnect you to "who you were before your parents were born."

Portal #4: Animals

While the depth in a child's eyes is a portal to another time and another place, an animal's presence grounds us, not beyond time and space, but *TO* time and space. They ground us to the very Earth itself and remind us that we are simply another link in, what's been called, the "Great Chain of Being."

Animals remind us that we are part of an ever-evolving planet and not to become too self-absorbed in our own problems. When your love life is in turmoil, nothing else seems to matter. It feels as if the world is coming to an end. We spin emotionally out of control, losing our balance and our perspective. An animal's presence grounds us to our ancestral history saying, "All is well. All has *always* been well. Everything is unfolding just as it should. Relax and trust the Invisible Presence guiding it all."

Portal #5: The Arts

As should be obvious by now, I have a man-crush on integral philosopher Ken Wilber. He is the most brilliant psycho-spiritual thinker and writer of our time, in my opinion. Rarely does someone have a mind like Einstein and yet speak so warmly and eloquently from the heart. Here, he speaks of the power of a painting to open us to another dimension in ourselves, but he could just as easily be writing about any of the arts, whether it's painting, poetry, literature, music or dance.

> "When I directly view, say, a great Van Gogh, I am reminded of what all superior art has in common: the capacity to simply take your breath away. To literally, actually, make you inwardly gasp, at least for the second or two when the art first hits you, or more

accurately, first enters your being: you swoon a little bit, you are slightly stunned, you are open to perceptions that you had not seen before...Great art grabs you, against your will, and suspends your will. You are ushered into a quiet clearing, free of desire, free of grasping, free of ego, free of the self-contraction. And through that opening or clearing in your own awareness may come flashing higher truth, subtler revelations, profound connections. For a moment you might even touch eternity."

If you are fortunate enough to live in a big city like Los Angeles, San Francisco, Chicago or New York, be sure to take advantage of their amazing museums, playhouses and concert halls. Yet, even if you live in a smaller city, most have art galleries and other opportunities to allow the arts to expand the bounds of your spiritual awareness.

Dig Your Well
In conclusion, I'm going to tell you (and remind myself!) something I've told hundreds of golfers after giving them a golf lesson. It applies perfectly to our discussion here. To my former students, I would say, "If you don't regularly practice what I taught you, you will never improve your game." And sure enough, those who practiced improved very quickly and enjoyed the game immensely. Those who didn't, stayed stuck in the same patterns they originally came to me to fix.

The same holds true here. You've been exposed to five incredibly powerful and life changing portals that can help you discover who you truly are. If you actually "practice" these portals, your addiction will dissolve quickly. If you don't commit to them, your recovery will take a long time, as mine did. You will continue to look to your partners to quench your thirst, which will continue to produce the drama and heartache it always has.

These portals help you "dig your own well" and discover the "rivers of living water" present in your innermost being. Your spiritual identity is *not* discovered intellectually. It's discovered by practice and through personal experience. Ken Wilber describes the absolute beauty and freedom reserved for those who walk through these "Portals of Presence":

96

"Suddenly, you do not have an experience, you are every experience that arises, and so you are instantly released into all space: you and the entire Kosmos are one hand, one experience, one display, one gesture of great Perfection. There is nothing outside of you that you can want, or desire, or seek, or grasp—your soul expands to the corners of the universe and embraces all with infinite delight. You are utterly full, utterly saturated, so full and saturated that the boundaries to the Kosmos completely explode and leave you without date or duration, time or location, awash in an ocean of infinite care. You are released into the All, as the All—you are the self-seen radiant Kosmos, you are the universe of One Taste, and the taste is utterly infinite."

CHAPTER 8

Exorcizing the Demon of Loneliness

All man's miseries derive from not being able to sit quietly in a room alone.

—Blaise Pascal

The agonizing year that followed my break up with Julie felt like some evil spirit had entered my body and took over. I'm not kidding. I felt possessed by a demonic, vampire-like creature named Loneliness. I say "vampire-like" because I could resist him when the sun was up, but when the sun went down, it was a completely different story. During the day I was busy giving golf lessons, playing tournaments and being around friends. I also talked multiple times a week with my coach and I was making tremendous progress with her, awakening to my "bar-hopping" patterns, learning of my addiction and processing my grief. I was okay during the day, I could function.

As the sun was setting, though, things would change. Driving home each night to no one, a spirit of despondent isolation would slowly arise in me like an approaching storm. Within minutes the dark clouds would envelop me and drench me in Loneliness. I could not escape this evil commute. Like the irresistible gravitational force of a black hole, Loneliness sucked me in and possessed me.

By the time Loneliness arrived home (I seemed to disappear and Loneliness became me), the feelings were so intense and the pressure was so overpowering, that I felt like a vampire, craving and thirsting for blood. Loneliness needed to sink his "teeth" into the soft, fleshy neck of a woman to quench his thirst and satisfy his craving.

The Internet became Loneliness's salvation as he joined multiple dating sites and spent hours scouring profiles, sending emails and arranging dates. When he wasn't on-line, Loneliness prowled around at pick up bars and even hit on women in malls, grocery stores and health clubs. There was even one time when this demonic vampire brazenly appeared in broad daylight, hitting on one of Roy's female golf clients, something Roy vehemently objected to, seeing that it was completely unprofessional and borderline unethical. But Roy, it seemed, could not summon the strength to resist Loneliness. It was as if he was bound and gagged and forced to watch, in horror, as this demonic being took over his life.

The following day when I regained control of myself, I would tell Loneliness that he was out of control, that his desperate acts were embarrassing us both and that if he'd just stay with the pain and breathe through it and not react to it, he'd find it would pass. But my voice was no match for the overwhelming power of the evil spirit called, Loneliness. For that night, as I drove home, the process would repeat itself.

The Dangers of Loneliness

Loneliness is the inner demon that torments and tortures the relationship addict. If we want spiritual freedom and the ability to create a healthy, intimate relationship, we must exorcize this demon. He must be cast out of us, because when it's all said and done, he is the driving force that governs our lives. He's the one behind the scenes pulling the levers and turning the knobs. He must go.

I am not going to spend time discussing why we're possessed by this demon called Loneliness. What difference does that make? What's important is relief—now! If I tell you that we addicts didn't properly attach to our primary caregivers as young children and that our addiction is an attempt at repairing that damage, does that knowledge make loneliness go away? In my experience, it does not. I'm also not going to spend any more time describing how loneliness feels. You know exactly how it feels. But we definitely need to talk about the insane things it makes us do and how to cast it out.

Loneliness in Action

Loneliness makes us do the craziest things. We date people we shouldn't; we have sex before we're ready; we stay in dead-end relationships far too long; we give second chances to those who hurt us physically or emotionally; we make stupid financial decisions; we expose our children to losers and we don't follow our dreams. The list could go on and on. Loneliness makes us do insane things.

Freedom from Loneliness

When we look back on all the crazy things we've said and done in the name of love, it can all be traced back to this inner demon whose name is Loneliness. So, in this chapter, I want to perform an exorcism—but I promise there will be no spinning heads, no green projectile vomit, no holy water and definitely no screaming, *"The power of Christ compels you!"*

I promise no theatrics other than a simple process that will help you discover that you are, in fact, never, ever—not even if you are stranded on a deserted island—alone. Loneliness is an illusion. It's a real feeling, but it's a real illusion. You are never without love, you are never without companionship and you are never without support. For no matter what your life situation is— single, separated, divorced, widowed, friendless or in a dead marriage—you always have yourself. The end of loneliness occurs when you discover your Self.

Relationship addicts have no relationship with themselves. We are like parasites, who because we can not source life from within ourselves, we seek to attach to a host and suck life from them. And of course, because they're human beings, they are lousy life sources, and so we're constantly disappointed, let down and hurt. We feel alone, isolated, separate, detached, disconnected, deserted, unsupported and lonely because we don't have a love relationship with ourselves. The answer is not "out there." The answer is to know yourself, be your own best friend and fall in love with yourself. But the truth is we can't feel our own aliveness and we certainly don't know how to source it from within. We don't enjoy our own company and we aren't happy with ourselves.

One of my favorite *Seinfeld* episodes is the one where Jerry falls in love with a woman who is just like him. She eats cereal all the time, likes Superman and has the same sense of humor. But after a time, Jerry knows it won't work, saying, "I can't marry someone who's just like me. I hate myself!"

Mark Twain said, "The worst loneliness is not to be comfortable with yourself." Dr. Wayne Dyer echoes that by saying, "You cannot be lonely if you like the person you're alone with."

100

Imagine for a moment, that loneliness was not an issue for you. Imagine that you could feel, I mean really *feel*, deep in your cells, that you are never alone because you have a thriving love relationship with yourself, a relationship in which you source all your needs from within.

Without loneliness, would you ever be tempted to "settle?" Not a chance, right? And why do we stay in unhealthy or dead-end relationships? Because it's better than being alone, that's why. We even support people financially so that they are dependent on us, and therefore, less likely to leave us. And maybe worst of all, many addicts give up on their dreams or compromise their convictions just to keep from losing their partners.

For example, fatherhood was always a huge priority for me, but marrying Julie would have meant living over one thousand miles away from my then 12 year old son. Loneliness overrides even the deepest of convictions.

Think how amazing your life would be if you weren't lonely! And the good news is you don't have to be. The cure is not a relationship with someone "out there." The cure is a relationship "in here." You can cast out the demon of Loneliness by committing to the following process.

Sober Up!

This process is very, very simple, BUT, it will take you anywhere from five to ten weeks to complete. If you chose only one process to do in this entire book, this would be the one I'd most want you to do.

The process begins with a bizarre twist though, one that will make you think *I'm* the demon, not your loneliness. I want you to purposely and intentionally make yourself as lonely as possible. (No, I'm not kidding) Isolate yourself to the point where you feel withdrawal symptoms kicking in. The closer you are to the edge, the more profoundly this process will change your life. Let me be specific about this.

If you are not in a committed relationship, stop dating altogether for the duration of this process. Stay off the dating sites, no phone conversations, no emailing or text messaging. Don't meet anyone for coffee, stay out of bars and pick up places, don't attend any singles functions in church and no sex— definitely no sex. I know what I'm asking is a big deal. Your life's purpose has been to avoid feeling lonely. But you can't feel your own presence when you're out "drinking."

If you're dating someone and it's casual, or if you've got a couple "live ones" on your hook, cut the line. Tell them you're taking some personal time and that you'll call them in a few weeks. Don't worry about losing them. You're wonderful. They'll wait. (Then again, after this process, you won't care if they wait or not!)

If you are in a committed relationship this is a bit more complicated. Ask your partner for a relationship "time-out." Tell them about your "exorcism" and that you need to be alone for a month or more. If you're not living together, that means stop going out with them, seeing them or having sex with them. You can call them (if you must) to see how they're doing, but the idea is to be single and alone. (I realize this is a drastic step to take, but do you want to be liberated from your addiction or not?)

If you are living together, create as much separateness in your home as possible. Move into a separate bedroom and limit your interaction as much as possible. This may be tough if you have kids or other mutual commitments, but do what you can. The purpose is to surface your loneliness issues.

You may be wondering, "What if my partner won't support this "time-out?" Read this carefully. If your partner will not wholeheartedly support your spiritual growth and personal development, which is what this process is all about, you are with the wrong partner! Period.

Once you have made yourself lonely (if you weren't already), you are ready to begin.

1. Make a list of specific qualities you most want in a friend. Not a partner, or a lover or a husband or wife, but a friend. A best friend. What qualities or characteristics do you most want and appreciate in a great friend? I'll help you get started with five, but try to come up with ten.

- **Companionship.** A best friend is someone to keep you company. Whether it's shopping, working out, going to a concert, trying a new restaurant or attending a sporting event, having a companion means not doing things alone.

- **Support.** Best friends are great listeners. We can share our experiences, worries, fears, feelings and desires with them and they listen attentively.

- **Acceptance.** Judging, belittling, condemning, criticizing or attempting to change you are things a best friend never does. They see you as you are and love you for who you are.

- **Challenge.** Best friends want you to live your best life. They're great accountability partners, they dare us to take risks, they push us beyond our boundaries and urge us to take care of ourselves physically, relationally and spiritually.

- **Trusted Advisor.** One of the best perks of a friend is that you can go to them for advice on a problem, a decision, or some challenge you're facing. They know you well and they want the best for you, so their advice is extremely valuable.

2. Prioritize your list. After you've identified ten qualities of a best friend, arrange your list from most important to least.

3. Be your own best friend. Here's where the life change happens. If you put a little creative thought into each quality on your list, you'll find that you can give every single one of them to yourself. You can be your own best friend. You can source them from within to such an extent that you no longer "thirst" for them from without. You will find that there is nothing on your list that only another person can give you.

I'm not saying that if you are your own best friend you won't want a "real" person in your life. Of course you will. We are relational creatures. But you'll want one for an entirely different reason. You'll want a friend or partner so that you can give what you've discovered you are, not to get what you think you lack! You'll be in the relationship to give love, not to get love. As Bill Gates doesn't need money, so you don't need love. You're full. Your needs are met. You are complete, happy, your thirst is quenched.

4. Give each quality to yourself, daily, for a week. Take the first one on your list and give it to yourself every day for an entire week. Source from within. Work through your list. This will take you as many weeks as you have qualities on your list. Ideally that's ten weeks. Love yourself, discover yourself, source from within all that you previously looked for your partners to give to you.

In the event that you are confused as to what this would look like, let me walk you through each of the five qualities I listed and show you what I mean.

Companionship. This one is pretty obvious. Take yourself to any activity or to any place you want to go. Is there a new movie out that you want to see? Take yourself to it. Go with yourself to that new restaurant you've been dying to try. Take yourself shopping, to the beach, to get coffee, to a sporting event or a concert. Don't go alone—take yourself.

It will feel weird at first, maybe boring and definitely lonely. But slowly, if you breathe and don't resist the anxiety that's likely to occur, but simply welcome it and allow it to naturally dissolve in the moment, what you'll discover arising from within is a presence you never knew was there—YOU!

Next, pick out seven things you love to do, but that normally you'd do with your best friend. Commit to doing one of them every day for a week. Go to a movie Monday night, "alone." Tuesday, stop for a drink after work by "yourself," and so on. At the end of seven days, you will no longer feel terrified of being alone, because, well, you aren't!

Support. As for support, having a friend sit with you over a cup of tea and listen attentively as you pour out your heart to them about what you are feeling is, for many, the best part of friendship. However, you can source this from within. We don't need another physical body to be there with us. We can always sit with ourselves and listen attentively as we share our feelings. In week number two, commit to sitting down each and every morning for seven straight days and pour your heart out to yourself with pen and paper. "Talk" to yourself. Communicate with yourself by writing out your thoughts. This you may have done as a young child, writing in your diary. It was brilliant. Do it again.

Acceptance. While a great friend would never judge or criticize us, we can accept ourselves like that too. You can stop criticizing you; you can love you as you are; you can stop rejecting yourself. Be the friend that says my love is not dependent on you becoming thinner, richer, smarter, more patient, successful or enlightened. Be your own support group.

Take out a piece of paper and write out the top seven things that you reject about you, but that a best friend would accept in you. Write your thought and then write your friends loving response. For example, "I hate my lack of patience," becomes, "I accept my impatience." And, "I hate these 20 extra pounds I'm carrying," becomes, "I accept these 20 extra pounds I'm carrying." What would a great friend say to you if you shared your inner critic with them? Speak that to yourself. Love yourself that way. Do that for all seven days on your list. Focus on one per day, posting it on your bathroom mirror or refrigerator door. Love what is. Be comfortable in your own skin. Be your own best friend who accepts you as you are. At the end of seven days, you will no longer be "thirsty" for someone to accept you. You will accept you.

I'll go more quickly through the fourth and fifth ones. I think you're getting the hang of this.

Challenge. Be your own accountability partner. Source the motivation necessary to fulfill your goals from within. This week, choose a goal that you want to achieve and do something toward it every single day for a week. If a best friend would call you and challenge you to stay focused on your goals, source that from within. Kick yourself in your own ass.

And lastly, be your own trusted advisor. Just as you can be your own source of companionship, support, acceptance and challenge, you can also source from within all the wisdom you need to lead an amazing life. You don't need an external source of wisdom. Confusion arises as a result of being disconnected from your inner source of wisdom, guidance and knowingness. You don't have to go outside yourself for answers; you know exactly what's best for you. We are made of the very stuff of the Universe. "The kingdom of God is within you," Jesus said, meaning if you want God's opinion, look inside you.

Of course it's wise to seek advice when it's a subject you truly know nothing about, such as a financial or medical matter. But when it comes to you, your life, your relationships or your family, everything you need can be sourced from within. As a relationship and personal coach, my role is not to tell a person what to do, but to point them inward, so that they can hear and heed their own inner voice and knowingness.

Come up with seven things you would commonly ask a best friend about. Maybe it's how to discipline your kids, what to do about the "red flags" you see in your partner, how to handle your boss or your in-laws, if you should get married, find a new job or sell your home. Focus on one per week and seek your own advice and follow it. Act on it. Trust yourself. You know what you want and you know what to do.

Loneliness—Be Gone!

If you diligently live this process, and repeat it if necessary, you will cast the demon named Loneliness out of your experience and in its place you'll discover a Presence that never leaves you, never abandons you and is always there for you. Loneliness will vanish and you'll see that it was a horrible illusion all along. You are your companion, and although you'd love a partner, you are quite alright because you have yourself. If you're in a relationship, you express the love that you are without a hint of requiring anything in return, for you have learned to tap into the bottomless well of Living Water within you, sourcing support, love, inspiration, security and wisdom from within.

Welcome to Narnia.

Narnia is simply the awareness of who you are.

Now, as you move into the world, you move with an entirely different energy and purpose. Life is no longer a desperate search, for you know who you are. Margaritaville, the "bar-hopping," the "drinking binges," all of it is comical to you now. It cracks you up. How could you have been so blind? How could you have missed all that you are and all that is within you for so many years? It doesn't really matter, though, for you now know, deep in your cells, that you never lacked anything, that life as you knew it was a complete and total illusion. You were never separate or isolated, disconnected or alone. You just thought you were.

You are now comfortable in your own skin. You seek nothing, need nothing and thirst for nothing. No longer striving, craving and thirsty for a love that will make you feel special and alive, there's a relaxed ease and flow about you. You're liberated from seeking something "out there," realizing the abundance you are "in here," thus you are now grounded in Being, and therefore, free. And you're a joy to be around. Your clingy, desperate days are behind you. Whereas friends, partners and potential partners used to feel overwhelmed, turned off or even scared by your neediness, now people can't wait to be around you. Your aliveness and wholeness is sexy and attractive. Ironically, the less obsessed you are, the more attractive you become. You used to be the initiator in relationships, the one who had to make the first move, send the email, pick up the phone and make the arrangements. Now that you can reliably source your needs from within, you find others pursuing you! In the most bizarre of twists, you have to work on setting boundaries so that others don't suck the life out of you!

PART THREE

"Some people say there's a woman to blame…"
From the Darkness of Drama to the Dawning of Intimacy

CHAPTER 9

The World's Oldest Profession

"It's not whether you win or lose; it's how you place the blame."

—Oscar Wilde

Sometimes on late night talk shows, comedians will do a funny bit where they play an actual sound bite from a politician or some other public figure, and then "interpret" their words, telling us what they are *really* saying. It can be pretty hilarious.

I'd like to do that here. I'm going to play an "audio clip" of a conversation that Julie and I had only two weeks into our relationship and then I'll "interpret" what we were *really* saying to one another. (I apologize in advance for this not being very funny.) In order to fully understand this "audio clip," I should remind you of a few key events that led up to this moment.

You'll recall that about thirteen years prior to the conversation you're about to hear, I had quit my life long dream of playing on the PGA Tour to start a church in St. Louis. At the time, I was convinced God wanted me to quit golf, but in reality, I left with my tail between my legs, having been thoroughly embarrassed and humiliated by my performance on Tour. In my desperate attempt to bolster my sense of self through golf, quite the opposite had happened. I left the Tour feeling small and insignificant and looking for something that could repair my damaged ego. Enter God—or better put—church.

Being a pastor of a high profile mega-church was to be my salvation. Finally I'd be seen as *"Mr. Somebody Special."* But when the church didn't grow and people weren't responding to my vision, my management team lost faith in my abilities. I left the church as I did golf: humiliated and defeated.

Running concurrently in the background of both of those events was a deeply discouraging relationship with my wife. I felt she wasn't interested in me as a man but only as a father and a provider. We didn't do much together as a couple and we had no real physical relationship to speak of either. When we did have sex, I had to beg for it. It was horrible. I felt undesirable and emasculated.

I visited strip clubs in an effort to feel some sort of connection to the feminine (I told you this wasn't going to be funny). But, of course, that only diminished my masculinity further. The message I was sending to myself was, "Roy, if you want a woman to desire you and think you're special, you have to pay for it."

Given that context, you're now ready to hear the conversation between Julie and I, and you will quickly notice that what is said is fairly typical for new lovers. Early on in the romance phase of a relationship, each person tells a little bit about their former relationships and what they're hoping they will experience in this new relationship. That's what we were doing in this conversation.

Roy:
"Julie, I'm not that complicated of a guy. I want two things from a relationship with a woman. I want to have fun together. My marriage was so stale; we never did anything together. We just co-parented our son. And I want someone to have sex with me! I was in a passionless relationship for nineteen years and I want a woman who loves sex and loves sex with me. That's all I want, Julie. Nothing else really matters. Play with me and have sex with me—and I'll be a happy man."

Before I translate, telling you what I *really* meant, let me play you her "audio sound bite."

Julie:
"Roy, I've never been all that important to the man in my life. I wasn't really on his radar screen and my needs weren't paid much attention. I guess what I'm saying is that I've never been a man's priority. I'm not looking to be your number one priority, just somewhere in your top ten."

So, those were the actual words we spoke to each other. I wanted to be active with my woman, both in bed and out; she wanted to appear somewhere on my priority list. No big deal, right? It sounds reasonable—even doable. Except for one thing.

110

That is absolutely *not* what we meant. Of course we weren't aware of it at the time, but this is what we were both *really* saying to one another.

My actual meaning:
"Julie, I feel lonely, empty and undesirable. I don't have any aliveness in me. I need you to abandon your two children and put your full and undivided attention on me and our relationship because that will make me feel alive. And I need you to make love to me continuously because it makes me feel special and like a man. *If you do these two things, then I will make you the center of my life.*"

Julie's actual meaning:
"I am so overwhelmed by life that I need you to take care of me. Between my two boys, my home and my demanding 60 hour-a-week job, I need a man willing to make his life be about taking care of mine. *If you will do that, then I will be the woman of your dreams.*"

Unconscious Agreements

So that day, just two weeks into our relationship, Julie and I made a deal, albeit an unconscious one. Like two business partners, we signed our relationship contract, which was this: If I spoiled her, she would devote all her attention and affection to me. And that's what we did for about two solid years. I made her life easy by being her nanny, masseuse and housekeeper, and she made me feel like a man. We, of course, didn't verbalize this agreement exactly like that because, honestly, neither of us was aware of the real meaning behind our words. We just thought we loved each other and were perfect together. We felt like cookies and milk. But what we thought was incredible chemistry, was in actuality, beautifully compatible addictions.

Not only were Julie and I both relationship addicts, we had *complimentary* addictions. Though we expressed them differently, she was my "drink with legs" and I was hers. I looked to her to quench my "thirst" with her affection and attention so that I could feel special, desirable and manly; she looked to my devotion and support to make her feel special and worthy. We were quite literally co-dependent.

But notice something else about our unconscious agreement. It was utterly *conditional*. I would make Julie the center of my life *IF* she would be the woman of my dreams. And Julie would be the woman of my dreams *IF* I made her the priority of my life. We not only had an unconscious agreement at the core of our relationship, it was a conditional agreement! This is why I mentioned back in chapter 6 that addicts never truly love anyone. Love has no agenda; it has no *IF*. It's unconditional. Our relationship was based upon on an *IF*. I would be the man she needed *IF* she was the woman I needed, and vice versa.

I realize how ugly this sounds. I'm making the two of us sound like two completely insane, evil, selfish, manipulative bastards who deserve one another. But if you look closely at your relationship history, which I'll ask you to do at the end of this chapter, you'll see that you and your partners have been doing the same thing, though maybe in different ways. Frankly, we're all singing the same melody. Unless you've done an enormous amount of spiritual growth work you've got this dynamic going on in your relationships, because:

All relationships have, at their core, an unconscious, complimentary and utterly conditional agreement.

Okay, *all* might be a bit of an overstatement. I have to admit that I know of a few couples (maybe five) who have discovered their relationship's unconscious agreement and through an enormous amount of introspective work with a wise coach or therapist, have learned to source their life from within and gone on to create beautiful, authentic intimacy. But even they would agree that *originally* they were attracted to one another because their unconscious needs complimented each other like cookies and milk. These five couples simply saw the unconscious agreement, learned to meet their own emotional needs and created something wonderful. Most other people, however, still have unmet emotional needs and are unknowingly looking for their partners to meet them, which is the essence of relationship addiction.

I hate to sound cynical, but what most people consider chemistry and romantic attraction is actually two addicts whose addictions compliment one another with cosmic precision.

The Roots of Drama

Follow me now, for if you get what I'm about to say, you'll understand why your relationships have been so filled with drama and heartache.

If you have an unconscious, conditional agreement to meet each other's emotional needs at the core of your relationship, and I'm saying you do, and if one or both people *don't,* for whatever reason, hold up their end of the bargain—what happens? That's right. Drama! If the conditions of the agreement aren't being met consistently, the parties go crazy! Call it conflict, fighting, arguing, pain or heartache, whenever someone doesn't do what they've (unconsciously) agreed to do, the darkness of drama breaks out.

The five couples I referred to above—get this!—they do *not* have conflict anymore. They don't fight, they don't argue, they don't blame or criticize. And it's not because they stuff their feelings and don't communicate truthfully. There simply isn't anything to fight about! I suppose they might get annoyed with each other when one of them forgets to stop and get milk on the way home from work, but that's not what I'm talking about. When I say drama, I'm talking about those dark, ugly moments when one or both people feel lost, hurt and utterly disappointed by the relationship and then blame and criticize each other for their pain.

When you don't have unconscious agreements in your relationship, no one can be disappointed when their partner isn't holding up their end of the bargain—because there *IS* no bargain. If there are no unconscious agreements, there will be no drama—ever. Conversely, if there *are* unconscious agreements, there is ALWAYS drama, because no one can consistently and impeccably meet your unmet emotional needs.

Julie and I flowed beautifully as a couple as long as we each kept up our end of the bargain. But when we were no longer willing or able to take care of each other, we manifested the world's oldest profession: Blame.

The World's Oldest Profession

Prostitution is not the world's *oldest* profession—being a blamer is! Way back in the Garden of Eden we see the "first" couple caught in drama, blaming each other, their pet snake and even God! Yes, blaming is the world's oldest profession. (It's unfortunate that we aren't compensated for this, for if we were, we'd all be rich!)

As crass as this is going to sound, this is what is going on in relationships: There is an unconscious agreement to be each other's *hero*—to satisfy, heal and rescue each other from our unmet emotional needs and wounds. When that deal is broken, each person claims the *victim* position and makes their partner the *villain*, blaming them for failing to be the partner they need or once were.

In that paragraph, you see the three points on what's called, *The Drama Triangle*: Hero, Victim and Villain. (I sometimes call this the Bermuda Triangle because when your relationship "flies" into this area, it usually disappears and dies there.) All is well when we are each fulfilling our role as "hero" for the other, but when one or both of us fail to be "Superman" or "Wonder Woman," look out. We sprint for the victim position and blame, criticize and accuse our villain partner for "not being there for us." Let me give you an example of the Drama Triangle at work—in all its dark glory—in my relationship with Julie.

As you know, we mutually agreed early on to unconsciously be each other's hero—I spoiled her; she screwed me—to put it crassly. It still amazes me that it took two years for this arrangement to break down. But eventually it did—it always does. Here's what happened.

The day before Julie broke up with me, she asked me to drive her to work because she was so exhausted from working 80 hours that week. She didn't feel it was safe for her to drive and she was probably right. I was not happy about this at all, partly because I thought she was a workaholic and killing herself, but mostly because we hadn't had sex in over a week! She was too tired. She wasn't holding up her end of the bargain! I didn't think of it that way at the time because I didn't have the understanding that I do now. I just knew that I was upset, feeling like she was taking advantage of me, because I was still holding up my end of the bargain.

I picked her up that evening in a dark mood, and as we were talking on the way home, she casually mentioned a conversation she had with a co-worker that day. She was raving about how wonderful I was because I did 70% of the work around the home, spoiling her rotten. Normally I would have loved that and said something sweet to her like, "Oh baby, your life is so tough, I'm

114

glad to be able to help." But this time I drove in silence, my head spinning with anger and fear. Anger, because it was more like 90%, and fear, because I felt embarrassed that she was describing me as "Mr. Mom" to her co-workers. Was that me? Did I exist to take care of her and her kids? As incredible as it sounds, I really had not seen it as clearly as I did in that moment. I thought to myself, *this ends right here!* In an effort to rectify this one-sided relationship, I said, "I want to have sex tonight." (Stop laughing.) She went ballistic. She blamed and criticized me for being inconsiderate and selfish, seeing what kind of week she was having. I began blaming her for not having any time for "us" and for turning our relationship into a one-sided affair.

In this story, it's easy to see us both race for the victim position and turn the other into the villain. We had been having some drama in the months prior to this fight, but after this one, our relationship ended. It had to. We were no longer willing and able to fulfill the reason we were together, which was to be each other's hero. I didn't want to take care of her life *IF* she wasn't going to take care of mine. And she was too committed to her career to devote herself to meeting my insatiable need for attention and affection. The deal was off. The contract breached.

The Power Struggle

Julie ended our relationship the next day but many couples don't split up like we did. They instead spend years living on the Drama Triangle, blaming and criticizing each other in an effort to get their partner to recommit to the original reason they came together. They may be miserable, but they're hell bent on getting their partner to love them the way they used to. They'll blame, badger, whine, complain, criticize, threaten, shame, manipulate, control or guilt-trip the other person so that they will return to being "the person I fell in love with." (I recently worked with a client who had filed for divorce multiple times in an effort to coerce their partner to change.) This is called The Power Struggle phase of a relationship, and for many couples, it lasts for years, even decades. Blame is most people's favorite "power tool" in this phase and it's used, always unsuccessfully, to restore the relationship to how it felt and functioned in the beginning.

The Big Picture

This section of the book, *"Some people say that there's a woman to blame,"* is designed to help you move your relationship experience from the darkness of drama to the dawning of intimacy. So, let's take a bird's eye view of relationship drama, summarizing what we've said so far.

1. *Attraction.* The first stage in a relationship is when two people meet and find that their unmet emotional needs match with perfect compatibility. They, of course, mistake this for chemistry and fall in love at the speed of light.

2. *Romance.* In stage two, our love birds make an unconscious deal to be each other's life-source, quenching each other's emotional "thirst" by hero-ing for one another. But it's a precariously balanced arrangement based on a conditional, though unconscious, agreement. The lovers are actually in *IF* with each other; they're not in *love* with each other.

3. *Drama.* In this stage, one or both of the partners prove to be lousy life-sources, failing to adequately and consistently meet their partner's emotional needs. In other words, they fail as superheroes. All hell breaks loose when the unconscious relationship agreement is broken and they run for the victim position, blaming each other all the way there.

4. *Choice.* Stage four is where angels hold their collective breath. What will the lovers do? How will they react to their drama and disappointment? The honeymoon is now over. They are at a critical choice point. What will they do? They have three choices:

> a. They can break up, believing they simply had the wrong partner, fall in love again with someone else and *undoubtedly* repeat the same pattern. (I estimate that just under half of all people choose this option.)

> b. They can become curious about themselves, hire a coach or therapist, wake up to their addiction, "lose faith in love," learn to source their aliveness from

within and *undoubtedly* create a beautiful, new authentic relationship. (Congratulations! By reading this book, it appears that you've chosen "b". I estimate that about 5% of people choose this option, and that may be generous.)

    c. They can move on to stage five. (This option is chosen by about half of all people also.)

5. *Power Struggle.* Here, while still oblivious to their addiction, each partner grabs their favorite "power tool", blame, and begins the long, arduous task of hammering their partner into submission. They pound away at them until he or she recommits to meeting their unmet emotional needs—like they used to. This stage can go on for years and drama becomes cyclical and a way of life. However, occasionally one or both partners returns to stage four (Choice), and they again are faced with the same three paths. As I mentioned earlier, the universe continually offers you opportunities to wake up and end the insanity that is your life.

Sober Up!

Before I move on to the next chapter where I'll talk about how to rid your relationships of unconscious agreements and create authentic intimacy, I want to help you make your current or past unconscious agreements, conscious. I want to help you see what you've been up to. This is a vital step in your journey to relationship sobriety. What did you *really* want from love? What was the deal, the arrangement? In an effort to help you see it, here are some questions to ask yourself.

First, and foremost, what was your Addiction Type, the one that you identified back in Chapter Two? You will, undoubtedly, yet unconsciously, be expecting your partner to impeccably meet the need of your particular Type.

Second, what has been your life-long fantasy concerning intimate love and/or marriage? What do you want to get from love? Is it to never be abandoned or to always be cherished? Do you want to feel admired, attractive, smart, special, listened to, provided for, respected, trusted, wanted or spoiled? Your fantasy reveals what you'll unconsciously require from your partner(s). Of course many of these things are present in great relationships, but they're not the *reason* for the relationship. That's what we're getting at here, the *reason* for the relationship, its deep, underlying purpose.

Third, in one word, what did you *not* get in your childhood from your primary care-givers? You will be expecting your lover to heal that wound. (It's probably very similar to your fantasy. Can you see that?)

Fourth, what are your complaints concerning your partner(s), past or present? We complain when something isn't the way we want it, so with a bit of introspection, our complaints can reveal our unconscious needs. I used to complain about Julie working so much. If I thought about it, I may have seen how much I needed her presence to make me feel alive. I also complained when she ate fattening foods. Again, if I had inquired into my complaint I may have noticed how much my sense of self was derived from how she looked. So ask yourself, "What do my complaints reveal about my unconscious needs?"

Fifth, if you "lost faith in love," what would you be letting go of? What would you be afraid you'd never experience? (Do you see that you can give that to yourself? If not, go back and reread chapter 8.)

Your Agreement

After you have considered those questions and even written out your answers, compose your personal unconscious relationship agreement. As an example, mine would be this: *I need the attention and the affection of a woman to make me feel special, alive and manly.* Now write yours.

_____

_____

Extra Credit

The above exercise was about your *personal* need in a relationship. For extra credit and a gold star, expand what you've written to include the unconscious agreement between you and your partner(s). Put it in a conditional format using the word, "IF." For example, here is the one between Julie and me, plus a

118

couple other popular ones. *I will be your nanny and housekeeper IF you give me all your attention and affection.*

Some other popular ones are:

- I won't ask you to face your alcoholism IF you don't ask me to face my obesity.
- I will ignore your affairs IF you keep me in the lap of luxury.
- I won't unleash my anger IF you don't ask me to help parent the kids.
- I won't cheat on you IF you keep yourself fit and have sex with me.
- I'll stay married to you IF you stay famous and successful.
- I won't say "no" to sex IF I get free reign with the checkbook.

_____

_____

Extra, Extra Credit!

When you clearly see that your relationships have been mired in unconscious, complementary and conditional agreements, it dissolves resentment with past or current partners. Does that make sense? Can you see why? You both "loved" the only way you knew how. Seeing myself and my relationship with Julie the way I do now, how can I blame her or have any resentment toward her? Forgiveness arises with the awareness of your unconscious agreement. All I have left for Julie and our relationship is warmth. There is no fault, only fondness. Can you let go of your past hurts?

CHAPTER 10

From Insanity to Intimacy

"In my book, 'If You're Happy and You Know It, Think Again,'
I speak of intimacy or Into-Me-I-See."

—Guru Pitka
From the Movie, *The Love Guru*

In the last chapter, we focused on the darkness of drama and now I want to turn our attention to the dawning of intimacy. In other words, we've seen our "Relationship X-Ray" and it shows a dreadful dark spot that's been diagnosed to be a "cancerous tumor" called an unconscious agreement. If it's not dealt with, our relationships will die a slow death—if they're not dead already.

We know that this tumor, this unconscious agreement, has to be cut out of our relationships if we want any chance at real intimacy. But how? Is there a cure or a "surgical procedure" that can remove the tumor and give us a chance at relationship health and happiness?

Of course there is. In fact, there are a bunch of them. It seems everyone has an approach to transforming drama and creating intimacy. Authors, television personalities, psychologists, coaches, therapists—even you and your friends have theories.

In fact, even his Holiness, the Guru Pitka, has a theory. I know it was a stupid, silly movie, and I also know that if I tell you that I think his Holiness was on to something, it may shred any credibility I have with you. But frankly, the "Into-Me-I-See" approach worked for me and completely changed my relationship life. I now enjoy a thriving, satisfying relationship with my wife because I used his approach and so, believe it or not, I'm going to recommend that you try it as well.

But before I tell you about Guru Pitka's approach and how it can work for you, I want to briefly touch on five other approaches I've used that have spectacularly *not* worked in my attempt to end the insanity of drama. They are very common; perhaps you've tried them as well.

The "Gone Fishing" Approach

The most common approach to ending drama is to go "fishing" for a new partner. If we believe that our partner is to blame for our relationship drama and pain, then it stands to reason that the solution would be to find a new partner. This was the belief that created my double life and subsequent divorce. My ex-wife was the problem, so I went "fishing" for a new one. In fact, my password on my email account back then was, believe it or not, "fishing621"! (The numbers represented the exact date, June 21, that I began my double life.)

The major problem with this approach is that if your partner *was* the problem, then life should be blissful with your new partner. But it doesn't work that way because we take our addictive needs with us and recreate the same problems with our new partners. Trading in one partner for another is as insane as being a driver who is accident prone yet trying to solve the problem by getting a different car!

For that reason, I rarely counsel my clients to get divorced or split up. While there are times when a relationship is broken beyond repair (especially if there's abuse), I usually encourage them to stay together and work on their unconscious agreement rather than projecting it onto their next relationship and ending up in the exact same place. Remember, wherever you go, there *you* are. Stop "fishing" and start fixing—yourself.

The "Mr. Goodwrench" Approach

Another common approach to ending drama is to take your partner to a "mechanic" and get them fixed. This approach, too, is based on the belief that your troubles are your partner's fault, but here, instead of trading him or her in for a new model, you take them in for major repairs.

Before I began my double life, I took my ex-wife to a number of therapists, because frankly, she was screwed up! Since my years of blaming and shaming her for being a shitty wife were not producing the desired results, I decided to enlist a professional to fix her. My thought was that we'd gang up on her, joining forces like some wrestling tag team and body slam her into submission. You can imagine how well that worked.

When couples enter therapy, they usually show up, one as victim and the other as villain. The victim drags the villain in to see "Mr. Goodwrench," seeking to have them repaired. Strangely, if the villain even shows up at all, they're usually willing to take responsibility for their end of the drama as long as the victim does as well. But often, the self-righteous victim won't even entertain the idea that they might have an equal role in the drama and so ironically, it's the person initiating counseling who usually stands in the way of it being successful! Couples therapy or coaching won't work unless *both* people are willing to take 100% responsibility for their particular relationship dynamic. Don't bother going for counseling until both people are curious about their role in the drama.

The "Moses" Approach
This is one of my old favorites. I used this approach to shame my ex-wife into making me happy. I call it the "Moses Approach" because I'd tell her how God wanted her to behave by quoting Bible verses like, "Wives, submit to your husbands", and, "The wife's body does not belong to her alone", and my personal favorite, "Let her breasts satisfy you at all times". My message to her was this: "God said it, you do it, that settles it!" This sort of manipulation is used by many devoted, well-meaning, yet unconscious, church-goers today. Instead of using a therapist or a coach, they use God as a means of getting their partners to recommit to meeting their emotional needs.

The "Putting Lipstick on a Pig" Approach
While this fourth one is not the most dangerous approach used to end drama (the next one is), this one is, in my mind, the single most popular method of dealing with relationship problems today, especially for those of us interested in self-help.

The saying, "Putting Lipstick on a Pig," has been a cliché for years (you probably heard it used in the Presidential campaign of 2008). It refers to the misguided attempt to fix a problem at the surface level. If you put lipstick on a pig, as beautiful as the lipstick might be, it doesn't change the fact that the pig is still a pig! The phrase speaks to the importance of attacking a problem at the root level, where the real problem lies, and not simply making cosmetic changes. Let me give you a few examples of this from my life.

There was a time when I thought my drama and heartache was the result of not being able to understand and communicate with the opposite sex. So I picked up John Gray's book, *Men Are from*

Mars, Women Are from Venus. I quickly learned how to speak Venusian—*as an addict.*

Then I thought my relationship trouble was because I wasn't in touch with my deep masculine core. So I read books like *Iron John*, by Robert Bly, *Fire in the Belly*, by Sam Keen, and *King, Warrior, Magician, Lover* by Douglas Gillette and Robert Moore. I even went to some all male retreats and pounded on some drums. I embraced my power—*as an addict.*

Then I wondered if my childhood was somehow to blame for my relationship disappointments. So I did a little therapy and I read all kinds of psychology books. And through that journey, I learned to love my wounded inner child—*as an addict.*

Then I began believing my painful love life was because I didn't understand personality types and temperaments in myself and others. So I studied *Please Understand Me*, a book that details the Myers-Briggs personality typing system. I also dove into the *Enneagram* personality system, learning from Helen Palmer, Don Riso and Russ Hudson. Great stuff. Soon, I understood myself and others—*as an addict.*

Single women are often extremely frustrated with men and dating. So they pick up, *He's Just Not That Into You.* Another good read. Now you understand men—*as an addict.*

Are you getting my point? All these things don't transform our relationship experience because they don't address the root issue—addiction. Most of us are "Lipstick Lovers," learning techniques, tools and tricks on how to *manage our addictions rather than transform them.* We're trying to *cope* with our unconscious agreements, rather than expose them for the insanity that they are. We're trying to learn *skills* to control relationships *on* the Drama Triangle, rather than opting out of it altogether.

I'm as guilty of this as anyone. I have more lipstick on me than all the hookers on Hollywood Boulevard combined! I've tried all the cosmetic changes and yet the root problem was never being addressed. I was looking to a woman to alleviate my fear of abandonment and validate my worth as a man. I had "faith in love." I was an addict and no amount of lipstick could pretty me up.

We've got it backwards. We're detailing a car that won't start. We're "Putting Lipstick on a Pig." There's nothing wrong with detailing or lipstick. The books and tools I referred to are wonderful. I mean no disrespect at all. Read and study widely. But don't lose sight of your root issue. You're a pig! (smile) So go ahead and learn to communicate with the opposite sex, learn about personality types, delve into your childhood (we will at bit in chapters to come), embrace your inner goddess or warrior, but don't miss what's really causing your drama, heartache and pain. The root cause is that we suffer from a severe case of spiritual amnesia, having forgotten who we truly are, and consequently look to our partners, and love itself, to alleviate loneliness and make us feel special, alive and whole. Our addiction—our "pigness"—is the problem. And if the root problem isn't addressed, we will never experience relationship bliss.

The "Imago" Approach
The final ineffective approach that I've used to end drama in my life and create healthy intimacy comes from the New York Times best-selling author Harville Hendrix (not to be confused with Gay Hendricks, whose work I greatly admire and quote often in this book). Hendrix has sold over a million copies of *Getting the Love You Want: A Guide for Couples*, and while his intentions are admirable, in my opinion, it is a dangerous book. His "Imago" system, while claiming to create a "Conscious Marriage," actually *creates* relationship addiction! Even though his book was originally published in 1988, it's still quite popular today and so I feel it necessary to discuss it briefly.

Hendrix's view is that we enter adulthood with wounds from our childhood and that we are unconsciously looking for a partner to love us in a way that heals those deep wounds. In order for this healing to take place, Hendrix says, we instinctively seek a partner who is like our parents (This is where he gets the term "Imago," which means *image* in Latin). Once you find your new "mommy" or "daddy", then you want them to love you in the way you originally needed your parents to love you, thereby healing you and making you whole. Eventually though, your partner/parent will fail you and when they do, the result is drama.

I basically agree with him up to this point because most people do seek to be re-parented by their partners. What concerns me, however, is his *solution*. I find it particularly dangerous because:

- He does not urge each person to turn their attention inward, to discover that in the present moment, there are no wounds, there are no needs and there are no problems. Our childhood wounds only exist today if we identify with them and keep them alive by reacting to them as if they were happening in the present.

- Hendrix doesn't believe you can let go of your past. You must relive it until your partner's love heals it. But this way of thinking keeps you stuck in your story because whatever you put your attention on grows.

- He does not encourage each person to recognize who they truly are, that they are whole, complete and have access to Rivers of Living Water that flow from their innermost Being. We are damaged goods, in his view, in need of significant repair.

Hendrix's system says that healing must come from "out there," and more specifically, it must come from your partner who is the spitting image of your parents. (In his system, single people are basically out of luck. They must find a partner willing to re-parent them if they're ever going to be a healthy and whole.) The "Imago" system creates dependency and requires partners to function as rescuing heroes.

If Hendrix were to counsel Julie and I, this is how it would sound:

- "Julie, Roy's mother wasn't available and affectionate to him and you're like that too. You need to be his mommy and give him the attention and the affection he needs to be healed of his wounds. Besides, Julie, being less obsessed about work is just what you need to do anyway."

- "Roy, Julie's dad was absent and never made her the center of his world. You need to be her daddy and prioritize her, allowing her to flourish in your loving care. Besides, being less self-absorbed is just what you need anyway."

"Imago" therapy is dangerous because it encourages us to rely on someone external for our happiness and growth. That is exactly what it means to be an addict.

The Guru Pitka's Approach

Enough of what didn't work for me (and what won't work for you). Let me tell you what did. And again, I don't come to you with a message from God or from years of scholarly research while sitting in some ivory tower, nor am I even going to share a bunch of stories from my clients lives. I come to you from the trenches of my own life and personal experience—and that's why I don't *think* this works, I *know* it works. And what worked for me was the "Into-Me-I-See" approach, espoused by none other than the His Holiness, The Guru Pitka.

Here's the question before us. How do we end the darkness of drama and experience the blissful dawning of authentic intimacy? We know that the answer is not found "out there" in our mulligan mommy or daddy, nor is it found in a new or improved partner or even in a new shade of "lipstick."

You already know the answer—it is found by looking within. In-sight or as Pitka put it, "Into-Me-I-See," is the commitment to Self-knowing, or as the ancient Greeks put it, "Know Thyself." Drama ends and intimacy dawns the moment we see ourselves clearly, when we wake up from our spiritual amnesia and see our Original Face, recognizing our deepest Essence and our oneness with Source.

Addiction, and all that comes with it, dissolves in the awareness of who we are. Drama, conflict, loneliness and dependence dissolve with the discovery of our true nature. Jesus said, "Is it not written…ye are gods?"

Waking up from your spiritual amnesia, you realize that you are not an addict…

**You are love. You are peace. You are joy. You are free.
Ye are god.**

You and I just don't see it. Hardly anyone sees it. That's why there's so much unhappiness, heartache and suffering in our world. It's the lack of true Self in-sight that causes addiction, and of course, addiction always results in drama.

126

So finding or creating a love-life to die for is about seeing your Self clearly. Your spiritual evolution is the key to the dawning of intimacy in your life. If you're One with Source, you're one with everything. Authentic intimacy is not about your partner or finding the right partner. That's the big, deceptive lie. The answer is not "out there."

Authentic intimacy is not about who you see in front of you, it's about who you see within you.

"Into-Me-I-See" brings intimacy—first with yourself, then with everything and everyone in your life.

The problem is we that we don't know who we are, we can't make out our Original Face. It's as if the mirror is all steamed up. Something is blocking our view. The reality is there; our true nature is there. Our essence is shining like the Sun but its rays are obstructed by clouds.

Michelangelo's David

Someone once asked the great painter and sculptor, *Michelangelo*, how he was able to perfectly sculpt *David* from a huge piece of marble. His answer was so simple, yet astounding. He said he simply chipped away everything that wasn't *David*.

David was there within, shrouded, veiled, shelled in marble, concealed from view. But he was there. All that was necessary was for Michelangelo to remove what didn't belong and the beauty of *David* would be displayed.

It is exactly the same for us. Our beauty is there. Our Spirit, our deepest Self, our shining, radiating Essence is within but it's shrouded in fog, veiled and shelled from our view. Our work is to chip away all that isn't authentically us.

This is the path I took to liberate myself from the bondage of relationship addiction and create authentic intimacy: I went looking for what was real in me and chipped away everything that wasn't. And for the next few chapters, I'm going to help you do the same. Get your chisel. Let's get to work chipping away what isn't authentically You.

CHAPTER 11

Stuck Between A Rock and a Hard Place

If I had a prayer, it would be:
God, spare me from the desire for love, approval or appreciation.
Amen.

–Byron Katie

April 26, 2003, started as a routine Saturday of climbing for 27 year old Aron Ralston, an avid outdoorsman and mountain climber. Needing some time alone and without telling anyone where he was going, he spent the day canyoneering—rappelling between very deep and very narrow canyon walls—at Bluejohn Canyon in southeastern Utah.

As Ralston made his final rappel, an 800-pound rock shifted several feet, pinning his right arm. He tried ropes and anchors to move the boulder, but it wouldn't budge. He even tried to chip away at the rock with his knife, but after ten hours, he managed to produce only a small handful of rock dust. He was alone and trapped.

Five days later, knowing he would soon die of dehydration, he realized his only chance at survival was to cut himself free by amputating his own arm. Knowing that the blade was not sharp enough to cut through bone, he leveraged his body weight and snapped both bones in his forearm. The pain was excruciating. Once the bones were broken, he applied a tourniquet to his arm and used his dull knife to cut through the nerves and muscle tissue, amputating his right arm below the elbow. Ralston then administered first aid to himself from the small kit in his backpack and rappelled the last 70 feet to the bottom of Bluejohn Canyon. Hiking five miles, he encountered a family on vacation and his life was saved.

Could you do such a thing? Do you have that kind of will to survive? Yes you do, and so do I. In fact, we've done a similar thing. Ralston's amazing story of survival is a story that every relationship addict has lived. For each one of us has faced a point

128

in our lives where we've been caught between "a rock and a hard place," knowing that unless we took drastic action, we too would die of thirst, all alone. You've read his story, now read ours.

Your Original Shine

Human beings, from the worst of us to the best of us, are essentially made of the same stuff—Spirit. Beyond our actions and egos, beyond our DNA, molecules and atoms, we are all the same—formless, eternal, Spirit Beings, "made in the image of God." All the great wisdom traditions teach this.

In order to make this incomprehensible truth somewhat understandable, think of human beings as light bulbs. Each bulb has the same Light (Spirit), but each bulb has a different color casing, and so each bulb *appears* unique. I call this our Original Shine, our individual essence. It's what makes you—You. Your essence is different from mine, from everyone's, though at the Spirit level, we are all the same. Your essence is the combination of your gender, personality, temperament and giftedness; it's the well from which your interests, passions, preferences and life's purpose spring.

So, keeping our light bulb analogy going, we can sum up like this: Our Light (Spirit) "shines" through our unique casings (essence), creating magnificent and unique shades of glory for the entire universe to behold. Furthermore, as Spirit shines through essence, our essence shines through our bodies and our bodies, in turn, shine with feelings. So this is the human condition up to this point:

Spirit > Essence > Body > Feelings

Are you with me? This is your story; this is my story; this is everyone's story. We are Beings of Light graced with amazing and unique essence qualities housed in a beautiful body that has a wide range of incredible feelings. This is the story of what it means to be human, but as you well know, it's not the end of the story.

Picture a small child at about six years old. In fact, let's make her a little girl with pig-tails, a runny nose, a beautiful smile, scraped up knees and an infectious laugh. Can you see her? Her "light bulb" is shining like the sun. Her glorious Being is on display. Life is good for her. Her imagination is off the charts,

129

she never stops talking and she plays with reckless abandon, hence, the knees. She is trusting, honest and filled with wonder and love for everything from birds to animals to trees to people. And if you had to use only one word to describe her you'd definitely choose *authentic*. *This little girl is real.* She doesn't hide anything. When she's happy, she beams and dances. When she's sad, she heaves in pain and cries a river. And when she's angry, look out! Everyone in your zip code is going to know it. This magnificent little girl is uncensored, authentic and alive.

And then the most bizarre thing happens to her. The little girl experiences some form of rejection. Sometimes it's by her siblings, friends or teachers, but usually it's by her parents or her primary caregivers. And when I say "rejected" I don't mean she's dropped off at a Fire Station and abandoned. The rejection isn't that overt. Rather her father (for the sake of discussion) doesn't like aspects of who she is, her unique way of "shining," *and wants her to be different.* She may frustrate, embarrass or disappoint him because she doesn't fit the mold of how he thinks his girl should be. For example, he does not like that she talks all the time. He tells her, "Children should be seen and not heard." And when she expresses feelings like sadness or anger—especially anger—he yells at her to quit whining and then leaves the room. Sometimes it's worse—she may be punished or even physically hit.

At this point, a completely new thought enters her mind. It dawns on her that her father doesn't like her the way she is, being so verbal and emotional. She doesn't know why. She just notices that he doesn't want to be around her when she's "being a brat." What is she going to do with the rejection she is experiencing, this feeling of not being the girl her daddy wants?

I wish the little girl, at this crucial moment, somehow knew the truth, that she really doesn't *need* her Father's love and approval. It would be great if she knew that she was made in the image of God and that all she needed was to love and approve of *herself!* When her Father scolded her for being so emotional and turned to leave the room, I wish she could have said, "Dad, wait a minute. I feel like I can't breathe right now. I feel so sad when you walk away from me when I'm emotional. I want you to find the strength to stand in my "storm" and be present with me as I process my feelings. But I know if you can't do it, it's not that I'm too much, but that you're too little."

Wouldn't that be awesome?! I would stand up and cheer: YOU GO GIRL!! But seriously, she's six! (Most of us don't find that voice until we're 40 and maybe not even then.) She simply wants to be seen and loved. She wants to be "daddy's little girl," but the girl she is, daddy doesn't want. So she's being rejected and it feels like she's going to die.

Between a Rock and a Hard Place
Can you feel her dilemma? She's between "a rock and a hard place." She's stuck. Her authentic "shine", her *Spirit-Essence-Body-Feelings* is being rejected. What is she going to do? As we've seen, she doesn't have the maturity to differentiate from her father, so with the belief that her very survival is at stake, she comes up with a brilliant idea:

She decides she will "cut off" the parts of her that he doesn't like and add the parts he seems to want.

She will conform to his image, and "shine" the way he wants her to, in an effort to secure his love. This is the next step in our developmental story: the creation of a fictitious self.

Remember how I said that we were just like Aron Ralston in Bluejohn Canyon? Dying of thirst, the thirst for love and approval, we did exactly what Ralston did for exactly the same reason— survival. He amputated his arm, and then days later put on a fake arm, a prosthetic limb, in order to function in the world. This is the human experience.

In order to survive as children, we "amputated" the parts of ourselves that our primary caregivers (and a host of others) didn't like, and in their place, we put on fake "limbs" that would help us function and get the love we believed we needed.

This is the beginning of what I call the "Unenlightened Dark Ages of the Human Condition," or more succinctly put, "Hell," because that's exactly what it is. The real, authentic You, your Original Shine, is slowly but surely disappearing, and what is emerging in it's place, is a brilliantly-crafted, yet utterly fictitious self, a self that is foreign to you, but one that the people around you are absolutely crazy about.

Bare in mind that you didn't know that you were "cutting and pasting" a new version of you into the world. This process is totally unconscious. You didn't say to one of your friends in the

131

sand box, "Hey, my Dad's been avoiding me lately. He can't handle emotional women. So I'm going to stuff my emotions and not express them and then he'll love me and want to be around me." That's ludicrous. You had no choice but to create a fictitious self. Remaining the magnificent Being you were born to be would have led to greater and greater wrath and rejection and neither you, nor I, nor anyone, has the ability to stay true to themselves at that early age. So, in order to survive, we surrendered our authentic, radiant and "shining" selves for a life-saving, but utterly false self.

Breathe!

Take a deep breath. We covered an enormous amount of territory and you may be experiencing very strong emotions right now. This story is about you, isn't it? I know, because it's about me too. It's about all of us, addicts or not. So feel your feelings in the moment. This may be the first time you've clearly recognized the wound you received as a child and what you did to survive it. Can you love the little girl (or the little boy) who so brilliantly found a way to survive? Aren't you amazed at yourself? You did what you had to do, just like Aron Ralston. Love yourself for your bravery and creativity.

And remember that our parents did the best they could (or the vast majority of them anyway). They raised us in a way that perfectly reflected their stage of consciousness at that point in their lives. They really could not have raised us in any other way. They were not Buddha or Jesus, though they may have been their followers. They were just people, wounded by their parents as well, unknowingly "visiting the sins of their fathers upon their children."

Recall what Jesus said on the cross as they were driving spikes into his wrists and feet: "Father, forgive them, for they know not what they do." While he felt the incredible pain of their actions, he knew they were simply doing what they thought was right. And so did our parents (and so are we—with our children!).

You Are A Survivor!

Having said that, the reality is that our parents (and others) do become frustrated, embarrassed or disappointed with our essence qualities, our physical appearance and the way we express our feelings. And we are told, verbally or nonverbally, that they would prefer us to be different than we are. This is emotional

132

abandonment. It sounds harsh, but when this happens, they've rejected us, they've abandoned the real Being that we are. They want a different child.

For example, they may have wanted a boy rather than a girl; a passive child rather than an aggressive one; a quiet, polite, introspective kid rather than a loud, extroverted party animal. They may have wanted us to be athletic rather than musical, logical rather than emotional, brilliant rather than average, compliant rather than strong-willed, careful rather than risk-taking. These "rathers" are each forms of abandonment.

But while both parents are a part of this rejection of our Original Shine, I've found that for love addicts, we've felt this rejection especially from our *opposite sex parent*. This is not to say that boys don't have issues with their fathers or that girls don't have issues with their mothers. Of course they do. But as far as relationship addiction goes, my experience indicates that the wound is tied to our relationship with our opposite sex parent.

Let's look at girls first.

Besides not liking their daughters the way they are, as we've mentioned, dads abandon their girls in other, equally devastating ways. When dad is an alcoholic, incapable of closeness, preoccupied with work or hobbies; when he disappears after a divorce and has little or no involvement in his girl's life, he leaves the girl "thirsty" for masculine love and energy, and she will search for a "drink", desperately, throughout the unenlightened dark ages of her life.

For boys, the situation is slightly different but equally devastating. While it's unusual for a mom to disappear from her son's life after divorce, moms *do* want their boys to be different than they are. And moms can also be alcoholics or be preoccupied and obsessed with work or men. Additionally, many moms never wanted to be moms in the first place, or at least not when it happened. And some moms also have unresolved anger with men that they project onto their sons.

These issues create a distant, disconnected relationship between moms and their sons. And when that happens, the boy can see his mother, but he can't "have" her. She's unavailable, out of his emotional reach. As a result, the boy will become a man who feels alone and "thirsty" for feminine energy, and he'll search for a "drink" throughout the unenlightened dark ages of his life.[*]

Sober Up!

So, here's where we stand in the story of how little boys and girls grow up to be relationship addicts:

**Spirit > Essence > Body > Feelings >
Rejection > Formation of Fictitious Self >
Unenlightened Dark Ages >**

We are Spirit Beings graced with unique essence qualities living in a body that has feelings. And then something happens. We're rejected and emotionally abandoned for who we are. In order to be loved and survive this trauma, we create a fictitious self, what psychologists call a Persona. We do all of this to be loved.

This entire process is unconscious and is the genesis of relationship addiction. When we're not loved for who we are, we spend the next 30 or 40 years of our lives trying to find someone who will. That's relationship addiction: The reliance on someone else to give us the love we didn't get in our childhoods.

I'm getting a little bit ahead of myself, however. At this point in our story, we are only between 6 and 12 years old. That's the age range, give or take a few years on either side, where the rejection of our authentic Being is replaced by a fictitious/persona self. But there is much more to our story and we will go deeper into it in the following chapter.

Take some time now, though, and reflect on your childhood. I want you to write about your relationship with your opposite sex parent. How were you rejected? How did he or she abandon your true essence? What wasn't *okay* with them? How couldn't you *be*?

---

[*] Note: A man's involvement in strip clubs is usually an unconscious attempt at healing this distant, disconnected relationship with Woman. And a strip club dancer is similarly, yet also unconsciously motivated. She may be there to repair an abusive or abandoning relationship with Man. I believe that spiritual liberation is being sought by those in clubs, both by the men and the dancers, but unfortunately neither party is conscious of what they're up to or how they could support each other's development. In a strange but beautiful way, strip clubs could become "church," a place of personal development and mutual awakening.

Recall situations, conversations and experiences. When did you feel his or her love the most? When did you feel it the least? In your family, what was valued and championed? What message did he or she give you about your body's size, shape, athletic ability, sexuality? What couldn't you talk about with your opposite sex parent? What feelings weren't allowed? What feelings were you supposed to feel? Use an extra sheet if paper, if necessary.

_____

_____

_____

_____

_____

_____

_____

CHAPTER 12

Casanova: The World's Greatest Lover

"The moment you are born, you bring a truth in your being. And unless that truth is expressed you will not feel contented. You have to sing the song of your heart. You have to dance your dance. You have to be utterly individual, not an imitation, not a carbon copy. You have to bring out your original face. The moment you are able to reveal your original face to the world, your life will be fulfilled."

–Unknown

In European history, the period between the fall of the Roman Empire (c. 500 A.D.) and the Renaissance (c. 1500 A.D.) was called the Dark Ages. It was a time of barbaric warring, rebellion, chaos and difficulty. Sounds a lot like the teenage years!

The Unenlightened Dark Ages of our *personal* history (12-40 years of age, or so) begins after a "fall" of sorts as well, when our authentic Being, our Original Shine, was rejected and abandoned in our early years. In a brilliant, Darwinian, survival-of-the-fittest moment, we unconsciously created a false self to get the love and attention we felt we needed to survive. This process is basically completed by the beginning of our teenage years.

But since this persona self hasn't been in place for long—we're still pretty young—there remains within us a flickering of awareness about what's happened. Though very few teenagers can verbalize this, they can feel that something is off, that something within them is out of alignment. This is, in large part, why so many teenagers are depressed, withdrawn, angry and rebellious (not to mention chemically and non-chemically addicted).

Usually, the teenager doesn't have a wise confidante to explain what's happened and to help him or her rediscover their Original Shine. So over time, that flickering light of awareness darkens completely, leaving only the pseudo, persona self in place. For the next 25-30 years, they will completely identify with this fictitious self, thinking that it's actually who they are.

Thankfully, the story of human spiritual development does not end here. I want to dive a bit deeper into these "dark ages," this unenlightened period of our lives. I want to be your "wise confidante," the one you (and I) needed when we were teenagers and help you discard your persona self and rediscover your authentic and Original Shine. For true intimacy is impossible if we're still living as our persona self.

Personas

The word *persona* means "mask". It means to wear a facade in order to satisfy the demands of a situation or an environment. It is not the real you, but a "person" you believe you have to become in order to survive a threat, satisfy a need or be successful at something. We have an amazing ability to figure out who we have to be in order to get what we need. In that sense, we are like chameleons, changing the color of our "skin" in order to survive situations.

While I have dozens of personas (as do you), three are relevant for our discussion here. Recall that in chapter five, I identified my three primary "bars" as golf, God and girls. I wanted to be successful in those areas of my life because I believed my sense of self and my worth as a man depended on it. Without conscious knowledge of it at the time, I used my amazing chameleon-like abilities to discern who I had to become in order to succeed at those endeavors.

For example, in golf, I believed that I had to try harder than anyone else in order to get good enough to qualify for the PGA Tour. So I became the guy who had an incredible work ethic. He was my golf/career persona and I called him, "Mr. Avis," because he tries harder.

As a pastor, in order to be successful and build a big, growing mega-church, I became the guy who appeared to be impeccably holy, truly caring and aggressively evangelistic. He was my spiritual persona and I called him, "Dr. Billy," short for Dr. Billy Graham.

Now it gets interesting.

What did I think it took to be successful with girls? Well, my answer to that question came from the relationship I had with my opposite sex parent, the first "girl" in my life, my mother. What did I have to do to be successful with her? What actions created harmony and closeness? Answer: You did what made her happy.

137

The old cliché, "If momma ain't happy, ain't nobody happy," was certainly true in my family. All was well if everyone fulfilled mom's agenda, including dad. In fact, I think I learned "Casanova" from him, which is the name I gave my "girls" or relationship persona. My dad warned me about going against the grain and upsetting mom. You just didn't go there. You did it her way if you wanted to have any sort of close relationship with her.

Therefore, I learned that if I wanted a woman's attention and affection, I was to set aside my agenda and totally focus on making her happy, following her agenda and making her life easier. What I wanted was beside the point. I learned to make the woman the priority, to be a "good boy." I learned to be *Casanova*. Let me tell you what he was like when he became an adult.

Casanova

As I write this part of the book, it's Christmas time and there's a really funny television commercial running for *Helzberg Diamonds*. There is a guy giving a bath to a very cute, but utterly "girly" little dog. The commercial makes it clear it's not his dog. But he's being very sweet and gentle with the little thing. After gingerly toweling her dry, he puts a cute little pink bow on her collar and then cradles her in his arms. (At this point, if the commercial is creating the desired effect, women are swooning and men are barfing!)

While he's holding the little dog, the camera cuts to a beautiful women walking in the door. He puts the little dog on the floor and she runs over to the woman. As she picks up the dog, she has a look on her face that says she can't believe what she's seeing. In disbelief, she says, "Did you give *Toodles* a bath? I thought you were going to watch the big game with your friends?" to which he replies, "Na, it's just a game."

As the camera cuts back to the guy, the announcer's voice sarcastically says, "Because you're not *THAT* guy, there's Helzberg Diamonds."

But Casanova *IS* that guy! Casanova acted like that all the time, especially in his relationship with his Julie. Let me explain.

After my double life was exposed in the papers during the 2003 U.S. Open, Julie and I briefly broke up. But within a few days, she forgave my lies and deceit. We resumed our romance as I proceeded with my divorce, and nine months later, we moved in together. At that point in my life, Julie was everything I ever wanted in a woman. She was my "drink with legs", a Margarita: sweet, salty and sexy. Casanova loved her so deeply and so desperately that he used all of his considerable charm to ensure that she was happy and that her life was easy.

For example, even though I had two jobs (playing golf competitively and instructing), Casanova found time to clean the house, do the dishes and all of the laundry. He was the primary care taker of *her* two boys (ages 9 and 12), getting them up each day, making sure they ate breakfast and taking them to school (Julie chose to go to work at 6:00 am and return home at 7:00 pm). Casanova helped the kids with homework, washed their sheets, made their beds. When Julie's mother, who lived just down the street, wasn't able to come to our home and cook dinner for the kids, Casanova came home early and cooked (frozen crap—I'm Casanova, not Rachel Ray). He took the boys to baseball practice and to tutoring appointments. He took care of the dog, did a little shopping and ran interference when the boys wanted to kill each other.

Casanova also made sure that the house was peaceful when Julie arrived home and that the boys wouldn't crowd her the minute she walked in the door. Casanova was like the Secret Service to the President. You had to go through him to get near her. Once she arrived home, Casanova would feed her if she was hungry, get her medicine for her frequent headaches, listen to her talk about her day and massage her shoulders. She was madly in love with Casanova and sexually "told" him so every night and every morning before she left for work.

That was Casanova, the world's greatest lover, and he "loved" her that way for about two years.

Full disclosure compels me to say that she didn't verbally insist that I do all of that, though on more than one occasion, she did actually say, "If momma ain't happy, ain't nobody happy." She said it humorously, of course, but she believed it and so did I. That said, Casanova had an agenda too. Being the world's greatest lover ensured that she had nothing else to do but spend all of her non-working time in bed with him. Casanova took care of her life so she could take care of his.

But by the end of the second year of our relationship, and having been engaged for six months, I began getting tired of being Casanova. I was her hero, rescuing her as if she was a damsel in distress. I didn't want to run her household and be her nanny.

That was not my sole purpose in life. Our lifestyle was beginning to bother me. She brought work home and often worked through the weekend, regularly working 60-80 hours a week. In my view, I was enabling her to be a workaholic—in exchange for our nightly sexual escapades. I began realizing that this was how my life was going to be if I married her. This is what I had set up. I was living my future.

As I began expressing my displeasure about our lifestyle and suggested we make some changes, our relationship went on "tilt." It didn't work anymore. (I've mentioned this but it bears repeating because it's so central to why our love lives don't work.)

Our relationship worked as long as both of us remained caught in our relationship personas. I took care of her and she had sex with me. We never said it that way, but that was the deal. It worked as long as we both held up our end of the bargain. But as time went on, I didn't want to keep being Casanova, playing the role of hero and that created drama between us.

In his best-selling book, *A New Earth,* Eckhart Tolle writes as if he knew Julie and Casanova.

"In the early stages of many so-called romantic relationships, role-playing is quite common in order to attract and keep whoever is perceived by the ego as the one who is going to 'make me happy, make me feel special, and fulfill all my needs.' 'I'll play who you want me to be, and you'll play who I want you to be.' That's the unspoken and unconscious agreement. However, role-playing is hard work, and so those roles cannot be sustained indefinitely, especially once you start living together."

Our role-playing *was* sustained for quite a time, but soon after we moved in together, neither of us wanted to continue to fulfill our respective roles. We argued and fought for the first time in our relationship. We were starting to make each other miserable and soon Julie ended our relationship.

Please understand that I don't have anything against a guy being "Mr. Mom." There are some men whose life purpose is to be the primary care-giver in his family. It's a wonderful calling, a tremendous gift to children and the world. But it must be something a man (or a woman) authentically feels called to do. It wasn't for me. I did it from fear; I did it to *be* loved, not *because* I loved, though of course, I didn't know it at the time.

So, throughout most of my life, "I" have been Casanova, this sweet, thoughtful guy devoted to spoiling his woman, making her the absolute focal point of his life. Casanova's mission was to make her life easier and happier. But it was motivated by fear, rather than love. Casanova thought he had to be that way in order to attract and keep a woman. He learned that from his mom.

It should be pointed out that today, I still treat women like goddesses (that is who they are, after all) because, in my essence, I am a loving, considerate and passionate man. But when I ignore my needs, silence my voice and lose sight of my life's purpose— all to secure affection and avoid abandonment—I am in the grip of my relationship persona, Casanova, and eventually everyone suffers.

Sober Up!

Now it's your turn to begin the process of discovering, and therefore discarding, your relationship persona. Remember, we cannot have authentic intimacy until we are authentic people. Up until now, your relationships have been unconscious, persona-to-persona arrangements rather than Original Shine-to-Original Shine intimacies. Awareness is the key to making this shift. Our definition of enlightenment was to "see yourself clearly." In order to help you see yourself clearly, I want to take you through a process, a guided mediation of sorts.

1. Write Your Relationship Pattern

How do you function relationally? How do you behave in order to attract and keep a partner? Write your pattern in one concise sentence. For example, mine would be this: *I prioritize the woman and ignore myself.*

_____

_____

2. Name Your Persona

Thinking of that pattern, come up with a name. Try to come up with something fun. Fictional characters from cartoons, comic

141

books, television shows or movies are great because, well, your persona *is* fictional! But don't be afraid to use cultural icons or famous people either. The idea is to pick a name that embodies your pattern perfectly. Mine, of course, are "Mr. Somebody Special," "Mr. Avis," "Dr. Billy," and "Casanova"—to name only a few!

This is a very important step. Author Debbie Ford has written extensively on the fictitious self. In her excellent book, *The Dark Side of the Light Chasers*, she writes:

> "Examining our [personas] can be a tool to help us reclaim the lost parts of ourselves. First we must identify these parts and then name them, then we'll be able to disengage from them. Actually naming them creates distance...In a funny way, as soon as I name these aspects of myself, I feel fondness for them. I can then stand back and look at them in an objective way. This process starts to loosen the grip these behaviors have on your life."

So, take some time and come up with a really fun name for your pseudo, love-thirsty self.

---

3. Interview Your Persona

One of the ways we can "feel fondness" for our personas, as Ford says, is to let them speak. So, let's interview them. Ask your partner or a trusted friend to interview your persona-self.

The following six interview questions are taken from the work of Gay and Kathlyn Hendricks. They suggest two things to make this process transformative.

First, as much as possible, fully "become" your persona. Take a moment, close your eyes, breathe a few times and put on the "mask." Get into character. Fully embody it, which might mean putting your body in a certain position or contorting your face in some way. Really get into it, go all the way with this.

The second piece of advice they give is to have the interviewer address you by your persona's name. The real you does not exist right now. Only the persona is present.

142

Then, have your interviewer ask you the following questions.

- _____, what's the most important thing to you?
- _____, what are you most proud of?
- _____, when did you make your first appearance?
- _____, who did you learn your style from?
- _____, what are you most afraid of?
- _____, what do you most want?

4. Exaggerate Your Persona

Another way to get to know your relationship persona and break its grip on your life is to exaggerate it. Play with it, dramatize it, act it out in a big, nearly embarrassing way. If you are currently in a relationship, it's best to do this with your partner. If, however, you're not in a relationship, a trusted friend will work just as well. You'll know you're exaggerating enough when the whole thing becomes hysterically funny.

Even to this day, if I feel that I'm slipping into Casanova with my wife, I'll call my coach on the phone in character—*as* Casanova. I'll call Diana and she'll answer normally, "Hello?" and I'll just start in with a sweet, romantic sounding voice:

"Oh, Diana, you're the most wonderful coach in the whole wide world. You're so smart and enlightened! Oh my God, Diana, where would I be with out you? You're amazing, you're beautiful! Is there anything I can do for you? I can fly out to California (I live in Florida) and do your laundry and take care of your kids? I can be there in a few hours. Maybe you need a back rub. You just name it and I'll drop what I'm doing and come take care of you."

She'll immediately know what I'm up to and play along.

"Oh, Casanova, I neeeeeeeeeeed you! Life is so tough right now. I'm exhausted and overwhelmed. The kids are driving me crazy and the house is a wreck. There's laundry piled up all over the floor and the fridge is empty. Could you come save me, Casanova? Could you come rescue me in my distress? I'm helpless and I can't survive without you! Oh, Casanova, come quick!"

By the end we're both laughing hysterically. Most importantly, however, by exaggerating Casanova and being playful with "him," I quickly shift and return to my real self.

5. Persona Call-Outs

The final way to discard your persona is to ask your partner and/or your friends to call you out when they see you in unconsciously caught in the trance of your relationship persona.

One of my wife's primary personas is "Little Ms. I-Don't-Want-To-Be-A-Bother." Her family of origin had a lot of financial and emotional difficulty so she learned to stay in the background and not make her needs known because everyone had so much on their plate already. She learned not to be a bother.

We have a commitment in our relationship to tell each other, playfully (that's critical—playfully!), when we see each other caught in the trance of our respective personas.

For instance, we'll be making dinner together and discover that we need something from the store. It never crosses her mind to ask me to make a quick run to the store for her. She'll simply reach for her car keys and head for the door. I'll say, "Honey, I'll go." And she'll say, "No, I'll go. It's no trouble," dismissing my offer as if she didn't even hear it (which she didn't because "Little Ms. I Don't-Want-To-Be-A-Bother" can't hear support). I know something's up.

I'll address her persona directly, in a playful voice, "Hey 'Little Ms. I-Don't-Want-To-Be-A-Bother'? Will you allow me to go to the store—it's really not a bother."

She'll smile at me and say, "Oh, I'm doing it again, aren't I? Yes, that would great if you went. Thank you." As I head for the door she yells, "Hey, if Casanova is going to the store, tell him he isn't getting laid for this!"

That simple interaction calls us to be fully present with our authentic selves as we relate to one another. As I bring her persona to her consciousness and she checks to see that I'm not unconsciously channeling mine, our Original Shine becomes that much brighter. The real her and the real me are present *and that is authentic intimacy.*

144

CHAPTER 13

Loving a Love Junkie

"Roy, I'm bored and tired of hearing about Julie. It's been a year since the two of you broke up and if you want to continue to rehash your relationship and whine about how much you miss her, fine. But you won't be doing it with me anymore. I'm not ending our friendship, but I'm telling you that if you want to talk about her, you'll have to find someone else. The next time I hear her name, I'm going to get up and walk away. I'm done hanging around in Margaritaville with you."

—Michael Wright
One of my best friends

Since this section of the book is about how to end drama and create harmony and intimacy, I would be remiss if I didn't address those who love the love junkies. Love addiction, like any other addiction, impacts many people in an addict's life, often creating significant drama and collateral damage. *Alcoholics Anonymous* is a wonderful and famous organization devoted to supporting the sobriety of an alcoholic, but equally significant is *Al-Anon*, which is devoted to supporting those who are affected *by* alcoholics. So this is an *Al-Anon* type chapter, as is the next one. Here I want to address three groups of people who interact with relationship addicts: friends, potential partners and current partners.

Friends

Friends of relationship addicts usually make one of two related mistakes. They either withhold their authentic truth or become enablers. My friend, Michael, whose words appear above, gave me an incredible gift by resisting the temptation to commit either one of those two mistakes. He was authentic with me and told me his truth, which was that he was sick of hearing about Julie. And he also refused to be supportive in a way that was enabling, deciding to walk away if I ever talked about her again.

If you are a friend of someone who is a relationship addict, they need to hear how you feel about their life. If you are bored with their sad stories; if you are sick of hearing how disappointing their marriage or love life is—tell them how you feel. If you're exhausted by the continual drama and the soap opera that is their life; if it breaks your heart to see your friend stay in a relationship that *they* know isn't good for them—tell them. If you want to scream when they bitch about their husbands—go ahead and scream! If you don't want to hear about another dating disaster or how some guy or girl never called or stood them up, or lied, or whatever—tell them! Tell them exactly how you feel. Why? Because...

Your authenticity is the voice of God

Michael's "harsh" words played a big part in my recovery. Yes, at first I was really angry and felt betrayed. I mean, what kind of friend tells you they no longer want to hear about your broken heart? (Answer: A good one!) We have to redefine what it means to be a friend. It doesn't mean being "nice." At a minimum, it means to want the very best for someone and to be honest with them about how you feel. Could they get mad at you? Yes. Might it even threaten your friendship? Yes. But could hearing your authentic feelings shake some sense into them? It did for me.

A short while after Michael shared his new commitment with me, I calmed down and said to him, "Is it that bad?" And when he said, "Yea, dude, it's *that* bad," I sunk in my chair with a deeper realization of how addicted I was. His courage to be authentic with me got my attention in a very powerful way and I will always be grateful to him for it.

The other mistake friends make is to become enablers of their relationally addicted friends. By that I mean, their friendship actually helps them to *continue* in their addiction rather than truly loving them in a way that calls them to come out of it. Since the concept of enabling is not easy to understand, I'll describe it this way:

In professional boxing, each fighter has both a trainer and a cut man in his corner during a fight. Do you know what the cut man's job is? He patches up a fighter's bleeding, beaten face between rounds, so that he can go back in the ring and continue fighting!

It's so easy for a well-meaning friend to unwittingly be a love addict's "cut man." Expressing compassion, empathy, comfort, sensitivity and caring can become a means of "patching them up" so they can continue in their addiction! Again, we need to ask ourselves what being a friend means. Does it mean to support them so they can continue to live in insanity or does it mean to hold up a mirror and say, "Look at your "face!"? "Look at your life! You're a mess. If you want to go back in the "ring," that's your choice. But I'm done being your 'cut man.' I'm done supporting the madness."

I'm not saying that the first time a friend complains about their love life that you should walk away. Coming to the conclusion that you are, in fact, enabling someone rather than supporting their freedom, often takes a considerable amount of thought and even advice from trusted, enlightened friends. Just bare in mind that what we often call "friendship" is sometimes being a very nice, very supportive—enabler.

Potential Partners

If you are single and you would like to meet someone and have a loving, committed relationship with them, you will undoubtedly bump into relationship addicts. The Internet, bars, health clubs, churches, grocery stores—any place that single people meet—are swarming with people looking for a "drink." How can you spot them? How can you tell if someone is a relationship addict and looking for you to end their loneliness, make them feel special and alive or complete them?

Well, first of all, in my opinion, about 90% of the population is, to some degree, looking for love to do that very thing. You probably are as well. As you know, when I use the word "addiction," I use it to describe an extremely common and normal state of mind concerning relationships. It simply means to have "faith in love," to believe that a partner's love can end loneliness and bring happiness. This mindset is reflected in nearly every romantic comedy, soap opera, television drama, woman's magazine, romance novel and song. Relationship addiction is deeply imbedded in our culture's consciousness. We've all got it to some degree or another. It's like the nose on our faces. We all have one, though some are bigger and more noticeable than others (smile). Likewise, almost all of us have "faith in love" to some degree or another. So give up thinking that you're going to find someone completely "healthy."

Having said that, there *are* signs that someone is *deeply* addicted and I want to share some of them with you. And the best way to do that is to let you meet Casanova, face to face. If he was alive and kicking today, this is what you would experience on a date with him or maybe when first meeting him:

- **Casanova Is Just Totally Into You—*Immediately*.**

If there is one thing you will feel, in spades, when meeting Casanova is that he is totally into you—*right away.* He will not talk about himself much, but instead will ask you meaningful, thoughtful questions about you and your life. He will be truly interested in who you are. This is an important point. Casanova is *NOT* a "player." He's not looking for another notch in his belt, nor will you feel any phoniness in him. He's honestly into you. He wants to fall in love with you because he's hoping you are "The One!" Consequently, you will feel understood, valued, seen and heard, and it will feel real because—it is! Casanova is complimentary, nonjudgmental and extremely attentive. When you are with him, you will feel like the only woman (or man) on earth.

Now, you may be asking, "What the hell's wrong with *that*? That sounds wonderful!" Well, the problem is not that Casanova is totally into you, it's *the speed at which it happens.* That's the sign, that's the red flag—the speed. Of course you want your man (or woman) to be totally into you, but Casanova gets there at the speed of light, like within the first ten minutes of meeting you! Watch out for "love at first sight" types. They're addicts.

- **Casanova Is Romantic—*Immediately***

Everyone likes to get cards, gifts, flowers, calls and texts from their lover. It's great to go to fancy restaurants or to take expensive vacations. We all like to hear the words, "I love you." But if those kinds of things happen on the second date, that's a red flag, don't you think?

Casanova (me) occasionally would bring a gift, something like a CD by *Sting*, to a *first* face-to-face Internet date—and then take her to a restaurant that would cost him $100! He was desperate for her to like him and so he went way over the top romantically.

148

And he'd utter "I love you" so soon that it would make any healthy woman get up and run!

Casanova, and relationship addicts in general, make extravagant over-the-top romantic commitments or gestures that are inappropriate for the stage the relationship is in.

- **Casanova Is Emotionally Intimate—*Immediately***

It goes without saying that Casanova wants physical intimacy as soon as possible. But that's not what I'm talking about here. Casanova wants *emotional* intimacy. He wants closeness, connection and communion. And again, who doesn't want their partner to open up his or her heart and share their feelings, dreams, hopes and fears? That is what intimate partners do. And that's the key word, *"partners."* You're not partners yet! You've only been on a date or two, for heaven's sake! And yet Casanova is acting like he's in a committed relationship, sharing very private, personal and intimate things with you.

A client of mine had one of those magical first dates. They didn't even sleep together and yet it lasted seven hours. When I talked to her the next day, she was euphoric, but surprisingly a little apprehensive. When I asked her about him, she said he was good-looking, really sweet and easy to talk to. Basically, she had a wonderful time. When I asked her why she felt a bit apprehensive, she told me that he told her all about his financial situation, describing in detail what was going on in his life. She said that while she loved that he was so open and honest, she felt it was "kinda weird that he'd get that personal on a first date." He was exhibiting a classic sign of relationship addiction: immediate emotional intimacy and transparency. Relationship addicts are deathly afraid of being alone, so in an attempt to connect, they get personal right away.

In summary, then, the problem isn't that Casanova is totally into you, or that he's romantic or that he's emotionally available. The problem is that he's (or she's) all those things—***too soon.*** It's a timing thing for Casanova. Because he's desperate, lonely and needing a relationship to make him feel safe, alive and happy, he moves too fast. His words and actions, while wonderful, are motivated by fear, and are inappropriate for the relationship's stage.

Current Partners

The last group of people I'd like to address are those who are currently in a relationship with a love addict. As you can imagine, the partner of a relationship addict is in the most difficult position of all. Friends don't live with the addict, partners do. And potential partners can simply not return a phone call and avoid the drama all together. But an intimate partner is right in the middle of everything. They feel the daily pressure to satisfy their partner's insatiable need for attention and affection and they live with the fear that if they don't continuously meet their needs, the addict will find someone else who will.

Now, how you live with a love junkie depends on whether or not they are aware of their addiction. There's a very different strategy employed for each scenario. So let's start with the assumption that the love junkie is *un*aware of their addiction. We'll call this strategy Path A. And, of course, if the love junkie is aware of their addiction, we'll call that Path B.

Path A: Loving an *Unconscious* Love Junkie

So, how do you love someone who is unaware that they are hooked on love? Well, it may surprise you, but your strategy has nothing to do with the junkie. If your partner doesn't believe they have a problem, then your total focus must be on yourself. Your role is not to wake them up. Of course you should share your opinions and feelings, and even tell them what you want, but when it's all said and done, if they doesn't see it, you must focus totally on yourself. So ask yourself the following questions:

- What is your life's purpose? You were not put on this earth to meet your partner's needs. Their needs are not your responsibility. You are not their life-source and you're not supposed to be. A healthy relationship is NOT where two people commit to taking care of each other. A healthy relationship is between two whole, differentiated, self-realizing people committed to the same overall path in life.

- What is your part of the unconscious agreement? Remember, the two of you are creating this. It's not just them, even though they're the junkie. Think of it like playing tennis. You can't play alone. They hit the ball, you hit it back. The game only works if you both play. Your role is to see how you've been "playing" and stop. Drop your racket and walk off the court.

Julie could have said, "Roy, I'm going to start taking care of myself and stop rewarding you sexually for spoiling me. I love you but you're clingy and needy and I'm tired of trying to satisfy you. I'm done playing the game where you take care of me and I take care of you. I want us to take care of ourselves and share our life together. If you want that, let's stay together. If you don't want that, let's split up."

- What do you want? Set Boundaries. Communicate how you feel when they're flirty and needy and tell them exactly what you want in terms of their behavior. Be specific. And tell them the consequence if it continues. Whatever that is, you must follow through. This is not giving an ultimatum. You are not trying to scare them or control them. You're simply taking responsibility for your life and what happens in it. They can do whatever they want. But that doesn't mean you have to put up with it. Those living with addicts need to be warriors in terms of setting and enforcing their personal boundaries. You must have your "sword." There is no other way to have a relationship function smoothly unless boundaries are defined and enforced.

Path B: Loving a *Self-Aware* Love Junkie
If your partner knows that they are a junkie and if they're willing to face it, you're more than half way home. Awareness almost completely dissolves the problem because your partner will no longer be asking you to be their "drink with legs." They'll know when they're "thirsty" and when they're slipping into their addict persona. So, again, if they know they're addicted, you're very close to relationship bliss. There are some other things you can do, though, to keep your relationship headed in that direction.

First, keep up with them. What's your persona? What's its name? How does it compliment theirs? What is your end of the unconscious agreement and what are you doing about it? In other words, you have a partner who is committed to their spiritual evolution. Are you?

Secondly, commit to at least a year's worth of intensive relationship coaching.

Third, make sure you both work through all the processes in this book, especially Chapter 12. Those persona processes should become a normal part of your everyday relationship. Play with your personas together.

Fourth, you also need to set boundaries. Even though the junkie is aware of their persona-self, that awareness doesn't mean they can get away with it if they slip into it from time to time. Again, you must protect your own aliveness and energy and decide what you are going to do if your partner slips into their addicted trance. One of the key characteristics of an enabler is that they don't have their own personal boundaries, or if they do, they don't enforce them.

A Final Word

If you are living with a relationship addict, no matter how much attention and affection you lavish on them, you will feel that it is never enough. This is how Julie felt. In fact, she said those very words to me on more than one occasion. You'll frequently have the feeling that although you are giving all you can, your partner is still unhappy and dissatisfied with you. And depending on the extent of your partner's addiction, they may go outside the relationship to meet the needs you can't or won't meet.

This is extremely important: If that happens, believe it or not, it's not about you. (That may sound crazy, but stick with me.) It has nothing to do with you. In other words, *don't take it personally.* It's so easy to believe that somehow you're an inadequate partner when you're with a relationship addict. The thought is, "If I were a better husband, a better wife or a better partner, they wouldn't be so clingy and needy, nor would they have any desire to go outside of our relationship for their emotional and physical needs." That's a lie. What's going on with them is not about you and has nothing to do with you.

Here is the truth. Their thirst is insatiable. And you can not, nor can anyone, adequately quench it. Read this closely. You *ARE* inadequate. Nobody is adequate to meet a relationship addict's needs. Is an alcoholic ever satisfied with the drink in their hands? Would they stop drinking if they found the perfect drink?

Of course not. Addicts "drink." I don't care how hard you try, there isn't enough water in your well to satisfy their thirst. You can not, ever, even on your best day, give them what they need—so don't take it personally.

Julie took me personally, and I don't mean that negatively. She was just human. But she felt so bad that she couldn't make me happy. She wanted to be the woman of my dreams. She loved me. And it killed her to know that I was unhappy, even when she was doing the best she could. And, of course, nobody wants to be in a relationship that feels like that, so she broke up with me.

But if you are aware that your partner has a problem, there's no need to feel horrible, guilty and like a failure. It's them. They have an insatiable need that you can't meet. And when you know this, you're more likely to make a decision about the future of your relationship from a centered, non-reactive place.

Too often today people are ending relationships not realizing that they're living with an addict, and that if they didn't take it so personally, but instead insisted they get help, relationship bliss would then be possible.

What I'm saying is that the darkness of drama *can* lead to the dawning of intimacy. I am living proof of this. My addiction has been my salvation and being the Mayor of Margaritaville opened the door to Narnia. So if you're living with an addict, as hurtful and horrible as it may be, don't take it personally because if he or she is willing to look at themselves and get serious help, it can become a happy ending.

I'll say it again: Your partner is an addict. He's not just a horny jerk and she's not just a needy bitch. They're love addicts with a legitimate, treatable problem. If they won't acknowledge that and take responsibility for it and get help, and if their neediness is sucking the life out of you, then by all means end the relationship. No one is called to be the host for a parasite. Your first responsibility is to protect your aliveness.

Lastly, if they won't commit to an exclusive relationship, which most of us want, then you have to cut them loose as well.

CHAPTER 14

The Difference between Sex and Relationship Addiction

You come to love not by finding the perfect person, but by seeing an imperfect person perfectly.

—Sam Keen

As you are well aware of by now, the issue I am addressing in this book is relationship addiction *NOT* sex addiction. The two could not be more different, though they are often confused. Knowing the difference is important for those of you who love and/or live with love junkies because it makes a huge difference in how you will support their "sobriety"—if that is a choice you are willing to make.

Sex addiction is a relatively rare, hard core condition that almost always requires a stay at a residential treatment center followed by long-term professional help. It is a very complex and difficult addiction to treat. If, after reading this section, you feel your partner, or someone you know, is a sex addict and not a relationship addict, your role is to insist that they seek immediate and intensive professional help. It is not something you treat with a self-help book and couple's counseling. In medical terms, sex addiction is more like cancer than a sinus infection. It requires radical treatment, not a simple antibiotic.

Relationship addiction, conversely, is extremely common and it's actually quite easy to treat. Usually a small dose of self-awareness, a good self-help book, a serious commitment to personal growth and a bit of relationship coaching will do the trick. And your role as someone who loves them is not to send them away to the *Betty Ford Center* to work things out on their own, but to join them and work through the issue together.

Remember, relationship addiction is *co*-dependence (with emphasis on the "co" part!). It's not a one person problem, but a co-addiction. In other words, if you think you have a healthy relationship to love and intimacy but your partner doesn't, your mistaken. While it is possible for only one person in a relationship to be addicted to sex, it's not possible for only one person in the relationship to have a problem with love addiction. So if you read through this section and have it confirmed that your partner is a relationship addict, look in the mirror. You are too. So your role is to *join* your partner in unwinding your relationship dynamic, not to encourage them to deal with it on their own.

Summing up then, with sex addiction you must support your loved one from afar; with relationship addiction your support is "up close and personal" because you are just as much of an addict as your partner is.

Let me also point out that the two addictions don't fall along gender lines either, with men being addicted to sex and women to relationships. While one would have to be blind not to notice that men can be "players," perpetual adolescent playboys (e.g., Hugh Hefner) or dangerous sexual predators, it is not uncommon for a woman to be a sex addict. The term "nymphomaniac" is a technical term reserved for *females*. And there are millions of men like myself who seek the attention and affection of women to validate their masculinity and make them feel alive and whole. Granted, male and female relationship addicts express their neediness differently, but the core element of love addiction, which is to source one's life and aliveness from an intimate relationship, is not gender specific.

Now, let's talk about the difference between sex and relationship addiction. I've designed **Table 16-1** (page 157) to help you see the difference between the two. However, I want to strongly caution you at this point. We're treading into dangerous waters here. After reading this section, be careful not to *definitively* label someone you care about as a sex addict based upon the chart I'm about to walk you through. Sex addiction is a very complex issue, as I said, and it can not be accurately diagnosed by simply reading a table. Sex addiction is not the focus of this book and it is definitely *not* my area of expertise. While I believe what I say about sex addiction captures its general essence, it should not be taken as gospel. My purpose in this section is to help you determine whether or not the person you care about is a *relationship* addict—period. Now, with that said, let's go through the table line by line.

Let's begin with the **pervasiveness** of each addiction. As I noted earlier, relationship addiction is extremely widespread, while sex addiction, comparatively, is quite rare. (You'll notice that the percentages don't add up. That's because I estimate that about 5% of people are actually healthy!)

The next element to notice is something that we haven't touched on and that is the **energy**, or the driving force, behind relationship and sex addiction. This is crucial to understand for the "sobering up" process. While both men and women have masculine and feminine energy, the relationship addict is overly identified with the feminine, meaning, they're obsessed with connecting and with love, while the sex addict is overly identified with masculine energy. They're obsessed with freedom.

Consequently, when it comes to **intimacy**, one is a "clinger" while the other is a "runner." A relationship addict is just what the name implies. He or she is obsessed with *relationships*. They may love sex but they're fundamentally *after* intimacy. Sex addicts, however, are after sex, plain and simple. They're not interested in "us," they're interested in "it."

The only point of commonality between both addictions, you'll notice, is that they share the same underlying and motivating **emotion**. Each is deeply driven by fear. But they fear different things. The relationship addict is afraid of abandonment and the sex addict is afraid of engulfment. Understanding what each addict is afraid of helps shed light on their feelings about **commitment**. The love addict is consumed by the idea, in fact, they feel naked without it, while the sex addict wants nothing to do with it.

The sex addict's "fishing" **mission** is to catch a partner, have sex with them and "throw them back." Their relationship **goal** is to stay single, being a committed bachelor or bachelorette. If they're married, they're committed philanderers; if **dating**, they are "players." Consequently, they have many short term flings with numerous **partners**.

The relationship addict also goes "fishing" for a partner, but they want to keep them, stuff them and mount them permanently in their lives! A relationship addict wants to get married (they are rarely out of a relationship) and generally they have long term relationships with only a handful of partners. When their addiction becomes extreme, they become stalkers.

Table 16-1

Comparing Sex Addiction to Relationship Addiction		
In Relation To…	**Sex Addiction**	**Relationship Addiction**
Pervasiveness	Rare (Est. 5%)	Widespread (Est. 90%)
Energy	Over Identified w/Masculine	Over Identified w/Feminine
Intimacy	Runner	Clinger
Driving Emotion	Fear	Fear
Commitment	Phobic	Consumed
"Fishing" Mission	Catch and Release	Keep and Mount
Relationship Goal	Single	Marriage
Dating	Player	Stalker
Nature & Number of Partners	Short Term and Many	Long Term and Few
Reason for Cheating	Physical Encounter	Emotional Connection
Sexual Activity	The Goal	Means to Connect
Communication	Conceals	Reveals
Developmental Disorder	Individuation Phase	Attachment Phase
Life Condition	Driven/Achieving	Drifting/Aimless

Sexual activity for a sex addict is the end game, the goal, but for the relationship addict, it's a means to an end, which is the emotional connection they so desperately desire. Sometimes, as in my case, a relationship addict loves sex. But often, a relationship addict only engages in sex because he or she feels they have to in order to preserve the existence of the relationship. It's not uncommon for a relationship addict to actually have little *real* interest in sex. They could take it or leave it. But they do "it" in order to secure "us." Sex is an insurance police against being alone. This, unfortunately, describes the purpose of sex for millions of people in committed relationships.

The **communication** style of a sex addict is to conceal. They aren't open, they aren't vulnerable, they aren't emotionally available. This is in part because sex is how they medicate and suppress their feelings. But in a more basic way, revealing feelings builds intimacy and connection, something the sex addict fears and is trying to avoid. For the relationship addict, as we said earlier, that's what they're after so they are revealing, tell-all types.

Child psychologists have identified many phases a child goes through on his or her way to healthy adulthood. And two of the most important ones are the attachment and the individuation phases. If these two phases are successfully negotiated, the child then grows to have a healthy relationship to intimacy, neither fearing it nor craving it. But if these two phases aren't navigated successfully, a **developmental disorder** occurs. If the child does not properly attach to their "life source," their parents or guardians, they enter adulthood feeling vulnerable, lonely and disconnected. A break down in the attachment phase is what gives birth to relationship addiction.

But if a child has properly bonded, the next major developmental phase is the individuation phase. Here, if the child is to become a healthy adult, they must be allowed to separate from their parents, spread their wings and become an individual. But many children are smothered and suffocated by controlling parents and grow up to be adults that fear and rebel against closeness. This is often the childhood story of a sex addict (e.g. Tiger Woods).

Finally, what's the **life condition** of each kind of addict? Well, usually, because the relationship addict is so obsessed with love and relationships, they neglect other important areas of their

158

lives (I did). Their ambition, energy, passion and creativity are all centered on their love lives. Consequently, their careers are stagnant and their life's purpose (other than being in love!) is unclear. They're not doing anything with their lives; they're drifting aimlessly through it, waiting for love to save them and make them whole. Relationship addicts are often quite boring people to be around. They don't have anything going on. We will talk more about this in chapter 26.

Conversely, the sex addict, being overly identified with masculine energy, is usually out to conquer the world. They can be driven, busy, successful and sometimes powerful people.* Intimacy and real commitment is a waste of time for them. They use sex to suppress their emotions so they can keep achieving their goals. They are hit-and-run "lovers" and often use prostitutes (there is less hassle) so they can get back to work. Tiger Woods, NBA superstar, Magic Johnson, and more recently, Elliot Spitzer, the former Governor of New York, are classic examples of this. My guess is that Bill Clinton would fall into this category as well.

These men illustrate, as do all addicts, that eventually their addiction, if not aggressively addressed, becomes their demise, ruining the mission they have been so committed to achieving. This is the saddest aspect of addiction: No matter what we're addicted to, we all end up, metaphorically speaking, in the same place—lying face down in a gutter, in a puddle of our own vomit. We end up in Margaritaville.

---

* The story of Tiger Woods and his "transgressions" hit the news as I was editing this section. While I have met Tiger, I don't know him. But from a distance, it appears he may have an issue with sex addiction, for he fits the profile.

159

PART FOUR

"But I know it's my own damn fault."
Leaving Margaritaville

CHAPTER 15

The 12 Steps to Relationship Bliss

Every man dies, but not every man really lives.

—William Wallace
From the movie, *Braveheart*

My all-time favorite movie is *Braveheart*. I think it's because the movie is about slavery and freedom, themes that powerfully resonate with my heart. When I first saw the movie and heard William Wallace (Mel Gibson) say, "Every man dies, but not every man really lives," it was as if he was speaking to me. For the vast majority of my life, I had not been "really living." I was addicted to my ego, seeking to establish it and enhance it through golf, God and girls. I was an addict and I was a slave. And, frankly, so are you. So is everyone who is hooked on love.

As we begin part four of the book, I want you to know that this section is about "really living." It's time to move beyond principle, beyond learning and even beyond awareness and begin taking direct, life-changing *action* to free ourselves from our addiction and make relationship bliss possible. For awareness without action leaves us stuck being very smart slaves instead of fulfilled, liberated beings.

The insights you've discovered about yourself and the processes you've completed as you've worked through this book have prepared you to take action, to take practical steps to free yourself from the prison of relationship addiction. And what would a book about addiction be if it didn't have a 12 step program? So, in the twelve short chapters that follow, I will outline the actual twelve steps I took in my life that allowed me to leave Margaritaville and take up permanent residence in Narnia. These steps are not theories dreamed up in some ivory tower, nor have they been gleaned from reams of research data. Frankly, they are more reliable than that. They are the steps I took to transform my life and so I know they work. I have absolute confidence that they will work for you because you and I are fundamentally the same.

Updating AA's 12 Steps

However, before I describe my 12 steps, I want to briefly comment on the original 12 Steps made famous by *Alcoholics Anonymous*. In my opinion, AA has been one of the most successful human development organizations the world has ever seen, yet I believe their 12 Step Program needs to be updated.

AA and the 12 steps were originally created in the early 1930's from insights gleaned from Christianity and western psychology. Since then, however, our collective understanding of psycho-spiritual development has evolved dramatically. In recent decades, it has become clear, both on a philosophical and experiential level, that the eastern wisdom traditions (e.g. Buddhism, Taoism, Hinduism) and the consciousness movement, espoused most recently by enlightened masters like Ken Wilber, Byron Katie, Gay Hendricks, Hale Dwoskin and Eckhart Tolle (to name only a few), have had extremely valuable things to say about personal development and it would be foolish to ignore them. AA needs to be updated to include this "new" wisdom. To disregard it would be akin to using a manual typewriter instead of a computer. Yes, a typewriter works, but not as efficiently or as quickly as does a computer. In like fashion, AA has three aspects of its recovery model that need to be updated and I want to discuss them briefly.

1. Mistaken Identity

When someone speaks at an AA meeting, they begin by saying, "Hello, my name is _____, and *I am* an alcoholic." That is a bold-faced lie! It's not who they are! They are Presence. They are Beingness. They are Unbounded Freedom, as are all of us. And what's really tragic, is that though such a statement is made in an effort to stay vigilant about sobriety, it actually makes it more difficult. For how long can anyone resist acting in accordance with who they believe, and publicly declare, themselves to be?

Imagine a little girl named Cindy and it's her first day of school. Last year, in third grade, she struggled in math. So as she stands up to introduce herself to her new fourth grade class, she says, "Hello, my name is Cindy and I am terrible at math." Wait,

162

it gets better. What if the teacher and the entire class *believed* her story and actually applauded her for her "honesty"? How do you think she's going to do in fourth grade math?

Frankly, it amazes me that anybody has ever stayed sober if they continually identify themselves as an alcoholic. All of our choices, decisions and actions are a reflection of our self image. We can only act in accordance with who we believe ourselves to be.

Don't misunderstand me. There is a time when it is absolutely necessary to say, "I am an alcoholic," and that's when, but *only* when, a person is first facing and accepting their problem. But in AA, this facing stage lasts forever! To me, this is slavery, not freedom. Once a person has faced and accepted their addiction, they need to begin choosing a new path and taking action. Otherwise an addict is perpetually facing and never *really living*.

The greatest contribution being offered to our culture from the eastern wisdom traditions and the consciousness movement is the emphasis they place on recognizing our deepest spiritual identity. (Christianity should also be a major player in this area, but they are lost in legalism and control.) We are called to look through, or beyond, all the personas, labels, stories and addictions that we think are real—that which we *think we are*—and see the unbounded, limitless Beings that we *truly* are. With just one glimpse of Presence, the Awareness that we are, every addiction would evaporate instantly. But if someone identifies with their personas and stories, which is what is happening when an addict continually says, "I am—*whatever*," then they will live in a constant battle with them. For again, *it's hard to resist being who you perceive yourself to be.*

2. Living in Present Time
Another extremely valuable contribution made by the "new age" movement, is the call to live in the present moment. The "I am..." statement made in AA meetings is spoken of, and thought of, in the present tense, as if it was happening *now*. But unless a person is attending a meeting with a real drink in their hand (or in our case, a human "drink" in our arms!) it isn't true in present time. It isn't here—NOW. This may sound like semantics, but it is enormously important. Addiction is a memory and lives only in the past. Addiction doesn't exist in present time. It's a story about the past, even if the past was last night. But by talking about

it like it was NOW, the past becomes present, and that perpetuates the struggle against something that can not be found in the moment. Yes, a person might have a sensation in the moment that they might label a craving. That can be present; that can be what's NOW. But if someone looks within, they will never find addiction present. It isn't real. It's a memory and a story about the past.

Now, I'm not saying that a person who was addicted to alcohol can drink responsibly once they know who they truly are. Chemical addiction doesn't seem to work that way. But I am saying if someone continues to identify themselves as an addict and declares it to be true *in the moment,* the struggle will never end and true freedom will never be experienced.

3. The Law of Attention

To make matters worse, many addicts continue to attend meetings even after years of sobriety. No wonder they often report living with constant cravings and the fear of relapse! They are surrounded by addiction. All they think and hear about is either drinking or not drinking. How could anyone expect the cravings to subside and the frequency of relapses to diminish when their whole life revolves around their addiction? AA needs to teach its members the Law of Attention, which says this: *What you put your attention on grows.*

Additionally, the whole point of AA, and recovery in general, is to let go of compulsive behavior and experience freedom of choice. If an addict is no longer drinking or using, but habitually attending meetings after years of sobriety, as is often the case, hasn't the addiction simply shifted from one expression to another? Isn't the addict persona still running the show? In my view, if someone has been sober for more than three years and still feels a need to attend regular meetings, they're still addicted, except it's to meetings instead of their drug! AA should be strongly confronting those who habitually attend meetings year after year after year. For this, too, is not *really living.*

It is time that the people who attend AA meetings be encouraged to say, "My name is _____, and I am Unbounded Freedom. And in the past, this body-mind used to be addicted to alcohol (or whatever). I've been attending meetings for a while and it is time that I let go of my past and begin to *really live.* Thank you so much for your support, but I won't be back again."

Roy's 12 Steps

Now, back to our regularly scheduled programming. I would like to make a couple of comments about my 12 step program. First, I had no idea I was working through these 12 steps when I was actually doing them. I was simply living my life as best I could, working with my coach and slowly "sobering up." There was no template that we were following. But looking back, I noticed that I did take 12 distinct steps and so I will share them with you in the order in which they unfolded in my life.

Is it important that you do them in the order in which they appear? Well, yes, at least the first seven steps anyway, and here's why.

When the Space Shuttle is launched, before it can even think about docking with the International Space Station, its ultimate mission and goal, it must first focus all of its energy and attention on escaping the Earth's powerful gravitational pull. Once it gets free, then it can turn its attention to docking with the Space Station. Likewise, before you can think about "docking" at Narnia, you must focus your complete energy and attention on breaking free from the powerful gravitational pull of Margaritaville. In other words...

Before you think about *finding love*, you need to break your addiction *to love*.

That is the whole point of this book. The first seven steps are all about breaking free from Margaritaville's powerful gravitational pull. Once it no longer has its hooks in you, which happens at the completion of step seven, then you can begin preparing to "dock" at Narnia. So work through the first seven steps in order. Then work the rest of the steps in any order you want. However, the way I did it proved successful, so why reinvent the wheel?

Second, I would advise you to read through all the steps and then come back and put your full attention on each one, staying with each step for as long as needed, until you and your coach think you've completed them impeccably.

Third, it may take you a while to work through the 12 steps (though the first four can be completed in a single day!). Relationship addictions can be mild, moderate or severe and the time needed to fully recover will depend upon how deeply you are addicted and how dedicated you are to getting "sober." While I was highly dedicated, my addiction, in my opinion, was in the moderate range and it took me a solid year before I felt free and capable of creating something healthy with a woman. If your addiction is mild, your journey may be shorter. If it is more severe, it may take you longer. Don't get stuck on the time frames, however, because everyone's journey is unique. My point is that this is a process. There are no quick fixes or short cuts.

Fourth, while leaving Margaritaville means that you stop "drinking," (sobriety, if nothing else, means you don't use anymore) that doesn't mean you can't be in a relationship as you work through these steps, nor does it mean you can not begin a new one during the process. I'll explain this more when we get to Step Seven. For now, just know that you don't have to become a monk or a nun for the next year!

So, are you ready? Are you ready to "really live?" Are you ready to leave Margaritaville and begin the journey to Narnia? If so, our first step is to make sure we have, indeed, hit Rock Bottom.

Grab your backpack. Let's go!

CHAPTER 16

STEP ONE:
First Things First—Hit Rock Bottom!

Are you willing to be sponged out, erased, cancelled?
Are you willing to be made nothing, dipped into oblivion?
If not, you will never really change.

—D.H. Lawrence

It is rare when someone's life substantially changes without hitting Rock Bottom. Yes, I have heard of people whose lives were changed because of a voice from the heavens or a compelling dream of a better life, but for most of us "normal" people, hitting Rock Bottom is what changes our lives. The raw and startling reality that our life is painfully and horribly out of control is usually the greatest catalyst for the deepest and most profound kind of life transformation.

Rock Bottom is a turning point, an end-of-an-era moment when we declare, "That's it! I am done with this!" Sometimes it occurs in a time of great drama and despair, other times in a quiet moment of solitude. But no matter the form, Rock Bottom is a whole-body commitment to forge a new path. Whether you want to lose weight, stop abusing drugs or alcohol, get out of debt, find a new career, improve your golf game or create relationship bliss, your life will not change unless you reach this point.

Let me put it this way. Many people *say* they want to change their lives; many think they *should* change their lives; many people *dream* of changing their lives; many people even *try* to change their lives, but only those who hit Rock Bottom actually *do* change their lives. So let's be crystal clear on what Rock Bottom is and what it isn't.

First, know that Rock Bottom's defining characteristic is not emotion. This is an important point, because many people confuse big emotion with hitting Rock Bottom. Being authentically filled with despair over some sort of relationship disaster does not mean your life will change.

167

Secondly, making dramatic promises or "never again" statements does not mean you've hit Rock Bottom. (I made a bunch of those.) No, Rock Bottom's chief characteristic and tell-tale sign is *awareness*. Rock Bottom is an awakening, a deep knowing, an understanding, a revelation, an "aha" moment—call it whatever you want—but when a person has truly hit Rock Bottom you'll know it because they will have become *aware*. Aware of what, you ask? Aware of what I call *"The 4 "R's" of Rock Bottom."* Read them carefully and when you finish, ask yourself, "Have I hit Rock Bottom? Do these four R's truly characterize me?"

Reality

The first "R" of Rock Bottom is seeing *Reality*. This means that you see the truth about yourself with jaw-dropping, smelling-salt clarity. *You* have a problem! A dysfunctional pattern exists in *you!* This kind of clarity is not necessarily emotional and it often leaves one speechless. It's an awakening; a kind of quiet inner knowing. It's what happened to me that night in the Caribbean. I *KNEW* I had a problem. And you, too, must have this kind of encounter with reality. This is the first authentic sign that you have hit bottom.

Responsibility

The second "R" is *Responsibility*, which is an awareness that says, "*I* did this." People who have hit Rock Bottom take full responsibility for their relationship history and experience. It's no one else's fault. They stop blaming others (partners, parents, fate or the gods) for their pain and they stop holding anyone else accountable for their heartache.

One of the reasons I love Jimmy Buffett's song, *Margaritaville*, so much is that as the song progresses, he takes more and more responsibility for his experience. He sings, "*Some people say there's a woman to blame,*" and he follows it with these three different phrases:

- *...but I know it's nobody's fault*
- *...now I think, Hell, it could be my fault*
- *...and I know it's my own damn fault*

Isn't that beautiful? He goes from *denying* responsibility to *wondering* if he is responsible, to *owning* it completely. A sure sign that you are done with your addiction is that you, like the song says, know that it's *your* own damn fault. When you talk about your troubled love life, there is only one name that comes up in the discussion—yours. It's not about anybody else. You no longer play the victim or point fingers at anyone other than yourself.

This doesn't mean your partner(s) had no part in the drama. Of course they did. It's just that they don't concern you anymore. It's not about them, it's about you. You simply recognize that without your unconscious needs and actions, none of it would have been possible.

Taking this kind of responsibility is not to be confused with self-loathing, guilt or shame. It's not dark or negative at all. It's actually quite liberating. It's simply about ownership. Julie wasn't responsible, Pam wasn't responsible, my ex wasn't responsible, my mother wasn't responsible, women in general weren't responsible—I was. I was responsible. It was my own damn fault.

Resist

The third "R" is the awareness of our inability to *Resist* our addictive compulsions. It dawns on us that we can't stop. In *Alcoholics Anonymous*, this is called powerlessness. A love addict who has hit bottom is aware that they do not have the inner strength to resist their crazy relationship impulses.

I knew that creating a committed relationship with Julie while I was still married was insane. I knew that it was nuts to go on a romantic vacation with Pam after I had broken up with her six weeks earlier. And I knew that having two, and sometimes three Internet dates a day was a clear sign that something goofy was going on with me. But I couldn't stop, I couldn't resist. The emptiness and loneliness were just too intense and too strong.

So a critical aspect of Rock Bottom is an admission that we, given the inner power that we currently have access to, are unable to resist our addictive impulses. We are powerless.

Notice, however, I wrote, "currently have access to", because in reality, we *do* have the power to resist our obsessive impulses. We just don't know who we truly are and what's available to us as Spirit Beings.

Let me illustrate. Large trucks usually have two fuel tanks. If you were driving the truck, but didn't know of the second tank, when the first tank ran dry, you'd say my truck is "powerless" and you'd be right. But that's only because you don't know of the second tank and you haven't learned how to "flip the switch" and access the power you didn't know you had.

But we have a "second" tank and we can only learn of *Its* existence when we realize that we don't have any power left in *our* tank. Rock Bottom breaks us and opens us to something deeper within us and that enables us to discover our connection to Source or Presence. When we're powerless, we look beyond ourselves, or better put, we look within ourselves and it's there that we discover Rivers of Living Water.

Re-Act

The final "R" is *Re-Act*. In the end, if you want to break free of your relationship addiction and experience bliss, you have to take action. Funny thing is, you've done that in the past, haven't you? Haven't you vowed to change, to do love differently? I know I did. But the problem, as we discussed in Chapter 10, was that our actions were misguided. We attempted to change our love lives by "Going Fishing," hiring "Mr. Goodwrench," or "Putting Lipstick on a Pig." We thought the problem and the solution were "out there."

But now we are going to take action again, we are going to *Re*-Act, only this time instead of finding a new partner or trying to change our current partner, we're going to focus our attention "in here," on ourselves, and take the "Into-me-I-see" approach espoused by His Holiness, The Guru Pitka. And in a nutshell, this Re-Action means to fully *commit*, with passion and tenacity, to the next eleven steps of your journey.

If you put your attention fully on your self and your spiritual liberation, I guarantee that in the end, you will have the most blissful, amazing love life imaginable. But you must commit.

Commitment is the act of gathering your energy and moving in a chosen direction. What direction is that? Narnia, via the next eleven steps. It worked for me and it will work for you—*if* you're fully committed to it. Your liberation must become your new obsession! Step 1, then, is absolutely the most important step. (In fact, it could be said to be the only step.)

If all four of the "R's" don't completely resonate in your being, then that simply means you're not done "drinking" yet. And there's no shame in that whatsoever. It took me a long time before I was ready to fully embrace each of these four "R's."

I tried to "sober up" because I wanted to set a good example for my young son. It didn't work. I tried to "sober up" because I knew I was wasting so much time and money on women. That didn't work. I tried to "sober up" because I wanted to impress my friends and especially my coach, Diana. That didn't work either. You only stop "drinking" when YOU want to stop "drinking." And if YOU don't want to stop yet, if you still want to cling to your faith in love, then I honor that commitment. You will continue to suffer, of course, but that may be what you need to do. So go "drink." When you're ready, when you've hit bottom, this book and the next eleven steps will be here waiting for you.

Finally, if you feel you have hit bottom, that the four R's are true for you, then I need to tell you one really important thing before we move on. Commitment does not mean that you never relapse or "fall off the wagon." You probably will. I did. If (or when) it happens, don't get discouraged and don't give up. Simply Re-Act again. Return to the twelve steps with even stronger determination.

Affirmation

My name is _____ **and I *was* a relationship addict.**

171

CHAPTER 17

STEP TWO:
Commit To Navel Gazing

"Your vision will become clear only when you can look inside your own heart. Who looks outside, dreams; who looks inside awakens."

—Carl Jung

One of the more interesting aspects of Internet dating is reading the profiles that people write about themselves. People will describe themselves as fun-loving, fit, kind, smart, successful, generous, honest, and so on. Having read literally thousands of profiles (not to mention those that I wrote about myself), do you know what term I never saw anyone use, including me? Navel gazing. No one describes themselves as a navel gazer. Why? Well, it's just not a sexy thing to say about yourself, right? I mean, how many responses would I have received if my profile read, "I am an athletic, funny, talkative, warm, successful man who is a committed navel gazer." That sounds a little creepy, not to mention, self-absorbed and egomaniacal. I doubt many people would respond to such a profile.

But, as you might have guessed, that's not what I mean by navel gazing. When I say navel gazing, I'm referring to being *curious about yourself.* Wondering about yourself is absolutely critical if you are going to create a blissful love life. To be curious means to turn your attention inward, not in a narcissistic, self-absorbed, the-world-revolves-around-me kind of way, but in a humble desire to understand yourself and what makes you tick. It's being inwardly inquisitive. It means to lovingly question your motives, beliefs, attitudes, actions and results.

Think about it. Most advancement in science, medicine, transportation and communication has occurred because someone was curious. Likewise, curiosity is the core value of relationship transformation. Conviction, curiosity's arch enemy, is what keeps us stuck repeating the same old patterns and experiencing the same old pain. While being a person of conviction may seem to be a positive quality (and in some sense it is), when it comes to personal development, it is deadly. Conviction means having a fixed and firm belief about something; it means you think you know the truth. And when you think know the truth about yourself, you close your mind to new insight.

Now, anyone who is reading this book is, by definition, curious and open to learning. So why am I stressing something you're already doing? Well, because it is easy to be curious when you're looking for something that is pleasant and desirable. For example, when you were a kid, curiosity came easy when you were looking for hidden Christmas presents, right? But when you thought there was a monster under your bed, was it as easy to search for that? Of course not. Unfortunately, when we commit to being curious about ourselves and our relationship dynamics, we may encounter more "monsters" than "presents."

When I discovered that my self-esteem was so low that I needed the affection and attention of a beautiful woman to make me feel like a man, to make me feel special and worthy, do you think that discovery felt like I found the Christmas stash? No, that was like finding a "monster" under my bed.

Your journey to Narnia is going to uncover some "monsters" under your bed as well. There will be painful discoveries (you've probably had a few already). Your eyes will be opened and it won't feel so good. Our instinct is not to look for something that is scary or potentially painful. *And so, it is essential that our curiosity be greater than our fear of what we might discover about ourselves.*

Dr. Gay Hendricks describes the importance of curiosity and wonder this way:

> "The path of conscious living is paved with stepping-stones of wonder. Your wonder comes alive the moment you shift from conviction to curiosity. The wondering sojourner reaps a singular reward given only to those who keep their curiosity alive: pure, raw, unfiltered experience. One moment the raw experience may be blissful, the next moment unbearably painful or unfathomably confusing, but it is always genuine, direct and all yours."

Wonder Questions

After hitting Rock Bottom, what's the first thing you should do? Answer: Commit to Navel Gazing. Let go of your convictions and beliefs and turn your attention inward. Become curious. Look for the path "paved with stepping-stones of wonder," for it leads to your liberation. Here's a few wonder questions to get you started. And remember, your responsibility is to open and wonder; it's the Universe's responsibility to show you the truth. Don't strive for answers. Just open your heart and listen.

- What does it mean for me to take 100% responsibility for my relationships and the drama I experience?
- What is the deepest need I am expecting my love relationship to fulfill?
- Is that need my responsibility, and if so, how can I fill it?
- What would happen if I wasn't in a relationship for a while?
- Do my lovers or partners have anything in common?
- Is there a pattern or typical cycle that my relationships take?
- What is my purpose in life? What am I about?
- How have I required my love life to be the way it is?
- What is the payoff for my addiction? What do I get out of it?
- Am I ready for intimacy?

Affirmation

I embrace curiosity and wonder and let go of conviction, allowing the Universe to show me the deepest truth about myself.

CHAPTER 18

STEP THREE:
Choose To Be A Stupid Dog!

"There is no birth of consciousness without pain."

—Carl Jung

I want to tell you a story about two dogs. They had everything in common except for one thing. One dog was smart, the other was really stupid.

These two dogs lived together in the same yard for years, and quite frankly, they were sick of it. They had each peed in their favorite places a thousand times and there was nothing new to smell and explore. It was boring and familiar. They wanted out of their yard. They were sick of the life they were living.

To make matters worse, they could clearly see a whole world of unexplored territory just beyond the boundaries of their yard. Their curiosity was killing them! It was right there in their face, cruelly taunting them. Everything looked as if it would smell so wonderful! They could see kids kicking a soccer ball—God how they both wanted to chase that ball! There were other dogs to play with, rabbits to chase and there was a bright red fire hydrant that had their names written all over it! Life outside their yard looked like absolute doggy bliss. Their lives, however, were going nowhere. They were stuck in their boring yard and frustrated that their life was being wasted. They wanted a new life in the worst way.

And, of course, these two dogs tried to leave their yard on many occasions. It seemed that every couple of months they would have an experience that would remind them of just how disappointing and frustrating their life was. And each time the stupid dog would say to the smart dog, "That's it. I'm done with this yard! I'm leaving." But then the smart dog would remind the stupid dog of what happens whenever they try to leave. You see, as soon as they took a step out of their yard, they would experience excruciating pain. They weren't really sure why or how it happened (even the smart dog didn't know), but whenever they left their yard, by even an inch, they would get an incredible jolt of pain in their necks. It felt like they were being stuck by lightening. It was indescribable pain. So they stayed in their yard, wanting a new life but turning back from pursuing it—*because of the pain.*

This went on for some time until one day—and there's no nice way to put this—the stupid dog allowed his stupidity to get the best of him. No one really knows why either. Maybe the wind blew a different direction and the stupid dog got a really strong whiff of what it smelled like beyond his yard; maybe he saw a little boy throw a Frisbee and his dog ran, leaped and caught it; maybe it was a rabbit that came close to the boundary of his yard and arrogantly smirked at him—no one knows for sure. But this day, the stupid dog made a commitment. He was leaving his yard.

This drove the smart dog insane. He scolded him, telling him that smart dogs have the good sense to avoid pain. Only a really stupid dog would go intentionally toward pain. *But the stupid dog had reached a point where the pain of staying was greater than the pain of leaving.*

So the stupid dog trotted back to the middle of the yard to get a running start. As he took off *toward the pain,* he heard his friend barking at him to stop. But he ignored his voice and ran as fast as he could, gritting his teeth, yet focusing his eyes intently on that awesome red fire hydrant and prepared to be struck by lightening.

And sure enough, the instant he left his yard, he was struck by a bolt of lightening. His neck became a ring of fire and he yelped and shrieked in agonizing pain. For a moment he thought his friend, the smart dog, was right. Maybe this was a stupid thing to do because the pain was beyond anything he could have imagined. But he kept his legs churning, refusing to stop. He wasn't going to give in to the pain this time like he had so many times before. He was not turning back. He was going to live a new life or die trying.

And then something amazing happened. It stopped. The pain completely stopped. Just like that. It was as if someone turned off a light switch. The pain just vanished. He couldn't believe it. He laughed and cried at the same time as he realized that he spent his entire life stuck in that yard believing that the pain would never end, only to find out it only lasted for a few feet. He went straight to that delicious looking fire hydrant, sniffed it and then drenched it. *Oh, life is good!* He spotted that rabbit with the attitude and took off after it. And as he did so, he thought to himself, "My friend, the smart dog, was right! I am a stupid dog—*and now I'm free!"*

If you have truly hit Rock Bottom and made the commitment to forge a new path, which is leaving Margaritaville for Narnia, your new commitment, coupled with your navel gazing curiosity, will quickly introduce you to incredible pain. *What you do in response to this arising pain is critical as to whether or not you ever truly change your life and enjoy relationship bliss.* This third step is about *willingness.* You must choose to be a stupid dog. You must be willing to fight for your freedom. There are three kinds of pain that will arise from your commitment to stop "drinking." If you want to *really live,* then you'll have to find the courage to fight through each of them.

Withdrawal
The first pain is *Withdrawal.* When I stopped Internet dating, going to pick-up bars and dating just about any woman who would go out with me, I had a lot of time on my hands and I began to feel desperately lonely. Here's what I want to warn you about. "Sobriety" is not going to be a picnic. It's going to be *initially* hard and painful. You're going to crave a "drink" something fierce and you will need a "fix." Withdrawal is part of the healing process. You will be very, very lonely; you may have panic attacks and sleepless nights. But like the stupid dog, if you keep going, your withdrawal symptoms will decrease in intensity and you'll be free.

The Unknown
The second pain you'll run into comes from the *Unknown.* More specifically, I'm talking about the crazy stories we create in our heads *about* the unknown, scenarios that feel so painful that they derail our commitment to staying "sober." For example, after Julie broke up with me, I remember thinking I would grow old with no one in my life. I told myself stories about spending Christmases and birthdays alone. I even wondered what I would do if I fell down and broke my hip when I was 70! Who would help me? Who would call for an ambulance? I imagined dying on

177

my kitchen floor and being found months later by a stranger who became curious about the awful smell coming from my home! Our minds create amazing stories when we're faced with the unknown. One minute my fiancée breaks up with me, the next I'm an old man—abandoned, forgotten, rotting!

Trust me. You will have crazy thoughts like that if you quit "drinking." And our natural response to such painful scenarios is to abandon our commitments and either stay in dead-end, unhealthy relationships or get hooked up again at the speed of light. But if you don't react to your painful thoughts, you'll soon find that they evaporate in the light of your emerging sanity.

Revelation
This final pain is arguably the most difficult to endure because it hurts the most. My guess is that it's the primary reason most addicts relapse or renege on their commitments. I call this pain "Revelation" because of what is *revealed* when an addict stops "drinking." Every addict, not only love addicts, uses his or her drug of choice to medicate something painful. An addiction is a type of psychological Advil, something we "take" to keep from feeling pain.

When we stop "drinking," what we're really doing is inviting everything we've been suppressing and avoiding to bubble up to the surface. And what we'll experience, maybe for the first time in a long time, are deep feelings of rejection, fear and abandonment from our childhoods. The smart dog wants no part of this! Why invite pain? But the stupid dog discovers that if he chooses to feel the pain by going toward it, rather than continuing the old pattern of avoiding it, he ends up liberated and "really living."

The bottom line is this: You are going to face some significant pain on your journey to Narnia. This journey may be the most difficult thing you've ever done. You will need to dig deep for courage and determination. How badly do you want it? Will you face the pain? Are you a stupid dog?

Affirmation

I am willing to face, rather than avoid, whatever pain arises from my commitment to relationship sobriety.

CHAPTER 19

STEP FOUR:
Retain a Rude Relationship Coach

"When the student is ready, the teacher will appear."

—Buddhist Proverb

Have you noticed that nearly every successful person, in any field or in any endeavor, has a coach or a team of coaches around them? Those who are committed to bridging the gap between their life and their dreams hire coaches. Why would we approach relationships differently? *If you want relationship bliss, you have to hire a relationship coach.*

You can't do it alone. You can't do it alone. You can't do it alone! You can't break free of your addiction alone. Discovering your unconscious agreements, getting off the Drama Triangle, identifying your personas and reclaiming your shadow, facing the pain that arises as you stop "drinking" and learning new tools to build a conscious, healthy relationship can't be done successfully without help.

I've been candid with my problems and personal issues in this book. But now I want to tell you one of my very best qualities. Besides being curious, I ask for help. I am not too proud to ask someone to help me achieve my goals. I've done it in every area of my life, including my love life. Without the love, support, guidance and the occasional kick in the ass from my relationship coach, Diana, I would never have unwound my issues with women and created the relationship I now enjoy with my wife. I could not have done it without her. She was my guru, my mentor, my guide, my sage, my cheerleader—my coach. If you don't have a personal coach, you are missing out on one of the most amazing experiences life has to offer.

But in order for it to work for you as it has for me, you must choose wisely. Your relationship coach is a lot like a golf instructor. If they don't know what they're doing, you will get worse!

179

So, based upon my experience, here are a couple of tips on choosing a great relationship coach. (By the way, if you choose to use a counselor or a therapist instead of a coach, that's perfectly fine. They are synonyms as far as this chapter goes. No matter what their title is, however, evaluate them the same way.)

The Rave Factor

First, ask around. Try to find someone people rave about. You're worth it. Talk to people you know and trust and ask them if they know of a good coach.

Experience

This is huge. Find someone with real, down-in-the-dirt, personal experience with relationship addiction. In other words, don't focus on the number of years they've been working with people and don't put too much stock in the letters after their name. You want to find someone who's lived your life and come out of it successfully. In other words, look for a reformed relationship addict! If you choose not to call me or someone like me, then at least look for someone who's been divorced (or at least been through some really tough times) and now has a great relationship. Failure is the best teacher. Put little emphasis on credentials. Put a lot of emphasis on their spirituality and what has occurred in their lives. When you interview them (and you should do that), ask them about their relationship history and the current condition of their love life. *You're looking for someone who can do it, not just talk about it.* If they don't have a great love life, how can they help you create one? Would you hire personal trainer who was highly educated, but fat and out of shape? Of course not. And let me go so far as to say that if a prospective coach (or therapist) won't discuss their personal life, if they won't talk about their successes and failures and what they learned because of them, then I wouldn't work with them.

Gender

I suggest you choose a coach of the opposite sex. There's a huge benefit in doing this. Here's why.

It would be the understatement of the century to say that I had issues with women. I did not know how to relate to a woman without being Casanova. I not only had to let go of "him," but I had to learn a whole new way of being with women. Diana, my

180

coach, became Woman for me, a feminine space in which I could experiment with a "new" version of my Self. I could practice being Roy with her; a fearless, authentic man who expresses his wants, needs and feelings in a healthy way and not a guy who simply exists to take care of her. I don't think that I could have done that as effectively if I was working with a male coach. While I didn't choose Diana because she was a woman (consciously), in the end, it was a gift from the universe that she was.

Eastern Philosophy
I would *not* recommend a coach or a therapist who rejects the principles found in the eastern wisdom traditions. In my opinion, you will be better served to find someone who has a more holistic and integral philosophy of life. Avoid those who are solely committed to either a traditional Western view of psychology and/or a fundamentalistic and evangelical view of spirituality. Look for someone who appreciates and uses the work of Eckhart Tolle, Deepak Chopra, Marianne Williamson, Wayne Dyer, Byron Katie, Elizabeth Gilbert, Sark, Michael Bernard Beckwith, Hale Dwoskin, Ken Wilber and Gay Hendricks in their practice.

Hire A Rude Coach
Finally, and most importantly, make it your intention to find a coach who won't coddle you or let you skate. Diana was an amazingly "rude" relationship coach. There were many times that I wanted to crawl through the phone and throttle her (we did all our coaching by phone, which works great, by the way). You need someone who is not afraid of losing you as a client but is willing to speak the truth to you as they see it. Ken Wilber, puts it this way:

> "When it comes to spiritual [coaches], there are those who are safe, gentle, consoling, soothing, caring; and there are those outlaws, the living terrors, the Rude Boys and Nasty Girls of God-realization, the men and women who are in your face, disturbing you, terrifying you, until you radically awaken to who and what you really are.
> And may I suggest?: choose your [coaches] carefully.

If you want encouragement, soft smiles, ego stroking, gentle caresses of your self-contracting ways, pats on the back and sweet words of solace, find yourself a Nice Guy or Good Girl, and hold their hand on the sweet path of stress reduction and egoic comfort. But if you want Enlightenment, if you want to wake up, if you want to get fried in the fire of passionate infinity, then, I promise you; find yourself a Rude Boy or a Nasty Girl, the ones who make you uncomfortable in their presence…who will suffer you not sweet comfort but abject terror, not saccharine solace but scorching angst, for then, just then, you might very well be on the path to your own Original Face."

Affirmation

I have a relationship coach to support my sobriety, my personal growth and the creation of a healthy, blissful relationship.

CHAPTER 20

STEP FIVE:
Go Public with Your Personas

"Therefore, confess your sins to one another...so that you may be healed."

—James 5:16

Quite early in your work with your coach, you will begin discussing your relationship personas. A persona, you will recall, is the fictitious "person" we became in our early years to ensure that we would receive the love and attention we needed and deserved. I named my primary relationship persona "Casanova" because that image best captured the way I thought I had to act in order to get women (originally Mom) to like me. The most important thing to keep in mind about personas is that they are a role we are playing—*unknowingly.* By that I mean we don't know that we are *playing* a role; we think we *are* the role. Therefore, they are deeply entrenched and ingrained. And as you well know, changing life-long patterns is anything but easy, but it's especially difficult if you don't know they are there! But through your work in this book and the work with your coach, you are waking up to them.

But how do you break free of them and actually stop acting as your persona? It's one thing to become aware of them, that's a crucial step, but what we're really interested in is actually getting free of them. Is there something practical and concrete we can do to set ourselves free, to stop showing up in love relationships as our persona self? Yes. Quite simply, go public with them. Tell everyone close to you about your relationship personas. This simple act is the quickest and most effective way to set you free.

To Speak or Not to Speak
There are two primary reasons why this is true. First, if everyone close to you knows about your relationship personas, you can't get away with it anymore! Early in my "recovery," I told my buddies all about Casanova. I told them what he looked

like, sounded like and acted like. I wanted them to be able to spot him in me even if I couldn't, which happened frequently. I wanted them to kick my butt if they saw me channeling him.

Even after I was sober for quite some time, I still went public. I told my wife about Casanova within in the first month of our relationship. I wanted her to know about "him" so that she could call me out if she sensed I was slipping into that sweet, but fear-driven, self. And many times in our relationship, I'd say or do something and she'd get a suspicious look in her eye and say, "That didn't feel right. Who are you right now—Roy or Casanova?" So the first reason why you must go public with your personas is that it creates a support and accountability system.

The second reason is that when you name something and speak of it openly and honestly, you break its spell over you. I spoke of this briefly already, but now I want to give you an example to bring the point home.

The first real sign that I had an addictive relationship to women came back in the early 90's when I was a pastor. (I mentioned this woman back in chapter 2.) There was a woman in the church, one of my wife's best friends, with whom I became totally obsessed. Nothing physical ever took place; we had what I would consider to be an emotional affair. She was in a disappointing marriage, as I was, and we gave each other a lot of emotional affection and attention. We either spoke by phone or in person for at least an hour every day. This went on for about six months. I was obsessed and in lust with her. I thought and fantasized about her all the time. I even arranged to have her hired part-time so I could "legitimately" be around her. But I also knew that I was in some dangerous waters. Things were headed in a direction that scared me.

On one occasion, when I was telling my best friend about my obsession and that I wanted to break free of my feelings for her, he said, "If you truly want to put an end to it, tell your wife. Tell her everything. Tell her the complete unvarnished truth about what's going on, including who it's with, what you talk about—the whole nine yards. And then tell your "mistress" that you told your wife. That will break the spell."

And so that is exactly what I did. I brought the whole thing out into the open—and my friend was right. The obsessive spell was broken. I confessed my "sins" and I was healed. The lust, the

184

fantasies and the emotional connection for the other woman evaporated the moment I went public.

Going public about your personas does the same thing. It breaks their spell over you. When you declare something openly, honestly and publicly, when you bring it into the light, its power over you is broken.*

Confession

What we're really talking about in this chapter is the spiritual practice of confession. Unfortunately, organized religion has corrupted the deepest nature of this ancient spiritual practice by turning it into a mechanical ritual rather than preserving it as the relationship-healing, intimacy-creating tool it was designed to be. Spiritual masters throughout the ages have known that keeping your "sins" private and secret, while healthy for your ego, actually keeps you a slave to them. So if you want to break your persona's hold on your love life and relate as your authentic Self, you must take your personas public and tell *everybody* close to you. That means telling your friends and it also means telling your partner. Whether you are married, living together or just dating someone exclusively, if you want to show up as the real You and live as your Original Shine, which is the key to creating authentic intimacy, then go public with your personas.

Affirmation

I am open and honest about my relationship personas with those close to me.

---

* Note: If you're wondering about what happened when I told my wife, I can summarize it like this: We handled it like we handled everything. We didn't have the courage to really face our deteriorating relationship, which is what this problem signaled, nor did I have the courage to face my own issues, which is what this problem *really* signaled. We instead swept it under the rug and moved on. Of course the issue crawled back out from under that proverbial rug and this time the woman's name was Julie.

CHAPTER 21

STEP SIX:
Complete With Former Lovers

Your task is not to seek for love, but merely to seek and find all the barriers within yourself that you have built against it.

—Rumi

If you were to talk to any sports psychologist and ask them to name the single greatest mental skill a player of any sport needs to master in order to perform at his or her best, my guess is that nearly all of them would say it's the ability to approach the next shot, the next pitch, at-bat, play or point with a clean emotional slate. This is often called, "staying in the present." I call it being complete. Being complete means to play without baggage, to approach your future without the slightest hint of negativity about the past.

As important as it is in athletics, it is exponentially more important in relationships. If you are incomplete with former lovers—and I'm going to tell you in a minute just exactly what that means—then you are self-sabotaging your ability to create future relationship bliss.

And at the outset, I want to tell you that this will most likely be the most challenging step of them all for you. It definitely was for me. Your ego will fight this one tooth and nail because this step asks you to deal with your former "drinks," the very people with whom you have experienced the most drama and pain. And I know that sounds scary. But I'm here to tell you that you can't move forward if you're chained to the past.

Relationship Incompletion

Being incomplete with a former lover means you still have a negative energetic charge toward them. Another way of putting it is that *internally*, you are still in drama with them. If you are holding a grudge, blaming them for your pain, speaking harshly or gossiping about them, you still carry an emotional charge toward them and you are incomplete.

So how do you end the internal drama, release the charge and become complete? Well, *NOT* by vomiting your anger and bitterness all over everyone around you or even all over them! Most people think that being complete with a former lover means giving them a piece of your mind, telling them what a shit they were and how much they hurt you! But dumping doesn't end drama. I tried that with Julie and it doesn't produce completion. It creates more drama and deepens your energetic charge with them, keeping you stuck in Margaritaville.

The only way to release the negative charge is to see that you required the relationship to be exactly as it was. I've touched on this a few times in the book, but I am going to briefly stress it again, because it is **the** most important transformation principle in the entire book. Taking responsibility is the whole enchilada. So here's what I mean when I say you required the relationship to be exactly as it was. As always, I'll use my life as an example.

Casanova occupies the "hero" point on the Drama Triangle. And like every hero, he needs someone to save, a victim, a damsel-in-distress. With that understanding, the night I met Julie in that swanky pick up bar in Chicago, there were dozens of beautiful and available women in the room. Why did I choose her? Why was I attracted to her? The answer: somehow Casanova could *feel* that she was his kind of woman, a damsel-in-distress. Don't ask me to explain how this happens—it's a mystical, energetic thing. My persona, Casanova, the false self running my life at the time, *required* a specific kind of woman, someone he could save, and Julie fit the bill.

So when I became aware of this dynamic, could I really continue to blame Julie for how our relationship unfolded? How could I? I set the whole thing up! This awareness ends the drama and releases the negative energy. I was responsible for the whole mess. There isn't a woman to blame; it's my own damn fault!

When you get curious about your relationships, you'll discover that the same dynamic was happening in you. You required your partners and your relationships to be exactly as they were because of your personas. And when you see this, you will feel a new spaciousness open in your heart. You won't need to forgive anyone for anything because no one did anything to you. The only forgiveness needed is self-forgiveness. Negativity dissolves and the drama is finally over—in you. However, you are still not *fully* complete because you're not complete with them.

Go Public—Again!

In order to be truly complete, you have to tell *THEM* what you now see about yourself and how it negatively impacted your relationship (Breathe...I told you your ego wouldn't like this). True completion requires a short conversation where you share the inarguable truth about *yourself*. You're not there to share your insights about them. I tried that and it doesn't work. Your conversation is limited to what you know to be true of you. This conversation should take no more than five minutes and should be done in person, if at all possible. If it's not, you can use the phone or write a letter. If they won't see or talk to you, or if you do not know where they are, or if they are deceased, you and your coach can role play.

This undoubtedly brings up a ton of questions. Let me answer a few of the more common ones.

1. How will they respond?

When people imagine meeting with a former lover to complete, most worry about what their former lover will say or do in response to what they hear. Will they respond angrily, saying, "I told you so" and dump all over you? Will they call you a psycho-babbling idiot? Or, will they own up to their part and their personas? The simple answer is this: It's none of your business AND it doesn't matter what they say or do with what you share. All that matters is that you complete the relationship. You're not there to have a two-way conversation. You're there to tell your truth and move on. Obviously, if they have something to say, you can listen. But you're not there to argue or debate. That's just more drama. This is about you taking responsibility, and showing them the respect they deserve by owning up to your part in the drama and pain between you. What they say, do or think is none of your business. Also, this is not about apologizing or saying you are sorry and it's definitely not about taking the total blame for what occurred between the two of you. As you know, it takes two to tango. You're just talking about your particular "dance" moves. Whether or not they recognize theirs is none of your business.

2. *Do I have to do this with every single one of my former lovers?*

No. Only those you have an energetic charge with, which are probably only those with whom you had a committed relationship. I had a number of relationships with women I met on the Internet. I have not tried to find them and tell them my story because I feel no energy around them. But I have had completion conversations with my ex, Pam and Julie.

3. *What do I tell them?*

Tell them your story. Tell them what you and your coach have discovered—in less than five minutes. I shared about golf, God, girls, Casanova and my relationship addiction. Each had their own reaction which I listened to and respected. I don't have any negative energy toward any of them anymore. I'm free. I'm complete.

A Completion "Coincidence"

(Note: The "coincidence" story that I'm about to share only occurred to me as I was actually writing the previous paragraph. I honestly had no awareness of it until just a few seconds ago. It was an "aha" moment and tears are streaming down my face as I write. I share this story with you because it is a powerful example of how completing with former lovers opens the space for healthy, authentic love to appear.)

When I met the woman who is now my wife, MaryMargaret, we had some twists and turns in the first month of our relationship. We weren't connecting somehow. We were physically attracted to one another, we enjoyed each other's company and we were spiritually compatible, but for some reason she just didn't seem emotionally responsive to me. She seemed a bit shut down, closed off and kind of lifeless. After a handful of dates, our relationship fizzled in an awkward and confusing way. Like a car running out of gas, we just drifted to a stop. It was very strange.

A week or so after that, I was having a phone session with my coach, Diana, and we realized that I still had some unfinished business with Julie. Though it had been 14 months since we had broken up, I still had some negative energy toward her. Diana said I needed to call her and get complete with this. And I did.

My discussion with Julie got kind of heated initially because I played the victim and blamed her for what she did to me. But then

I came to my senses, took responsibility and told her my story, even though she already knew most of it. The conversation ended beautifully with us sharing kind words of gratitude and appreciation for one another. It was actually a sweet moment between us. It felt like a tender exhale. We were complete.

A few days after that, I found myself thinking of MaryMargaret. I felt as if we were incomplete as well, and because I was so pumped about how good it felt to be complete, I called her as well. I told her that I wasn't comfortable with how our relationship had drifted to a stop and that I wanted to meet and get some closure. I had no thought of her and I being a couple again. None whatsoever. Nor did she.

We agreed to meet at a restaurant that was midway between where we both lived. It was *Cheeseburger In Paradise.* (The irony of that is so outrageously breathtaking that it brings tears to my eyes as I type these words.)

Anyway, initially, she was just as I remembered her: sweet, spiritual, beautiful—and distant. But a transformation in her energy and demeanor began occurring about ten minutes into our meeting. (No, it wasn't her drink taking effect. And no, she was not having a Margarita, smart ass. It was a Mojito.) Words can't really describe what was happening right before my very eyes. She was simply morphing. It was like her cells were rearranging, birthing an entirely new being. The woman I used to know was hidden in a shell, withdrawn, closed up and shut down. This woman was coming to life. She was luscious, vivacious, playful, warm, sensual, flirtatious and outright energetic. She lit up the room. She felt like a gooey vat of chocolate fudge that you wanted to dip your hands into and smear all over your face. She was delicious and I was dumbfounded.

I basically asked her, "What the hell happened to you?!" She knew what I was talking about and seemed as confused by her radiating aliveness as I was. I told her that I had no idea what was going on but that I was having second thoughts about "us" and was thinking maybe we ought to consider dating again. She beamed. We both did. Again, neither of us knew why, but we knew that something had fundamentally shifted between us. As we walked toward the restaurant door, this formerly shelled over, closed down woman grabbed my ass—right in public! We ended up making out in her car like a couple of teenagers!

We have since talked about that night many, many times. It brings a smile to both of our faces. But it was not until I was writing this chapter that I saw the "coincidental" connection between finally being complete with Julie and MaryMargaret's resurrected aliveness. She had no cognitive awareness when we first met that I was somehow still energetically stuck in the past, that I was still incomplete with Julie. But her body could *feel* it. Her deepest Self would not allow her to relax into me because she could feel that I was not fully available for her.

But within ten minutes of sitting and talking with me, again without knowing I had talked and completed with Julie, her body could *feel* that I was fully present, and she opened up like a flower. My incomplete relationship with Julie had shut down her heart. And when I closed the loop with Julie, her body told her that it was now okay to let go and take up residence in my heart, for now there was room.

The lesson is this: To create authentic intimacy with someone takes emotional space within your heart. Being on the Drama Triangle with a former lover dominates the space in your heart and makes genuine intimacy with someone else impossible. Your heart must be open and clear for something new and wonderful to occur. Complete with your former lovers. It was the best thing I ever did.

Affirmation

I have completed with my former lovers by sharing with them how my addiction negatively impacted our relationship.

CHAPTER 22

STEP SEVEN
Go Cold Turkey

It doesn't interest me where or what or with whom you have studied. I want to know what sustains you, from the inside, when all else falls away. I want to know if you can be alone with yourself and if you truly like the company you keep in the empty moments.

—Oriah Mountain Dreamer

A few years back I took my son hiking in the Grand Teton Mountains, near Jackson Hole, Wyoming. After about three hours of pretty intense hiking up the mountain trails and switchbacks, my son, who was twelve at the time, hit the wall. I couldn't blame him; it was a difficult hike. He said, "Dad, a few hours ago I was all excited to go on this journey with you, but it's turning out to be a lot harder than I thought it would be. This isn't very much fun. Is it going to be like this the whole way?"

I gave him a knowing and understanding smile because I hiked this very trail a year earlier and I knew the hard part was just about over. I said, "Son, hang in there. We've got about another half mile up and then we start going down the other side of the mountain. It's a breeze and it's way more fun. And on top of that, when you finish the hike and look back at the mountain you just climbed, the feeling is indescribable. So hang in there and just keep going."

I mention that story because I'm wondering if at this point in our journey to Narnia, you are feeling like my son did. Maybe you too were excited when the journey began but are now hitting the wall, realizing that this journey is a lot harder and a lot less fun than you thought it would be. If so, hang in there. This step, Step Seven, is our last challenging and uphill step and then the rest of the way, I promise you, is downhill and way more fun. Think of it this way. Steps 1-7 are like going to the dentist and steps 8-12 are like going for a massage. The difference will be that dramatic, so hang in there. Also, I can tell you based upon first hand experience, that if you muster the strength to keep going, there is an indescribable joy that awaits you at the end of the journey. It will have been worth it. I guarantee it.

Quit "Drinking"!

We all know that the phrase "going cold turkey" means to abruptly stop using your drug of choice, whether it's cigarettes, alcohol or some other substance. For relationship addiction then, going cold turkey would mean to abruptly stop using our partners and lovers as our drug of choice. In other words, it means to stop "drinking."

But that raises a few questions. For example, if a person is addicted to alcohol and can never drink again, not even in moderation, does that mean that a person who is addicted to love can never be in a relationship again? Well, obviously not. This is a major difference between chemical and non-chemical addictions. For example, if a person is addicted to work, and we all know workaholism is very common, would that mean, if they were in "recovery," that they could never have a job again? You see how absurd it is? So obviously, when I speak of going cold turkey, what I'm talking about is a fundamental shift in *how* we relate with our partners and lovers, not *if* we relate to them. Let me remind you of our definition of relationship addiction:

> *Relationship addiction is any <u>reliance</u> on another person to give you a sense of your self, alleviate a fear, create a feeling of aliveness, or to validate your worth.*

Going cold turkey means not doing *THAT!*

I underlined "reliance" because that is what we must quit doing and what we must forever quit doing. A relationship addict can certainly be in a committed relationship, but he or she must forever quit the habit of sourcing life from from their partners. Going cold turkey means to abruptly stop having "faith in love." Whether you are in a committed relationship or if you're single, never again will you drink Jerry Maguire's Kool-Aid. I want to share an example of this from my life.

New Year's Eve "Sobriety"

About 2½ months after Pam slapped me in the face and about 13 months after Julie broke off our engagement, I had a major breakthrough.[*] This moment proved to me that I was forever done with Margaritaville.

It was New Year's Eve and I had a date with a nice woman named Kathy. We had been out a couple of times. I liked her, yet I knew she wasn't right for me. Nevertheless, I asked her to not only spend New Year's Eve with me, but to spend the entire night with me. Our relationship had not yet become physical and we both knew that this date was going to change all that.

But a couple of days before New Year's Eve, I admitted to myself that to go out with her and sleep with her, when I knew she wasn't right for me, would not only be unfair to her, but it would be a return to relying on a woman to alleviate my fear of loneliness. It would be "drinking" again. Plain and simple. But as much as I knew she wasn't right for me, the truth was that I didn't want to be alone—not on New Year's Eve!

If you're hooked on love, you know that the thought of spending New Year's Eve alone is horrible (the same goes for your birthday and Valentine's Day). So cancelling this date was enormously difficult. But as I hung up the phone, I felt a surge of energy well up in my body and I yelled—out loud—"YES!!! That was the *right* thing to do, Roy. You are *done* playing these Margaritaville games!"

Going Cold Turkey

The observable and visible way my addiction manifested was that I would continue dating a woman long after I knew she wasn't right for me. That was my M.O. That is what I did many, many times. In fact, Pam is a perfect example of this. I knew she wasn't right for me two weeks into our relationship, yet I moved in with her and stayed with her for four months! And then six weeks *after* I broke up with her and moved out, I went on vacation to the Caribbean with her! That's my addiction in action. So going cold turkey, in my life, meant I had to quit doing *THAT!* I had to quit dating a woman the moment I knew she wasn't right for me. And that is exactly what I did on that New Year's Eve. Kathy wasn't

---

[*] I know these dates are confusing. So, again, for a chronological timeline of the events presented in this book, see Appendix I.

right for me and I chose to be lonely rather than be with her and "drink." I said "no" to "A Drink with Legs." It was a breakthrough moment in my life. The question for you is this: What is your M.O.? In the most practical, observable, real-life sense, how does your addiction manifest? What do you do? What's the action, the behavior, the way your addiction expresses itself? If you are single, my M.O. may fit you. Feel free to use it. If you're a guy in a committed relationship, you might say this: "I rely on my partner's physical affection to relieve my stress and make me feel alive." If you're a woman in a committed relationship, yours may sound like this: "I rely on my partner to listen to me, to be at my emotional beck and call, because it makes me feel safe and special." Give it some thought. What's your M.O.? Write it down in the space provided below. Don't describe a feeling, a fear or a belief. Describe, instead, an observable, visible action and behavior. Describe what you actually *DO*.

_____

_____

This observable action is what you must abruptly quit. Going cold turkey means never doing *THAT* again.

Affirmation

I know how my relationship addiction manifests and my intention is to never "drink" like *THAT* again.

CHAPTER 23

STEP EIGHT
Date Yourself!

I had just broken up with a man at the time and was feeling quite lonely. Instead of sinking into my sadness I decided to take on the project of falling in love with myself. Every night I'd make myself a beautiful dinner, even though I didn't cook very well...While I was eating I'd listen to music and light incense. After dinner I'd make a fire for myself and light candles all over my house. It was mood setting just for me. After a week or two, I couldn't wait to go home and be with myself. Instead of waiting to find someone to romance me, I romanced myself—and it worked.

—Debbie Ford

Step Eight is about *experiencing* your own completeness. It's about discovering that loneliness is an absurd and hilarious illusion because you are always in communion with the most amazing companion, the most devoted partner and the most intimate lover anyone could ever dream of—YOU! This step is about resting and relaxing into your own Being-ness, discovering that you *are* that which you have been forever seeking. And one of the most enjoyable ways of discovering this is by dating yourself.

As you know, a perceived internal lack is the fuel of relationship addiction. If we believe we are "thirsty," we will seek "A Drink with Legs." But when we realize that we are filled with "Rivers of Living Water," that perceived lack, that "thirst" which fuels relationship addiction, simply dissolves. It's much like a hurricane which dissolves without the presence of extremely warm water.

Step Eight, and indeed each of the remaining five steps, are all pleasurable and practical activities that I personally engaged in that exposed this perceived lack, or incompleteness, for the illusion that it is. And so we begin with the easiest way to see this, which is to simply spend time with you! Just hang out with you, all by yourself, and you'll see there is no lack, that you're never alone and that there is no emptiness to fill.

When I went cold turkey and no longer dated women who weren't right for me, I obviously went on fewer dates and had more time on my hands. I was terrified of how that felt and complained to my coach, "What am I supposed to do on Friday or Saturday night? Sit home and suck my thumb?" She said, "No. Date yourself." She asked me what I liked to do with my girlfriends and on dates. I mentioned the usual stuff like going out to eat, seeing movies at home or in a theater, talking over a drink, cooking out, attending concerts, playing golf, working out, having sex and so on. "So," she said, "Can't you do all those things by yourself? Go out with yourself, date yourself, be your own partner. Do it for a week and see what happens."

So I did. On one such "date," I was sitting at my favorite bar having a drink, like I did with many a woman, but this time I was alone. It was Saturday night and the place was packed. Normally, if I was alone on a Saturday night, I would have had my head on a swivel looking for "A Drink with Legs," but this time I stayed within myself and my experience. I wasn't looking for anyone because I was already *with* someone—me. And I won't lie to you. At first I felt awkward, lonely and self-conscious. I felt like a loser. But I didn't allow the initial wave of loneliness to scare me into dumping myself. I was tempted to hit on a woman, and somehow distract myself from the uncomfortable feeling I was experiencing, but I instead stayed with myself. And soon, I began to feel okay. In fact, I started to really enjoy myself. I had plenty to talk about! There were some decisions and challenges I was facing and I discussed them with myself (silently). During other moments, I sat with inner silence. I didn't have to fill the emptiness with inner conversation, I could just sit and be, sit and breathe, sit and enjoy my own company. I discovered something amazing that night. I wasn't alone. And even though I am now married, I still date myself. I still go to movies, restaurants and such by myself. It's amazing. I am never alone. Ever.

Now, for those of you who are in committed relationships, this chapter is for you too. You need to take yourself off "life support," which is your partner (I sometimes call him or her, "The Ventilator"), and discover that you can, indeed, breathe on your own. Date Yourself. Do things you like to do all by yourself.

197

Tell your partner what you're up to. This is very important. Even if you're living together, tell them that you've been "using" them like a drug and that you need some time apart from them, time to be with yourself. If they ask if the relationship is at stake, tell them if it is or if it isn't. Most likely it isn't. The point is to tell them exactly what you're doing. And if they love you, they will wholeheartedly support you, for to love someone is want for them what they want for themselves. Lastly, dating yourself is not a chance to spend more time with your friends. They are often "drinks with legs" too. Be alone, be with yourself. Give yourself the chance to *experience* your completeness.

For How Long?

People invariably ask, "How long should I date myself?" And my response is always the same: That is the wrong question. The length of time isn't the point. It could be a single instant, it could be a week, it could be a year. I only went a few weeks without dating someone. The length of time doesn't matter; it's the *realization* that matters. You need to date yourself until you get a glimpse of your own completeness, and if you're open to it, that can come in an instant. But more than likely, it will happen like this: When you go cold turkey, date yourself and quit "drinking," initially the withdrawal symptoms will come. But if you don't run from the pain and choose to be a "stupid dog," they will subside and what will emerge is a quiet inner peace, a relaxed open awareness of your own Presence. Your previously perceived internal lack will dissolve. No longer will you obsess about getting hooked up or staying hooked up, for you will know that you *are* hooked up.

The insightful and playful author, Sark, in her book, *Wild Succulent Women,* summarizes this step beautifully when she writes:

> One time, after a long-term relationship had ended, a friend challenged me and said, "Can you just spend some time <u>alone</u> now?" The idea of being alone terrified me. So I got a cat. This helped. I entered a long period of celibacy, therapy and learning to fall in love with myself...We don't commonly celebrate alone-ness the way we celebrate couples. Nobody says, "How's your love life?—with yourself?" For awhile, I noticed

couples everywhere. Everyone seemed to be "in love" except me. Then I began to realize the gifts that learning to love myself gave. *Finally, I wasn't waiting to be loved!* I took vacations alone, bought clothes for my taste only, read books undisturbed, and turned off the phone for days at a time. Then it seemed time to be in union with myself, so I performed a metaphorical marriage, and promised to love and honor myself until the end. What this meant was that instead of waiting to be married or partnered, I decided to marry myself in a ceremony by the ocean with a private ritual to celebrate. Try this: Marry your self." (Italics, mine)

So, who are you going out with tonight?

Affirmation

I know that loneliness is an illusion because by dating myself, I have experienced my own completeness and I know that I lack absolutely nothing.

CHAPTER 24

STEP NINE:
Have an Affair—with Mother Nature!

One way to define modernity is to trace the process by which nature has been desacralized and God has moved indoors.

—Sam Keen

In Step Eight, we committed to a permanent, exclusive, loving relationship with ourselves, forsaking all others. But in Step Nine, while we are still dating ourselves, we do the unthinkable. We have an affair—with Mother Nature.

If dating yourself was a simple way to experience the truth of your *completeness*, having an affair with Mother Nature is a simple way to experience the depth of your *connectedness*.

Loneliness, as you well know, is the primary felt need that drives relationship addiction. It's behind all the crazy things we do. Loneliness is the feeling or perception of being alone, both internally and externally. When Julie broke off our engagement, I felt both of those with an intensity that I didn't know existed. I felt inwardly empty, vacant and hollow, while externally I felt abandoned, isolated and separate.

But when I started dating myself, I discovered that *internally*, I am anything but vacant and hollow! Jerry McGuire *was* full of shit! I am already complete. I lack absolutely nothing. And when I had an affair with Mother Nature, I discovered that *externally* I was in communion, or "common-union", with all that is. Any sense of being isolated, separate, and abandoned becomes quite humorous when you are lying in the loving arms of Mother Nature.

As I alluded to back in chapter seven, nothing in the physical world teaches us about our deepest spiritual identity and our oneness with God more than nature does. The infinite night sky, the salty ocean air, a towering rocky mountain or a simple flower dissolves our perceived aloneness and helps us see that there is no separation. Mother Nature whispers a sweet something in our ear, telling us that there is no duality, there is only One. This is mystical and it can not be grasped by the mind. It is something that is felt, experienced and simply *known*. Yet, having said that, listen to how Ken Wilber describes it:

> "You might be looking at a mountain, and you have relaxed into the effortlessness of your own present awareness, and then suddenly the mountain is all, you are nothing. Your separate-self sense is suddenly and totally gone, and there is simply everything that is arising moment to moment. You are perfectly aware, perfectly conscious, everything seems completely normal, except you are nowhere to be found. You are not on this side of your face looking at the mountain out there; you simply are the mountain, you are the sky, you are the clouds, you are everything that is arising moment to moment, very simply, very clearly, just so."

During my mid-life crisis year, when I was an emotional mess, one of my favorite places to "hook up" with Mother Nature was on a golf course near my parent's retirement home in Florida. It was one of the main reasons I visited them. When I felt lonely, abandoned, and unable to sleep, I would take long walks on their course, usually near midnight. I especially enjoyed the times when it was warm enough to go outside barefoot, wearing only a t-shirt and shorts. The feeling of the warm, moist air and the cool, damp grass beneath my feet allowed me to feel a deep sense of connection and grounding. But even if it was cold, I would always be completely alone with Mother Nature, never seeing another soul. These were beautiful times for me. I was a hurting, lonely man in the infinite presence of a "loving woman" who would be with me, and welcome me, in whatever way I wanted to show up.

And sometimes these trysts would be filled with intense grief and despair. I'd look up to the heavens crying, complaining and pleading for relief. Other times I would vent my frustration by ranting, screaming, even cussing about the way things had unfolded. I would talk to Mother Nature as if she was my therapist, rehashing old conversations and painful memories I had of Julie and I (as if She didn't already know). I'd ask Mother Nature questions, and even discuss what I was learning from Diana. We had some amazing talks and I received some incredible insights walking those dew-drenched fairways. But the vast majority of these rendezvous' with Mother Nature were silent, tender moments. Strange as it may sound, we were like two lovers who had no need to communicate. We simply walked with each other in the quiet of the night.

No matter how I showed up: sad, angry, scared, talkative or silent, I felt "her" Presence. I was not alone. I was not abandoned. I was not separate and isolated. I was in communion with ultimate Feminine Energy. This may sound grandiose, but I remember thinking, "Oh, this is what King David meant when he wrote in Psalm 23, "Even though I walk through the valley of the shadow of death, I will fear no evil, *for you are with me.*"

Spend time with Mother Nature (call it God or Presence if you want). Rendezvous and be intimate with her often. Discover the absurdity of separateness. Allow her the opportunity to put her arms around you, to communicate to your Spirit that you are not a separate-self, left alone to fend for yourself, but are, in fact, in "common-union" with the entire Universe.

Find those spots where you feel her presence most powerfully, be it on a golf course, standing on the shores of the ocean, hiking in the mountains or gazing up the trunk of a Redwood. When you have vacation time, skip Disney World and go to a National Park. Pass on the mall on a Saturday afternoon and walk on a nature trail. Get outside. Go mountain biking, canoeing, golfing or skiing. Play in the snow, walk in the rain, sleep under the stars. Don't allow yourself to live exclusively in the world of concrete and commitments. Allow Mother Nature to put her loving arms around you, for in her presence, you will find your own.

Affirmation

I regularly rendezvous with Mother Nature. "She" always reminds me that I am One with the whole and never, ever alone.

CHAPTER 25

STEP TEN:
Live *As* the Eye of The Hurricane

"There is a holy nothing at the center of everything, and it is really something."

—Gay Hendricks

As I write these words it is summertime here in Florida and that means it is hurricane season. It's the time of year when the water temperatures in the Caribbean and the Gulf of Mexico reach the upper 80's, creating the ideal conditions for those beautiful, enormous and utterly destructive storms to form.

I have always been fascinated with hurricanes, partly because they are so gigantic and unpredictable, but mostly because they are such a study in duality. The outer bands of the storm are unbelievably chaotic and violent. They not only produce torrential rains, storm surges and tornadoes but they can have *sustained* winds in excess of 150 mph!

But while the outside of a hurricane is chaotic and violent, the center, what is called the Eye of the hurricane, is astonishingly still! There is no storm at the center, only stillness, quietness and calm. It's an extraordinary dichotomy.

A relationship addict, and indeed every human being, is a lot like a hurricane. Sometimes our life situation is a chaotic, spinning, unpredictable mess. But at the center of us, we too have an Eye, a "place" of utter stillness, quietness and calm.

But our task in this chapter is not simply to discover that we have an Eye, nor is it even to discover how to access it and live from it, as valuable as that would be. No, our task is much deeper. What Step Ten is all about is discovering that we *are* the Eye of the hurricane. It is not something we live from, but something we *live as*.

The Spin Cycle

As I mentioned a few chapters back, when I decided to be alone on New Year's Eve and not spend the night with a woman I really wasn't interested in, that was a turning point for me. I *physically* quit "drinking." I went cold turkey. And when the withdrawal symptoms of loneliness and abandonment surfaced, I dated myself and discovered the deep connection I had with myself. Then I had an affair with Mother Nature and discovered that I was intimately connected to the All. And doing those two things utterly transformed my life. They made a radical difference. I no longer spent every waking moment looking for a woman. I quit hitting on them in bars, restaurants, malls and bookstores and I also got off the Internet dating sites. By all *outward* appearances, I was "sober" and at peace, but inwardly it was a different story. It's one thing to look and act peaceful. It's another thing to *be* peaceful—on the inside.

Long after my relationship with Julie had ended, I was still spinning internally like a category 5 hurricane. I relived and rehashed our relationship incessantly in my head, having an internal conversation with her about things that had happened long ago in the past. It was insane. Although I was no longer physically "drinking," inwardly I was a mess. I was not at peace.

And this is when my coach and I began talking about the eye of the hurricane as a metaphor for the human experience. I needed to leave Margaritaville, not just outwardly, but inwardly as well. I needed to know what to do, moment-to-moment, when my mind would tell stories and torment me. I needed to know how to shift from stories to stillness. Basically, I needed to know how to experience *inner* peace.

Living *As* The Eye

The shift from stories to stillness begins when you realize that there is a difference between your stories and who you are. You have thoughts but you are not your thoughts. You have feelings but you are not your feelings. You have stories but you are not your stories. In this sense you are like a hurricane. Though your life situation may be chaotic and stormy, at your core you are calm and peaceful. You are not the stories, thoughts and feelings swirling around in your head. You are Peace.

The second step to inner peace is to then *witness* or *observe* your thoughts, feelings and stories—nonjudgmentally. Like watching kids playing in a park, you simply watch your mind "playing" between your ears. As the witness, you realize that you are not the stories, feelings and thoughts that are occurring; you are the Awareness that is watching them. *You are the Eye, that which is aware, but yet unaffected by that which is occurring.* This can be hard to grasp, so let me give you an example. When we go to the movies, there are a bunch of images being projected on the movie screen. If it's a romantic comedy, the images might tell a happy story. If it's a horror film, they may tell a scary story. But no matter what's appearing on the screen, the stories are **not** the screen. The screen is a still, unchanging "presence" on which the stories appear, and the screen is unaffected by what's appearing on it.

You are the screen. You are not the images—the thoughts, feelings or stories—that are occurring. They are simply appearing in or on that which you are. So the first aspect of *living as* the Eye is to know that you are the Eye, and then secondly, to allow yourself to rest as the witness of what's occurring.

The third part of the shift occurs when you take more interest in the "screen" than you do in the stories that are appearing on it. Don't pay attention to the thoughts, feelings and stories that are occurring. They are there, but so what? Pay attention to the Awareness on which they appear. If there is loneliness, anger, fear, sadness and/or crazy stories being told in your head, so what? You don't have to pay attention to them, obsess about them, allow yourself to be hijacked by them, believe them or attempt to figure them out. In other words, you don't have to react to them. In fact, you don't have to do anything with them. Why bother? Have you noticed that you don't have control over them anyway? Why put your attention on that which is beyond your control? And have you ever noticed how quickly they come and go as well? Why invest energy and attention in a thought or a feeling that came out of nowhere and will disappear just as quickly as it came? Just observe them and dial into that which is ever-present, the unchanging Stillness that you are. If something can be done and needs to be done, you'll know what it is and you can do it— peacefully. You don't have to get all caught up in the drama of what's occurring in the outer bands of your life and mind. Instead, take more interest in the Eye.

Now, that may sound easier said than done so let me give you an example. Have you ever had a really interesting conversation with a friend on the phone while the TV was on in the background? Probably all of us have. How could you talk with all that other stuff going on in the background? You tuned out the TV and paid attention to your friend on the phone. You were more interested in the conversation with your friend than you were with what was happening on TV.

The "TV" is always on in your life. It never shuts off. There is always something happening. But you don't have to pay attention to it. The trick is to become more curious and interested in the unchanging Stillness, the ever-present Eye that you are, than with the stories, thoughts and feelings that are occurring in the "outer bands" of your life.

And remember this: What you put your attention on grows. If you pay attention to your thoughts, feelings, stories and problems—they will grow in intensity and dominate your life. Haven't you found that to be true? If, however, you pay more attention to the Eye, then the awareness of the Stillness that you are will grow and dominate your life.

Meditation Moments

One of the easiest ways I've found to shift my attention from the stories in my head to the ever-present Awareness that I am, is to engage in what I call, Meditation Moments. It just so happens that during the couple of days it took me to write this chapter, my mind spun like a category 5 hurricane, telling me some amazing stories of doom. I won't go into detail about the actual story in my head, because frankly, I'm not all that interested in it. But I will share how I used a Meditation Moment to shift out of it, for I am interested in that.

I must be honest and tell you that before I used my Mediation Moment technique, I chose to believe in and get completely sucked into my mind's crazy tale of doom. The result was a substantial meltdown the night before I wrote these words. I felt alone, depressed and scared. I whined and complained to my wife and got only about three hours of sleep. But this morning I began to shift.

The shift began when I chose to be the witness of, rather than be a participant in, my mind's stories of doom. Once I did that, I welcomed what my mind was doing as part of the present moment, meaning I didn't wish it would stop. Why bother wishing something wasn't, when it already is? My mind was telling stories

206

and that was okay. But I focused my attention on my breathing and after a few moments, I looked for the "screen." I looked for what was at the center of the "storm." I stayed still and what emerged was an awareness of calm, empty, spaciousness—the Eye. The Eye was what I found and I rested as *That*.

Was the mind still spinning tales of doom? Yes, of course, that's what it does. But am I any of the thoughts or feelings? Or am I that which is aware, but yet unaffected by them? Well, you know the answer to that.

So here's a summary of the shift move I call The Meditation Moment. It is the process by which you can *live as* the Eye of the hurricane, and experience moment-to-moment inner peace. I invite you to try this right now or the next time your mind tortures you.

1. Witness. Observe the stories, noticing that they are not You.
2. Welcome. Allow what is to be.
3. Breathe. Ignore the stories and instead, focus on your breathing.
4. Look for the "Eye." Turn your attention inward and notice the Stillness that is there.

You are *That*.

Affirmation

I am the Eye of the hurricane, that which is aware but yet unaffected by any thought, feeling or story that is spinning around in my mind.

CHAPTER 26

STEP ELEVEN:
Get a Life!

"We're on a mission from God."

—Jake and Elwood Blues
From the movie, *The Blues Brothers*

As you know, I think my coach, Diana Chapman, is the best thing since sliced bread. I formally worked with her for over two years and during that time we unwound a lot of old stuff which enabled me to live and love in a healthy, fulfilling way. Much of who I am today can be attributed to our work together.

Without question, the absolute highlight of my week was when I had a phone session with her. The best way to describe those calls would be to say that they were like getting a great massage, only it was a massage for my soul. At the beginning of a session, I'd tell her some of the issues I wanted to cover and after listening and asking questions, she'd then go to "work" on me, using her "hands" to help me release a pent up emotion, experience an "aha" type of insight or make a new commitment. It was an awesome hour—*usually*.

I say "usually" because every once in a while, it felt like my wonderful "massage therapist" went to the dark side. Sometimes, when she "worked" on me, she'd find a "knot", an area in my life that she felt needed attention. She'd hone in on that "knot," even if I didn't ask her to, and proceed to dig her "thumbs" into my deep "tissue." And sometimes it really hurt. Let me tell you about one such time.

During one session, I spent the majority of our time telling Diana how frustrated I was by a couple of women I had met and liked, but who had not returned my calls. (I know. It's hard for me to believe too.) With Diana being a woman, I asked her to explain her crazy gender to me. I didn't understand what was going on. I said, "Diana, how can a woman meet you, like you enough to give you her number and then not respond when you call? I mean, what the hell is up with that?" She said,

"Well, she probably did like you and find you attractive, but maybe she could sense that your only mission in life is landing a babe! I mean, Roy, what do you have to offer a woman? What do you have going for you that a woman would want to be a part of? What's your mission? What are you about? As far as I can tell, the only thing that gets you out of bed each morning is the desire to find a woman. That's a turn off to a quality woman. My guess is that these women could sense that you are drifting through life. So I suggest you get a life, *then* get a girl."

That made me furious. I was outraged! How dare she? I screamed at her for about five straight minutes, telling her how wrong she was about me. But she wasn't wrong. She was spot on. When I finally calmed down, we began to discuss what she was saying and she added,

"Roy, you're a great guy. I'm not commenting on your person or your value, I'm saying you're in Margaritaville. You are desperate for a relationship and a quality woman can smell it a mile away. Men can sense this about women as well. A healthy man can tell when a woman is needy and wants to be taken care of, that her only interest in life is to be rescued by her 'knight in shining armor.' Non-addicts can smell addicts a mile away. You basically have it written all over your face. Your energy screams, 'I'm desperate and lonely. Love me and save me!'"

Though I understood what she was saying, I was still hung up on the idea of a woman giving a guy her number and then not responding. So she continued,

"Should she have given you her number if she wasn't really interested in you? No, of course not, but some women have a hard time cutting a guy loose face-to-face. But that isn't the point, Roy. This is about you.

Put the babes on the back burner and first put your life together. The most attractive thing in the world to a woman is a man on a mission *and* who is available for intimacy. If you get your life together, you won't have any trouble finding the woman of your dreams. In fact, she'll find you."

She's right. Get a life, *then* get a partner. Relationship addiction is an obsession with love and intimacy. And, of course, when you're obsessed with something, by definition, it takes over your life. This is easily seen with addictions like gambling or crack cocaine. The addict's life revolves around finding and using their drug of choice. And it's the same with love addiction. Life revolves around love. For a relationship addict like me, my life's ambition, energy, passion, and creativity was devoted to acquiring the attention and affection of women. That was all I was about. Whatever else I did in life was done to fill the time between dates.

And so, the rest of my life suffered from neglect. My relationship with my son grew distant because I was either on the Internet or on the phone with all my babes when I was supposed to be spending time with him! And I was treading water in my career. It was going nowhere. I wasn't doing anything with my life except looking for love. This is maybe the saddest result of love addiction. Your own life slowly withers and decays from lack of attention. The irony of this is staggering. The life we are so desperately trying to find through love is actually being destroyed by the pursuit of it!

Express Your Authentic Self

One of the final steps in my journey was to discover my life's purpose and start living it. I had to quit waiting for love and start living my life. But that was impossible when I was still the Mayor of Margaritaville. I had to break free of my addiction first and stop obsessing over where my next "drink" was going to come from, so that I could focus my attention on discovering my life's purpose. That is why getting a life appears as step eleven and not step one. It isn't possible when you're living in Margaritaville. But you're free now. You no longer have "faith in love." You know loneliness is an illusion; you can feel your completeness and your connectedness to the All. And so now you can answer

Diana's question for yourself: What are you about? What is your mission? How does your authentic Self, your Original Shine, want to be expressed in the world? For me, I felt called to completely reorganize my life. I moved across the country and went from being a competitive golfer and an instructor to being a relationship coach and an author. You may or may not need to be that dramatic. This step is not about engaging in some enormous life makeover. It is simply about discovering what you're passionate about (other than love!) and pursuing it joyfully. That might be diving into your career, becoming an activist, investing deeply in your kids, writing a book, training for a marathon, going back to school, traveling the world, joining Toastmasters, taking a cooking class, playing on a softball team or getting a pet! It doesn't matter. All that *does* matter is that you express your authentic, creative Self—Now!

For instance, what are you going to do today (or ten seconds from now when you finish this chapter), that is about *you* and not about *love*?

Get a life! Live it, enjoy it, express it, relish in it—and let love find you.

Affirmation

I know what my mission is and what I am passionate about and I am actively and joyfully expressing it in and through my life.

CHAPTER 27

STEP TWELVE:
The Ingredients for a Delicious Love Life

"BAM!"

—Emeril Lagasse

Imagine that you want to open an elegant restaurant in New York City. Before that momentous day, you will find an ideal location, hire an expensive interior designer to create your atmosphere, recruit a world-class chef and staff to ensure impeccable food and service, choose an amazing wine list and even hire a top advertising firm to promote your opening.

But when your elite cliental arrive on opening night, everything you've done to create this fabulous restaurant will have been a waste of time and money if your food isn't absolutely fantastic. For no matter how amazing your famous chef's recipes are, no matter how wonderful the atmosphere and service is, if the meals aren't prepared with the absolute freshest and highest quality ingredients, the food will be awful and your restaurant will fail.

The same is true in your love life. If you want it to be the most delicious romance imaginable, it will be because you too have committed to using the freshest, highest quality "ingredients" possible. In this, the final step in our journey to Narnia, I want to share with you ten ingredients, that when mixed together, form the recipe for a delicious love life.

The best way to think of these ten ingredients is to view them as personal commitments, for that is really what they are. They are the ways you are going to behave in your love life; the ways you are going to act and interact with your partner, or your potential partner, if you happen to not be currently in a committed relationship. They are the way you will *do* love.

My wife and I have been "cooking" with these ten ingredients and I can tell you that they do, indeed, create an amazingly delicious love life. But we aren't the only ones who "cook" with these ingredients. If you talk to anyone experiencing a truly healthy and fulfilling love life, you'll find them using these same ingredients too, though they might use different names to describe them. There's a good chance that you'll find one or two of them quite bitter to the taste, however, for they are very challenging. (Why do you think great relationships are so rare?). I ask you to resist the temptation to "cook" without the ingredients that are not immediately appealing to your palate, for they are *all* necessary for the recipe to taste just right. Finally, each of the ten ingredients could be an entire chapter unto itself. But what follows is a brief description of each of them and I invite you to make them a central topic of conversation with your rude relationship coach, because a little personal guidance will be necessary to fully and properly implement them into your life.

1. Seek Your Spiritual Evolution

Your complete development as an individual is critical if you desire to create a delicious love life. When it's all said and done, *you* are the main ingredient in the recipe. Everything else is secondary. You must be the "freshest, highest quality" person you can be if you want to be in a delicious relationship, for the key to intimacy is not *finding* the right partner, but *being* the right partner. Therefore you must be "sober" and committed to discovering and displaying your Original Shine. I won't say anything more on this since the entire book is devoted to it. *But understand that your relationship will never be healthier or deeper than you are, but it will, in fact, always and only reflect your spiritual maturity and depth.*

2. Stop Blaming and Take Responsibility

I'm going to sound like Nancy Reagan when I say this, but the second critical ingredient to relationship bliss is to "just say no" to blame. You will never have even a decent relationship, much less a blissful one, if you play the victim by blaming your partner for your feelings, problems, decisions or experiences.

This is no easy task because at times it will seem like your partner is, in fact, responsible for your pain or problems. When that happens, what do you do? Well, first, don't blame. Just don't

213

go there, as tempting as it is. Instead redirect that accusation energy and use it to fuel deep self-reflection and curiosity. Turn your conviction into inquiry and wonder. Ask yourself how you might be responsible for what's occurring.

I know how bizarre and illogical this may sound. When my coach first taught me this truth, that we are 100% responsible for our reality, I thought she had lost her mind. But when I deeply looked into what I thought was someone else's fault, I always found that I *allowed*, *invited* or *required* things to be exactly as they were. I had, in fact, set the whole thing up. As I previously have said, this doesn't mean that our partner (or anyone else) doesn't have their part, for they are 100% responsible too. It just means that without us, it could not have turned out as it has. Let me give you an example.

I once worked with a couple that was on the verge of divorce because the wife had found out that over their 20 year marriage, her husband had about a dozen emotional, but non-sexual affairs. When I first talked to her, she was, of course, terribly hurt, but she also saw herself as the total victim of his behavior and blamed him for ruining their lives. "How could he do this to me?" she said. After a bit of discussion, I asked the question that led to her breakthrough: "Tell me about the early days when you dated." She said, "Well, it was rough. We broke up three different times because I caught him flirting with and dating other women."

She knew exactly who he was before they got married! He was simply continuing to be the guy he always was. How then could she claim to be the victim and blame him for her pain? She set the whole thing up. She chose to date and marry a guy who was not a one-woman man. As Jimmy Buffet said, "Some people say that there's a woman (in this case, a man) to blame, but I know, it's my own damn fault."

Now, is he responsible for his Casanova-like, addicted behavior? Of course he is. He certainly had some issues to address and he did. But the point is that none of it could have occurred without her choosing to ignore who she knew him to be. Does this mean she should stay married to him? No! It means she can take responsibility for how she created the mess and for what she now wants to do about it. In the most literal sense, this is absolute freedom.

And this freedom is only available to those who "just say no" to blame and instead inquire, introspect and wonder about how

214

they set the whole thing up. This is, without question, the most challenging fundamental of all, but living it brings liberating, profound results.

3. Reveal Rather Than Conceal

In our former way of life as relationship addicts, we were so afraid of losing our partner's love that we hid and concealed anything that we thought might threaten the relationship. This pattern has to stop. Intimacy is built upon the pillars of honesty and transparency.

Now, I know that complete honesty is a scary thought. But if you conceal and withhold from your partner, what kind of relationship do you have? A safe one, but not a healthy, intimate one, that's for sure. In a healthy relationship, partners don't protect each other from the truth; they respect and value each other enough to reveal it.

Elizabeth Gilbert was recently being interviewed in Oprah's magazine. She was promoting her latest book, *Committed: A Skeptic Makes Peace with Marriage*. This is what she said about her commitment to being completely open and honest with her husband, Felipe.

"It was like a pre-consent form; a full disclosure kind of thing. What I was so interested in doing in this whole story of our marriage was making sure that we were living in as much of a delusion-free zone as possible, having cultivated and spread delusion for so much of my romantic life because it was so much more exciting and glamorous and thrilling than the truth. Certainly part of seduction is a masquerade, you know? One of the rules is that you don't show yourself. And I just didn't want that to be what was going on when we were preparing for this really big step. It's like, buyer beware. I'm 40; he's 57. We've been on the market a long time. And you should know; okay, a little termite damage. It's a pretty good house, but when it rains, it does flood the basement sometimes."

My guess is that they are experiencing relationship bliss.

I can tell you from personal experience that deceiving your partner is a terrible way to live. Even if you are not living a

215

spectacular lie as I was, to live incongruently, on any level, erodes your soul and saps your aliveness. (It can even ruin your chances in the U.S. Open!)

Now, if you reveal rather than conceal, might it get a little dicey? Yes, but what is the alternative? Living a lie just to keep the peace? Is that a love life worth celebrating? Remember there are only two paths in a relationship. The first is love, which calls you to reveal in order to relate; and the second is fear, which calls you to conceal in order to control. Those are the only two paths open to you. One leads to Margaritaville and misery, the other to Narnia and bliss.

Commit to the path of love. Refuse to withhold, hide or conceal. Reveal your feelings, thoughts, wants, fears, mistakes, needs, actions, dreams and decisions. If your partner can't accept and love the real you, then so be it. Remember, you aren't a relationship addict anymore and you don't fear being out of a relationship. Your primary commitment is to be yourself and if someone doesn't want to be with the person you are, then why would you want to be with them anyway? Only an addict would want that.

Live out loud. Tell the microscopic truth. Make your inner conversation public. Be transparent and open. Don't control your partner but love them enough to tell them the truth. And especially reveal those things you wish your partner would not find out about. Reveal what you have the urge to hide. In my experience, though it might get ugly for a time, revealing leads to freedom, intimacy and trust.

4. Protect Your Aliveness

Being selfish is essential if you desire to have a fulfilling and healthy love life. I know that sounds crazy, so let me explain.

I'm not championing self-absorption and the total disregard for others. That's what I call *narcissistic selfishness*. I'm talking about *sacred selfishness*. I am saying that you cannot have relationship bliss if you are not following your bliss. And your bliss is found in heeding your inner voice, being faithful to your creative path and engaging in activities that make you feel vibrant and alive.

When flying, we're told that in the event of an emergency, we're to put on our oxygen mask before we help anyone else with theirs. That's what I mean by sacred selfishness. As important as our partners, parents, friends and kids are, our aliveness must take precedence. You are the priority, for you are no good to anybody if you are "dead." You must not lose your self. (By the way, for those of you who are familiar with the Bible, when it says to "deny yourself," that's referring to your ego not your aliveness.)

Your aliveness is sacred, and you must protect it like a mother bear protects her cubs. If you put your partner or the stability of your relationship ahead of your aliveness, you will probably end up depressed, addicted or involved in an extramarital affair.

Many people believe that sacrifice and compromise are key fundamentals in healthy relationships. It's actually just the opposite. The purpose of a relationship is the growth and expansion of the individuals in it. A truly healthy and blissful relationship is one in which neither partner is giving up anything of importance in exchange for being in the relationship. Sacrifice and compromise are red flags. In most cases, if two people are willing to work at it, both partners can have what they want, for there are many creative solutions that can be found.

The best gift you can give your partner, your kids, your friends and your career is a Self that is in love with life. And that usually means being sacredly selfish about three areas of life:

A. Your inner voice. One thing I've always loved about Jesus was how he modeled this. Most of us see Jesus as a very unselfish being, and in the narcissistic sense, he was. But if you tried to distract him from following his inner voice, look out. On one occasion, his right-hand man, Peter, tried to do that and Jesus called him Satan! Before you listen to, or get distracted by any other voices in your life, i.e., your kids, partner, parents, boss, etc., hear and heed your voice. Give it priority.

B. Your creative path. Each of us has come into the world to make a contribution. We are here to express ourselves and offer our gifts. That is what I mean by your creative path. That may be anything from raising children to starting a business to being President of the United States. Your aliveness is intimately connected to how fully you live your creative path and you cannot allow anything or anyone to stand in your way.

C. Your activities. Engaging in activities that make you feel vibrant and alive is another crucial component to protecting your aliveness. Simply put, you have the right to do things that make you feel happy and joyful. Your role in life is not to help everyone else enjoy life, but to model joyous living for them.

I'm going to say something controversial here. The idea of spending quantity time with your children is bunk if it means you must cut out activities that rejuvenate and enliven you. Your kids are better off having one hour with a happy parent, than four hours with a depressed one. I'm not saying shirking your responsibility as a parent is a good thing. I'm saying quality really is more important than quantity.

5. Support Mutual Creativity

Ever been to a restaurant and ordered a meal based on the picture on the menu? (This may tell you the kind of restaurants I frequent!) Have you noticed that when the meal arrives at your table it doesn't look anything like the picture?

Well, I'm afraid you're going to experience that when you consider this fifth essential ingredient for creating a delicious love life. For at first, this one is going to look really, really yummy, but once you get a closer look at it, you might realize it's not all that it was cracked up to be. Let me tell you what I mean.

Imagine having a partner who is not jealous, scared or threatened by your expansion, aliveness and creativity, but actually willing to do what ever they can, short of abandoning their own creative path, to support yours! Isn't that a yummy looking dish? Don't you want to sink your teeth into a partner that is completely devoted to your full creative expression, to you being all that you were intended to be! Who wouldn't want to "order" *that* off the menu?!

But here's the catch. (There's always a catch, isn't there?) You, too, have to be that partner! You have to devote *yourself* to your partner's full creative expression as well. This can not be a one-sided affair. This ingredient means that both partners must *mutually agree* to support each other's full creative expression. And I know that sounds good, but consider this:

In many relationships, it is not unusual to have one person over-functioning while the other person is under-functioning. The

218

relationship is unbalanced. Now, for both people to support each other's full creative expression it will mean something has to give. The under-functioning partner is going to have to step up and take a more active role in the life of the relationship, so that the over-functioning partner can be freed up to pursue their fullest creative expression, if that is what they desire to do. This does not mean they simply flip-flop, however. It just means that the partner who has been skating and being taken care of by the over-functioning partner is going to be required to be a full participating partner in the relationship. And sometimes, they may not like that. Many under-functioning partners know that if they were to support their partner's full and complete creative expression in the world, they may have to spend more money, invest more time in the kids, do more chores around the house and generally have a little less "me" time. This dynamic is very common. Here's a couple of examples:

- A woman, while loving her role as a homemaker and wife, has always wanted to be a chef. But her husband doesn't think it's a good idea. Though he may come up with a "good" reason why she shouldn't pursue her dream, the real reason is that if she did that, he'd have to step up and do much more around the house and with the kids, spending less time on the golf course.

- A man making a six figure income wants to leave his career and start his own business. His spouse has enjoyed the fruits of his career, spending her time at the spa, having lunch with friends and playing tennis at the club. But if he does this, she'll have to go back to work or severely cut back on her lifestyle. She tells him, "With the economy like it is, I don't think it's a good time to take a risk."

So as much as supporting each other's mutual creativity *sounds* good, don't be naïve. Often, when one person decides to follow a dream, the other person is called to power, being asked to end the free-loading joy ride life has been and step fully into the relationship. What I'm describing is a co-committed, co-creative relationship, one that is equal, balance, mutual and ultimately blissful.

219

One last caveat. Certainly a couple can agree to an era (or even a lifetime) of imbalance. My dad started his company while he worked full-time at another job. He disappeared from the family for about three years and my mom stopped working to be home, compensating for his absence. But she did it willingly and gladly. It was her choice. What my dad was doing was *their* mission, not only his.

So imbalance is not necessarily wrong. If one person wants to let go of their dreams and desires to support their partner's, and if they do it consciously and without regret, then it can be a beautiful thing. I'm not arguing that two people should always be chasing their own individual dreams. But I am saying that relationship bliss is when both people commit to support each other fully, and then, from that space, they can decide on how their relationship should look at any given time.

Commit to being a person who supports, encourages, and even demands that your partner live the life that makes them feel most alive! This is what it means to love another person: You want them to have what they want for themselves.

6. Keep Your Agreements

As a life and relationship coach, I love working with clients who are confused, frustrated and disappointed with their life situation, yet they are deeply curious about themselves and willing to ruthlessly search their souls for answers. After weeks, or even months of gut-wrenching self examination, there is an "aha!" moment when they realize how an unconscious pattern or a self-sabotaging belief has been responsible for their misery. These defining, evolutionary moments, when a client discovers and releases a deeply hidden life-script, are the most rewarding moments in my work. The client's life is transformed right before my eyes! Although our sessions were filled with blood, sweat and tears, the client is now liberated and so every second of it was worth it.

And yet, for the vast majority of people who are stuck and frustrated in life, those kinds of dramatic realizations are **not** necessary. Often, for people to experience exhilarating results in their love lives, they only need to make one simple shift: Keep their agreements! They don't need to discover some complicated, deeply imbedded psychological issue to see their lives or love lives transformed. All they need to do is be impeccable with their word! That's it! It's no more complicated than that.

I admit that this sixth ingredient in the recipe for a delicious love life is not very sexy and exotic. But often, when a couple comes to me and says that they're fighting all the time and on the verge of divorce, what I find underneath the layers of hurt and heartache is a relationship riddled with broken agreements. Simply being impeccable with their word is all a couple needs to transform their life together.

We all know that breaking agreements around major issues like finances and fidelity leads to disaster. But even when "little" promises are not kept, trust is eroded. Relationships can't function if people don't keep their agreements. There is no predictability or reliability. If your word is worthless, it creates resentment and destroys respect.

Of course, you can always renegotiate an agreement if it becomes necessary, for they should always be mutual, but even this should be limited. Don't enter into agreements lightly. Make sure you get a full-body "yes" before you commit. And when you do make an agreement, keep it, for this is essential in the creation of a delicious love life.

7. Become a Conscious Listener

Another ingredient in the recipe for a delicious love life is conscious listening. As you might surmise, this is much more than merely hearing what someone is saying. To listen consciously means that you surrender your agenda and become the sacred space on, or in which, they can fully express what is true for them in the moment. You aren't preparing your response, mounting your defense, conceptualizing a solution or judging what is being shared. You are simply alert and present. Like the clean, white canvas that awaits the brush strokes of the painter, so you are the presence on which their words can be "painted." You are facing them directly, making eye contact, tuning into their energy and synchronizing your breath with theirs. You and your agenda have been set aside for the moment.

This kind of conscious listening is extremely rare because it requires two major shifts for it to occur. First, you must drop your ego and all of its wants, fears, defenses and problems. The ego is not invited to a conscious listening party. This is not about you, even if what is being said is! This is your essence being present

221

with another's, even if you are being taken to the woodshed! All judging, defending, explaining, dismissing and promising must be allowed to dissolve. The second reason conscious listening is so rare is that you must be able to be in the presence of powerful emotions and be able to handle it. Many of us are not comfortable with the expression of strong emotions so we distance ourselves by offering solutions (the tactic of many men), agreeing with the story being told (the tactic of many women), make jokes to lighten the moment (the tactic of yours truly), or we just call them crazy, tell them to get therapy and leave the room (the tactic of the soon to be divorced).

In my view, whether you are hooked on love or not, this is another really challenging ingredient to master. It is absolutely my weakest link. My ego is not inclined to take a back seat to anyone and I am very uncomfortable with a woman's anger, especially if it's directed at me. But I am committed to being the space in which those that I love, and those that I coach, can fully appear.

8. Cultivate an Affectionate Atmosphere
This eighth ingredient comes rather easily to most relationship addicts, being that we are so bent toward love and intimacy. But being an affectionate partner still needs to be stressed because it often gets lost as we live at the speed of life.

Blissful relationships are affectionate relationships. Hug, kiss, grab, caress, grope, fondle, squeeze, pinch, spank, spoon and tickle each other all the time. I make it a point to never walk by my wife without touching her in some wonderfully inappropriate way! Make out like teenagers (why should they have all the fun?). Give massages, back scratches and sponge baths. Wash each other's hair; sit next to each other, not opposite each other, in restaurants; choose movie theaters that allow the arm rests to be raised; hold hands while driving and slow dance as you tell each other about your respective days. Basically, do life in contact with each other.

Of course, if you have conflict, resentments and unresolved issues with each other, you won't be inclined to be affectionate, and rightly so. It would be inauthentic. That is why this ingredient is to be added late in the "cooking" process. Affection is natural in a relationship when two people are "cooking" with the other ingredients. They create an atmosphere where affection and non-sexual touching are nearly automatic.

Keep in mind that affection may lead to sex, but that's not the objective. There is no objective. You love him or her and you just want to touch them. You're not being seductive necessarily, nor are you attempting to turn them on. It's just your way of life. It's the atmosphere of your relationship, the environment in which the two of you exist.

I purposely have not talked about sex as an ingredient because it's *not* an ingredient that creates relationship bliss; it *reflects* relationship bliss. How can you not have a great sex life if you and your partner are in a relationship that is being prepared with ingredients like these? The real challenge is pulling yourselves apart long enough to get to work on time!

Finally, I understand that some people are not comfortable with public displays of affection. That's fine. Talk about it with your partner and make up for it in private! I also recognize that because of cultural heritage, personal preference or childhood experiences people vary in their natural inclination to give and receive affection. Again, talk about it and come up with something that will serve you both. However, in my experience, if someone is not comfortable touching and being touched, they probably need to address that with their coach or therapist because we are naturally affectionate creatures.

9. Replace Criticism with Appreciation

Appreciation is verbal affection. It is touching and caressing your partner's heart with your words instead of your hands. It says, "Hey, I see you, I am paying attention, I notice you and I am not taking you for granted. I am grateful and thankful for who you are and that you're in my life."

If you want to be in a blissful relationship, commit to being a partner who is generous with appreciation. Every day say something about your partner for which you are grateful. Admire, praise, thank and compliment them. Frankly, being critical, negative, harsh and judgmental makes you a pain in the ass to be around! Often times, we make romance overly complicated. Could it be as easy as being a person who is easy and fun to be with? Think of it this way: Would *you* want to live with someone who is channeling *Roger Ebert* all the time?

If you are critical, you will notice more and more things to criticize. And of course, when your partner constantly hears your criticism, they are liable to defend themselves by pointing out all the things you do that annoy them. Now you're in a power struggle for who's the biggest loser! It's a downward, vicious cycle. But if you regularly appreciate your partner, you will find more and more things to appreciate. And because they are moved and touched by your words, they will tell you something they appreciate about you. Now you've created an upward cycle. And this is because what you put your attention on grows. What you give, you receive; what you sow, you reap; what goes around comes around. This is basically what Karma means. And to a large degree, your Karma is created with your tongue. Lavish your partner with appreciation. Don't wait for them to appreciate you first. Sow appreciation and you'll reap the benefits.

10. Manage the Upper Limit Problem

This ingredient appears last on the list, not necessarily because it is the least important, but because it usually is only necessary when the first nine are being "cooked" with consistently. This ingredient isn't so much about how to *create* relationship bliss as it is how to *preserve* it.

One of the strangest dynamics in life is the tendency to self-sabotage ourselves when we are experiencing amazing amounts of love, joy and success. It's as if we can't stand too much of a good thing. This is called the "upper limit problem," a phrase coined by my mentor, Dr. Gay Hendricks. He says in his book, *The Big Leap*, that each of us has an inner thermostat setting that governs how much success and good feeling we can handle. When life is too good or "hot," our upper limit is triggered and we'll do something to "cool" things off.

Have you ever found yourself saying to your partner, "Why are we fighting? We had such a wonderful weekend! I've never felt so close to you, so in love, so connected. And now we're arguing! I just don't get it. It's like we can't handle success!"

And that's exactly right. You hit your upper limit and "cooled" things off. So the final step in a high-functioning, blissful relationship is to raise the thermostat setting so that you can experience ever increasing amounts of love and success. And you do that by intentionally allowing your relationship to breathe. Let me explain.

Most couples don't know that there is a flow in intimacy, akin to breathing, where an extremely intense experience of connection (inhale) is followed by a time of separation (exhale). This is how a blissful relationship stays blissful. It must be intentionally allowed to breathe.

Ironically, in order for a couple to expand their ability to experience greater amounts of love and closeness together, they need to honor their need for separateness. In a sense, then, there is an interval aspect to relationships, a rhythm of inhale and exhale, coming together and moving apart.

Interestingly, it's during the time apart—when you're with your friends, expressing your creativity or enjoying your hobbies—that your thermostat is being reset to a higher level. A relationship is much like a muscle. After an intense workout, the muscle needs time to rest—so it can get bigger. If it gets this "down time," it will be able to handle more weight next time.

So it is with our love lives. We must create time apart, especially after particularly intense moments of closeness, so that our inner thermostat, our capacity for love and intimacy, can grow and get bigger. Once you have mastered the first nine fundamentals, the upper limit problem becomes the only thing that can derail bliss. Balance your relationship. Let it breathe and flow from closeness to separateness to closeness again. In doing so, your capacity for intimacy will expand and you will reach heights of ecstasy that you never imagined possible.

Affirmation

I am committed to "cooking" with the ten ingredients that form the recipe for a delicious love life.

To sum up then, in my experience, these are the ingredients for a delicious love life. With a heartfelt commitment to the following ten ingredients your love life will "taste" just right.

- Seek Your Spiritual Evolution
- Stop Blaming and Take Responsibility
- Reveal Rather Than Conceal
- Protect Your Aliveness
- Support Mutual Creativity

225

- Keep Your Agreements
- Become a Conscious Listener
- Cultivate an Affectionate Atmosphere
- Replace Criticism with Appreciation
- Manage the Upper Limit Problem

Welcome to Narnia!

You made it! You have moved out of Margaritaville and taken up permanent residence in Narnia. Is it not everything I said it would be? Is it not a place of enchantment, magic, adventure and beauty? Isn't the idea of needing a partner to make you feel special, alive, happy and whole hysterical? Wasn't *Jerry Maguire* indeed, full of shit?

Take note of what you've been through. Recognizing your life was out of control, you turned your attention inward and intentionally chose to face your loneliness and pain. Hiring a coach, you identified your personas, completed with former lovers and went cold turkey. Turning away from external life sources, you dated yourself, had a affair with Mother Nature and discovered the Stillness that you are. Finally, you put your life together and committed to a whole new set of behaviors in intimacy.

Notice and celebrate who you are and the work you've done! Of course, be gentle with yourself if you wander away from Narnia from time to time. Drifting happens. If it does, simply identify which of the 12 Steps needs to be revisited and then recommit yourself to your "sobriety."

You now have the love life you have always wanted.

Now you have *yourself.*

EPILOGUE

The Love of *My* Life
The Caribbean, May 2008

"Do you want to meet the love of your life? Look in the mirror."

—Byron Katie

It is a beautiful, warm, breezy day in the eastern Caribbean. Not a cloud in the sky. The natives have told me that since Antigua does not have any high mountains, it hardly ever rains, unless of course, there is a hurricane. And the temperature today is basically like it is everyday—mid 80's. In January, the average high is 81° and in July the average high is 87°! My cab driver said, "Ya, mon, every day same in Antiqua."

Standing on the beach, chuckling as I remember his broken English and his thick Caribbean accent, I think to myself, "Well, every day may be the same for you, *mon*, but not for me. Today is my wedding day."

I am going to be married to MaryMargaret any minute now, right here on the beach of our beautiful, exotic, *non-au natural* resort. I honestly feel like I am an actor in a photo-shoot for a postcard company, it's that beautiful here. The sand on which I am standing is blinding me, its so white. And the calm, blue-green waters of the Caribbean are playfully lapping at my heels. Over my shoulder there is an old, beat-up fishing boat sleeping in the bay and further in the distance are sailboats that appear to be falling off the edge of the world.

I am wearing a bright blue *Tommy Bahama* shirt, linen shorts, a corsage, sandals and a smile. I am at peace as I wait for my woman to emerge from the flower garden so that we can say our vows to one another, vows we have written ourselves. Waiting with me is a videographer (that's partly why it feels like a photo-shoot), two beautiful young female resort employees who will serve as our witnesses, and the sweetest female minister you can ever imagine. You should hear her try to pronounce my name! Once the ceremony is completed, we will be taken to a small table

227

just yards from the beach to sign documents, cut the cake, enjoy our champagne toast and have our first dance in the beachside gazebo, dancing to music we have chosen. The whole thing is absolute heaven.

I had a general idea what MaryMargaret would look like today, since she asked me to be involved in picking out her wedding dress. I know it is supposed to be bad luck to see the bride in her dress before the wedding day, but one of the benefits of a second marriage is that you know marital success is determined, not by superstition, but by how diligently two people "cook" with the right ingredients. And besides, shopping with her was actually pretty fun. I got to see her in dozens of beautiful dresses and that led to many post-shopping romantic interludes. (I've never figured out why men don't like shopping with their wives or girlfriends, but I digress.) She finally decided on a short, rather sexy, slightly off-white sun dress. It looked great on her. (I playfully kidded her about the whole off-white thing.)

Suddenly, the music starts and all of us turned to see MaryMargaret appear from the garden. She's taken my breath away. Not only is she beautiful, but the stark contrast between the almost white dress and her tan skin weakens my knees. And in this speechless moment as she makes her way to my side, our eyes locked on each other in tenderness, I hear a silent whisper coming from within me. I immediately recognized it as the same voice, the same "fly on the wall" if you will, that spoke to me the last time I was in the Caribbean, the one that spoke to me when I was dragging Pam by her ankles to throw her out of our room. Back then, in the midst of that horrible moment, the voice shouted, "Look at yourself! Look at what you are doing? Look at what your life has become!"

Strangely, this time, the voice whispers the exact same thing. "Roy, look at your self. Look at what you are doing. Look at what your life has become."

Tears begin to well up in my eyes. And I know they are about more than the beautiful creature now holding my hand. Yes, she is the love of my life and I am the love of hers. But this moment, and the relationship I have with this woman, has only been possible because I stopped looking for the *love* of my life and instead went looking for the love of *MY* life.

For that is what our journey has been all about, friends. Never was it about finding a partner with whom we can experience exquisite intimacy and relationship bliss. It has always been about realizing that the love of our life has always been the one looking back at us in the mirror. Narnia has never been a place to go. It has always been the person you are! *For there is nowhere you need to go, nothing you need to do, and no person you need to have, in order to be that which you already are.*

Farewell

I leave you with the words from one of my favorite songs. When I first heard this song, I immediately went out and bought the CD. I think there was a four month period of time that I sang along with this song in my car every day, usually with tears streaming down my face.

The artist's name is Natasha Bedingfield and the song is, *Unwritten.*

I am unwritten, can't read my mind, I'm undefined
I'm just beginning, the pen's in my hand, ending unplanned
Staring at the blank page before you
Open up the dirty window
Let the sun illuminate the words that you could not find
Reaching for something in the distance
So close you can almost taste it
Release your inhibitions
Feel the rain on your skin
No one else can feel it for you
Only you can let it in
No one else, no one else
Can speak the words on your lips
Drench yourself in words unspoken
Live your life with arms wide open
Today is where your book begins
The rest is still unwritten

Appendix I

A Chronological Timeline for *A Drink with Legs*

Though all of the stories told in this book are true, they are not shared in chronological order. They are arranged to serve the book's ultimate purpose which is to help the reader understand and recover from relationship addiction. But for the "left-brainers" among us and anyone else curious as to how things actually happened in real time, I offer the following timeline.

GOLF ERA

June 1972	The first "G" was born. I played golf for the first time, paring my first hole. I was 12 years old. (Ch. 3)
Sept. 1983	I became a professional golfer, just five months after graduating from Louisiana State University.
March & June 1986	I played with my boyhood idol, Seve Ballesteros, and then saw him at the U.S. Open later that summer. (Ch. 2)
Jan. 1988-Dec. 1989	I qualified and played on the PGA Tour for two years.

GOD ERA

July 1990	I quit professional golf and became an intern at *Willow Creek Community Church* in suburban Chicago. "G" number two was born. (Ch. 5)
Sept. 1991-Feb. 1997	Co-created and was senior minister of *Windsor Crossing Community Church* in suburban St. Louis.
Feb. 1997-2001	Moved to Orlando and resumed my golf career playing full-time once again. This was the Strip Club era.

GIRLS ERA

April 1984	Got married to my first "drink with legs," Laurie, my ex-wife.

Sept. 1993	Had an emotional affair with a women in my church. (Ch. 22)
2001-2007	Led a gypsy lifestyle, splitting time between Orlando and Chicago. (Ch. 2)
June 2001	Decided to live a double life while sitting on my friends porch. (Ch. 3)
Sept. 2002	Got pulled over for DUI in Georgia (Ch. 2)
April 2003	Julie and I met and instantly fell in love. (Ch. 3)
June 2003	My double life was exposed in the *Daily Herald* during the U.S. Open Golf Championship in Chicago. Julie initially broke up with me and I asked my wife for a divorce. (Ch. 3)
July 2003-Oct. 2005	Julie I got back together about two weeks after my double life was exposed and we were together until she broke off our engagement. In all, it was a 30 month relationship.
Oct. 2005	Julie broke off our engagement and my one year mid-life crisis began. (Ch. 6)
Nov. 2005	I began working weekly with Diana Chapman, my relationship coach. We worked together for just over two years.
Nov. 2005-Nov. 2006	This was my Internet dating period.
June-Sept. 2006	I met Pam via the Internet and moved in with her two weeks later. I broke up with her in early September, but went to the Caribbean with her in mid October.
Oct. 2006	Pam bitch-slapped me all the way to Rock Bottom. (Prologue)
Oct. 2006	My friend, Michael Wright, refused to listen to my whining about Julie any longer. (Ch. 15)
Nov. 2006	I met MaryMargaret, my wife, at a personal growth conference in Chicago the day before I was leaving for Florida for the entire winter. We visited each other a few times, but it fizzled. I still wasn't ready. (Ch. 23)
Nov. 2006-Jan. 2007	I dated myself and had an affair with Mother Nature. (Ch. 25-26)

Dec. 2006	This was my final completion conversation with Julie. (Ch. 23)
Dec. 2006	I went cold turkey, spending New Year's Eve alone. (Ch. 24)

RECOVERY ERA

Jan. 2007	Met for closure with MaryMargaret at *Cheeseburger in Paradise* in suburban Chicago. (Ch. 23)
Feb. 2007	Diana, my coach, told me to "get a life." (Ch. 28)
April 2007	MaryMargaret and I fully committed to one another and became a couple.
Oct. 2007	MM and I became engaged.
Oct. 2007	I quit professional golf and the gypsy lifestyle. I moved to Orlando, where my son lives, and started my relationship coaching practice. MaryMargaret moved down with me in January 2008.
May 2008	MM and I were married in the Caribbean. (Epilogue)
Oct. 2008-Aug. 2009	I wrote *A Drink with Legs.*

Appendix II

Affirmations for Freedom

1. My name is _____ and I *was* a relationship addict.

2. I embrace curiosity and wonder and let go of conviction, allowing the Universe to show me the deepest truth about myself.

3. I am willing to face, rather than avoid, whatever pain arises from my commitment to relationship sobriety.

4. I have a relationship coach to support my sobriety, my personal growth and the creation of a healthy, blissful relationship.

5. I am open and honest about my relationship personas with those close to me.

6. I have completed with my former lovers by sharing with them how my addiction negatively impacted our relationship.

7. I know how my relationship addiction manifests and my intention is to never "drink" like *THAT* again.

8. I know that loneliness is an illusion because by dating myself, I have experienced my own completeness and I know that I lack absolutely nothing.

9. I regularly rendezvous with Mother Nature. "She" always reminds me that I am One with the whole and never, ever alone.

10. I am the Eye of the hurricane, that which is aware but yet unaffected by any thought, feeling or story that is spinning around in my mind.

11. I know what my mission is and what I am passionate about, and I am actively and joyfully expressing it in and through my life.

12. I am committed to "cooking" with the ten ingredients that form the recipe for a delicious love life.

ABOUT THE AUTHOR

Roy Biancalana grew up in suburban Chicago and attended Louisiana State University on a golf scholarship. After graduating in 1983 with a degree in marketing, Roy played on the PGA Tour and then co-founded and became Senior Pastor of *Windsor Crossing Community Church,* in Chesterfield, Missouri.

Roy is now a Certified Life and Relationship Coach (and author!). He has a 16 year old son and lives with his wife in Sanford, Florida. He works with clients in person or by phone and if you are interested in working with him directly or having him speak to your group or lead a workshop, you can reach him at:

www.coachingwithroy.com
roy@coachingwithroy.com
407-687-3387